P9-EEN-573

The Essential Guide To

CONTEMPORARY
HOMES

Over 340 Homes In Sleek, Modern Styles

- One-, 1½-, Two-Story & Multi-Level Plans
- Budget/Starter Homes To Luxury Estates
- Features & Details To Fit Your Lifestyle

HOME PLANNERS, INC.

Table of Contents

Published by Home Planners, Inc.

Editorial and Corporate Offices:
3275 West Ina Road, Suite 110
Tucson, Arizona 85741

Distribution Center:
29333 Lorie Lane
Wixom, Michigan 48393

Charles W. Talcott, Chairman
Rickard D. Bailey, President & Publisher
Cindy J. Coatsworth, Publications Manager
Paulette Mulvin, Editor
Paul D. Fitzgerald, Book Designer

Photo Credits
Front Cover: (center image) © 1992 Andrew D. Lautman
(top image) Roger Whitacre Photography
(bottom image) Laszlo Regos
Back Cover: © 1992 Andrew D. Lautman

First Printing, January 1993
10 9 8 7 6 5 4 3 2

All text, designs and illustrative material copyright © 1993 by Home Planners, Inc., Tucson, Arizona 85741. All rights reserved. No part of this publication may be reproduced in any form or by any means—electronic, mechanical, photomechanical, recorded or otherwise—without the written permission of the publisher.

Printed in the United States of America

Library of Congress Catalog Card Number: 92-074615

Softcover ISBN: 1-881955-02-8

Hardcover ISBN: 1-881955-04-4

On The Front Cover: Three fine examples of Contemporary style—Design W2894 (top), the home of Gretchen Carlson and Kent Hulet; Design W2781 (center), the home of Tony and Penny Wastcoat; and Design W2883 (bottom), built by Thomtech, Inc. of Rochester, Michigan. For more information about these designs see page 156 (Design W2894), page 6 (Design W2781), and page 235 (Design W2883).

On The Back Cover: The inside of our cover home (Design W2781) reveals an open, light-filled hallway, both upstairs and down. Additional information about this plan can be found on page 6.

Contemporary Design

Born of a mix of styles and cultures, Contemporary architecture borrows heavily from Modernist and International style. Large glass openings, geometric shapes, and bold yet elegant lines define the style and give it a special flavor. Elements from European, Early American and Later American architecture can be found in many of the dramatic facades. Closer inspection reveals details from the Cubism period. Combine these ingredients with traces of Tudor, Georgian, Salt Box and Cape Cod design and the true nature of Today's Contemporary home emerges.

Today's Contemporary homes suggest what must have been the slogan of their early designers—"form follows function," or later, "form and function are one." They are favored by those who like to spend time outdoors. Typical features include terraces, patios, large glass viewing areas and private balconies—all stashed in private rear and side yards. The fronts are reserved for window space that provides plenty of natural light to interior rooms.

Indoors, Contemporary homes are designed for convenient living, catering to busy lifestyles. Open spaces, efficient kitchens, many large bathrooms and multi-purpose rooms provide the space for various activities to take place simultaneously.

Though found throughout the United States, Contemporary architecture naturally varies from region to region. In the Northwest, Contemporary architecture reflects its woodsy surroundings. Many of these homes include extended wood beams, exposed rafter tails, heavy shake roofs, dark-stained exteriors, rough-cut siding, wide overhangs and balconies. As with all successful architecture, Northwest Contemporaries fit their settings and are built with materials readily accessible in the area.

Contemporary homes of the Southwest incorporate Spanish and Indian details into their design. Masonry walls and concrete block or adobe washed with stucco are often employed. These homes use roof decks, porches, sheltered ramada areas, shady overhangs and large blank walls that face west to tolerate scorching heat. Central patios feature fountains and plants.

The Midwest ranch house was introduced after World War II and combines design from both east and west with a practical substitution of Midwest materials. Long, low lines with a sense of mass and self-enclosure characterizes these adaptations. Less formal than earlier Contemporary homes, Midwest versions put emphasis on space, freedom and the outdoors. Brick is the most popular building material.

Because Early American architecture reigns strongly in the Northeast, adaptations of this style can be seen even in Contemporary homes. Simple Cape Cod cottages have been modified to include larger, more open rooms and various outdoor living spaces. Modern floor plans and wider windows lend Contemporary features to traditional renditions.

In the South, Contemporary architecture demonstrates a compromise between traditional styling and modern lines. These homes employ rough, natural materials and a variety of shapes in informal designs. Stone, stained wood and other natural materials are used for texture.

The homes presented here represent a fine collection of the many forms and variations of Contemporary design. They range in type from cozy one-story ranches to grand multi-level plans and provide the lover of Contemporary homes a vast choice of sizes and looks. Their livability and buildability are second to none. Their lasting appeal is evident throughout this volume.

Design W3408

Square Footage: 2,406

L

● Interesting angles make for interesting rooms. The sleeping zone features two large bedrooms with unique shapes and a master suite with spectacular bath. A laundry placed nearby is both convenient and economical, located adjacent to a full bath. The central kitchen offers a desk and built-in breakfast table. Meals can also be enjoyed in the adjacent eating area, formal dining room with stepped ceiling, or outside on the rear patio. A planter and glass block wall separate the living room and family room, which is warmed by a fireplace.

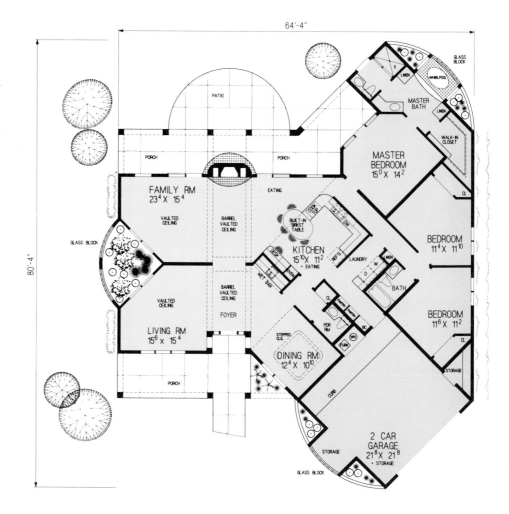

Design W3403

First Floor: 2,240 square feet
Second Floor: 660 square feet
Total: 2,900 square feet

L D

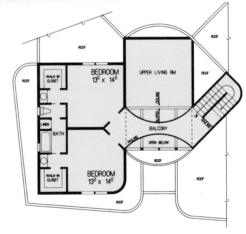

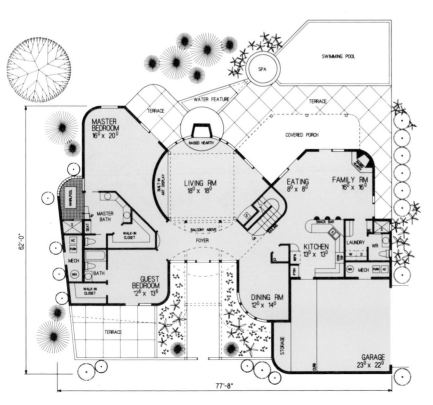

● There is no end to the distinctive features in this Southwestern contemporary. Formal living areas are concentrated in the center of the plan, perfect for entertaining. To the right of the plan, the kitchen and family room function well together as a working and living area. Also note the separate laundry room. The optional guest bedroom or den and the master bedroom are located to the left of the plan. Upstairs, the remaining two bedrooms are reached by a balcony overlooking the living room and share a bath with twin vanities.

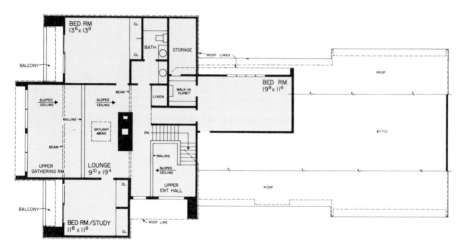

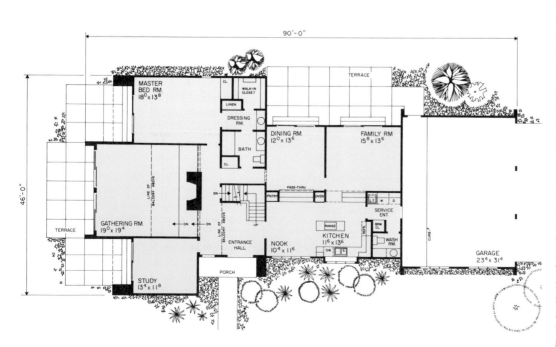

Design W2781

First Floor: 2,132 square feet
Second Floor: 1,156 square feet
Total: 3,288 square feet

L **D**

● This beautifully designed two-story has an eye-catching exterior. The floor plan is a perfect complement. The front kitchen features an island range, adjacent breakfast nook and pass-through to a formal dining room. The master bedroom suite has a spacious walk-in closet and dressing room. The side terrace can be reached from the master suite, the gathering room and the study. The second floor has three bedrooms and storage space galore. Also notice the lounge with sloped ceiling and skylight.

Design W3438

First Floor: 1,489 square feet
Second Floor: 741 square feet
Total: 2,230 square feet

L

● A unique farmhouse plan which provides a grand floor plan, this home is comfortable in country or suburban settings. Formal entertaining areas share first-floor space with family gathering rooms and work and service areas. The master suite is also on this floor for convenience and privacy. Upstairs is a guest bedroom, private bath and loft area that makes a perfect studio. Special features make this a great place to come home to.

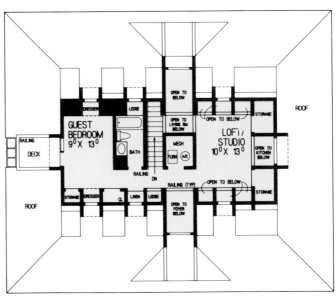

● This is most certainly an outstanding contemporary design. Study the exterior carefully before your journey to inspect the floor plan. The vertical lines are carried from the siding to the paned windows to the garage door. The front entry is recessed so the overhanging roof creates a covered porch.

Note the planter court with privacy wall. The floor plan is just as outstanding. The rear gathering room has a sloped ceiling, raised hearth fireplace, sliding glass doors to the terrace and a snack bar with pass-thru to the kitchen. In addition to the gathering room, there is the living room/study. This

room could be utilized in a variety of ways depending on your family's choice. The formal dining room is convenient to the U-shaped kitchen. Three bedrooms and two closely located baths are in the sleeping wing. This plan includes details for the construction of an optional basement.

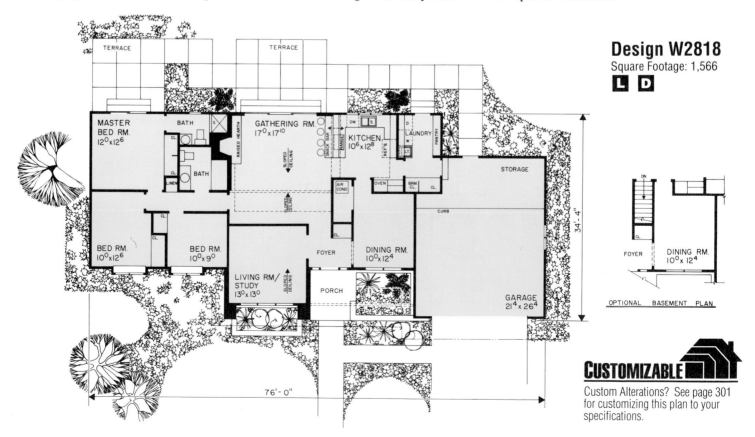

Design W2818
Square Footage: 1,566

L **D**

OPTIONAL BASEMENT PLAN

CUSTOMIZABLE
Custom Alterations? See page 301 for customizing this plan to your specifications.

● Something new? Something new, indeed!! Here is the introduction of two rooms which will make a wonderful contribution to family living. The clutter room is strategically placed between the kitchen and garage. It is the nerve center of the work area. It houses the laundry, provides space for sewing, has a large sorting table, and even plenty of space for the family's tool bench. A handy potting area is next to the laundry tray. Adjacent to

the clutter room, and a significant part of the planning of this whole zone, are the pantry and freezer with their near-by counter space. These facilities surely will expedite the unloading of groceries from the car and their convenient storing. Wardrobe and broom closets, plus washroom complete the outstanding utility of this area. The location of the clutter room with all its fine cabinet and counter space means that the often numerous family projects

can be on-going. This room is ideally isolated from the family's daily living patterns. The media room may be thought of as the family's entertainment center. While this is the room for the large or small TV, the home movies, the stereo and VCR equipment, it will serve as the library or study. It would be ideal as the family's home office with its computer equipment. Your family will decide just how it will utilize this outstanding area.

Design W2915
Square Footage: 2,758
L **D**

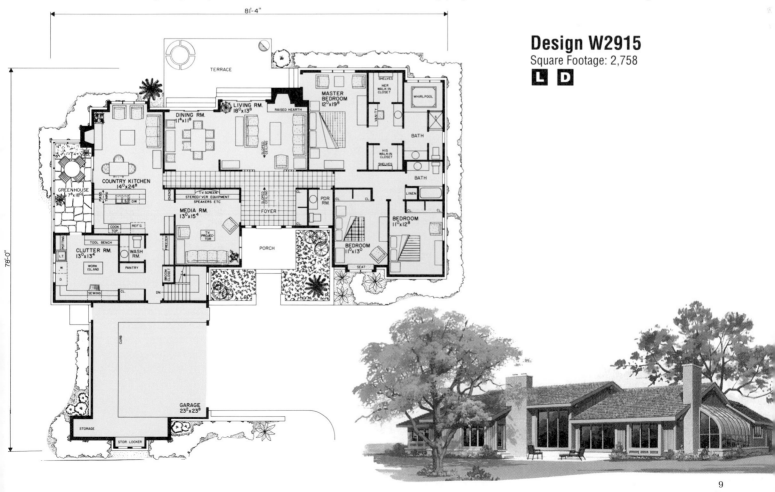

Design W3357

Square Footage: 2,913

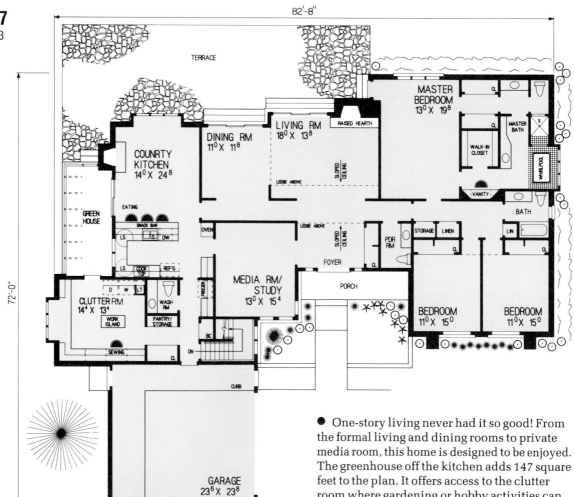

● One-story living never had it so good! From the formal living and dining rooms to private media room, this home is designed to be enjoyed. The greenhouse off the kitchen adds 147 square feet to the plan. It offers access to the clutter room where gardening or hobby activities can take place. A the opposite end of the house are a master bedroom with generous bath and two family bedrooms. Notice the wealth of built-ins throughout the house.

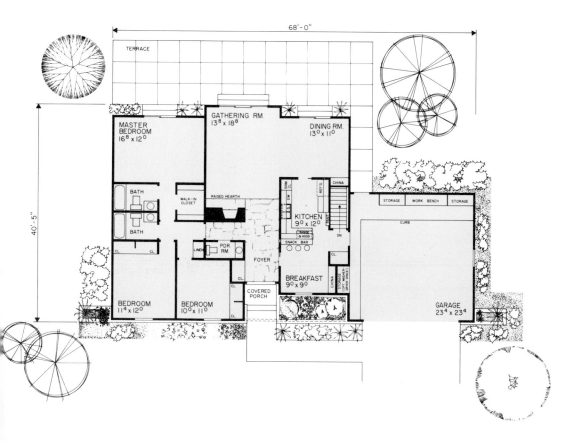

Design W2671
Square Footage: 1,589

L **D**

● The rustic exterior of this one-story home features vertical wood siding. The entry foyer is floored with flagstone and leads to the three areas of the plan: sleeping, living, and work center. The sleeping area has three bedrooms. The master bedroom has sliding glass doors to the rear terrace. The living area, consisting of gathering and dining rooms, also has access to the terrace. The work center is efficiently planned. It houses the kitchen with snack bar, breakfast room with built-in china cabinet and stairs to the basement. This is a very livable plan. Special amenities include a raised-hearth fireplace and a walk-in closet in the master bedroom.

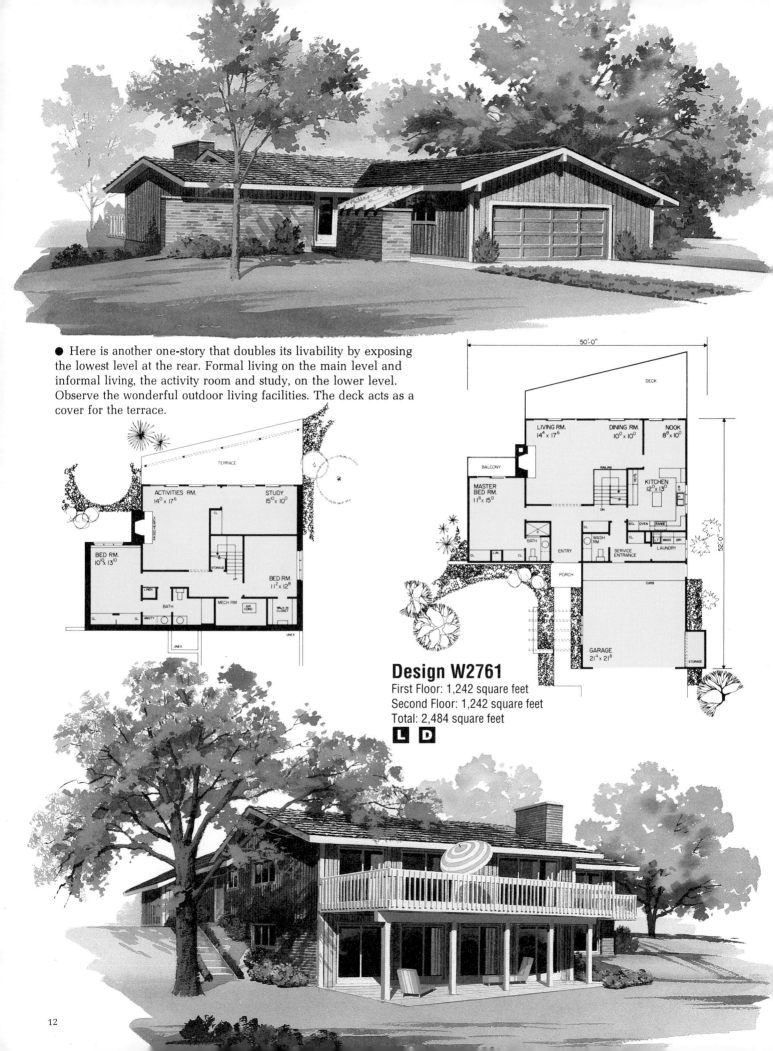

● Here is another one-story that doubles its livability by exposing the lowest level at the rear. Formal living on the main level and informal living, the activity room and study, on the lower level. Observe the wonderful outdoor living facilities. The deck acts as a cover for the terrace.

Lower Level Plan

TERRACE

ACTIVITIES RM.
14⁰ x 17⁶

STUDY
15¹⁰ x 10⁰

BED RM.
10⁰ x 13¹⁰

BED RM.
11² x 12⁸

CL.

STORAGE

UP

LINEN

BATH

MECH. RM.

AIR COND.

WALK IN CLOSET

VANITY

CL.

CL.

UNEX

UNEX

RAISED HEARTH

Main Level Plan

50'-0"

DECK

LIVING RM.
14⁴ x 17⁶

DINING RM.
10⁰ x 10⁰

NOOK
8⁸ x 10⁰

BALCONY

MASTER BED RM.
11⁸ x 15⁰

RAILING

REF'S.

KITCHEN
12⁰ x 13⁰

DN.

BATH

ENTRY

WASH RM.

SERVICE ENTRANCE

RECL.

OVEN

RANGE

WASH

DRY

LAUNDRY

CL.

LIN.

CL.

CL.

PORCH

CURB

52'-0"

GARAGE
21⁴ x 21⁸

STORAGE

Design W2761

First Floor: 1,242 square feet
Second Floor: 1,242 square feet
Total: 2,484 square feet

L **D**

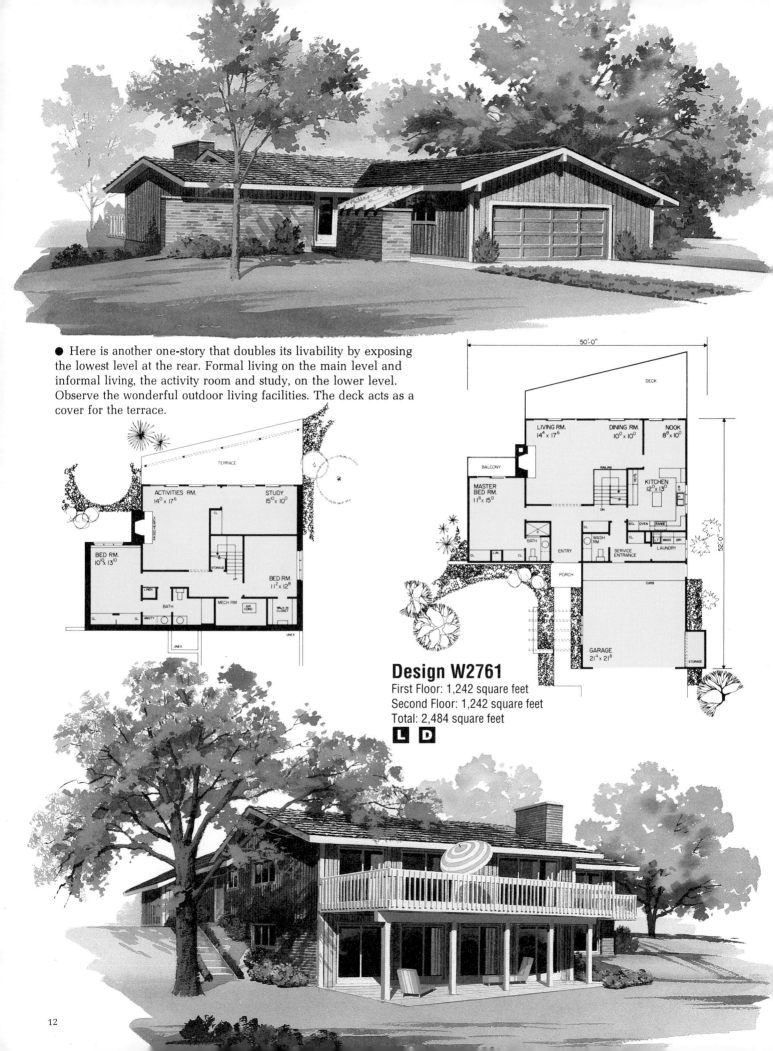

Design W2937 Main Level: 1,096 square feet
Upper Level: 1,115 square feet; Lower Level: 1,104 square feet; Total: 3,315 square feet

L

● This contemporary multi-level home features an extended rear balcony that covers a rear patio, plus a master bedroom suite, complete with whirlpool and raised-hearth pass-thru. Two other bedrooms and a second bath are on the upper level.

STORAGE 12⁸ x 8⁰

FUTURE BAR

ACTIVITIES RM. 23⁰ x 24⁸

STORAGE 12⁸ x 10⁰

FURN.

FURN.

UNEXCAVATED

CL.

UP

WASH RM.

UNEX.

BASEMENT PLAN

BALCONY

BEDROOM/ LOUNGE 10⁸ x 10⁴

BALCONY

MASTER BEDROOM 13⁰ x 21⁸

BEDROOM 13⁰ x 11⁴

SLOPED CEILING

SLOPED CEILING

OPTIONAL FIREPLACE

CL.

BATH

LINEN

SLOPED CEILING

SKYLIGHT

CL.

BATH

LINEN

CL.

CL.

SKYLIGHTS

SEWING/ HOBBIES

SLOPED CEILING

DN

UPPER FOYER

SLOPED CEILING

Design W2828
First Floor: 817 square feet-Living Area; Foyer & Laundry: 261 square feet
Second Floor: 852 square feet-Living Area; Foyer & Storage: 214 square feet; Total: 2,144 square feet

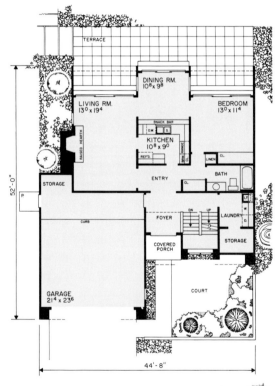

TERRACE

DINING RM. 10⁸ x 9⁸

LIVING RM. 13⁰ x 19⁴

BEDROOM 13⁰ x 11⁴

SNACK BAR

DW S

KITCHEN 10⁸ x 9⁰

RANGE

REF'S

LINEN CL.

RAISED HEARTH

ENTRY

BATH

STORAGE

CL.

P

52'-0"

CURB

DN UP

FOYER

LAUNDRY

W D

COVERED PORCH

STORAGE

GARAGE 21⁴ x 23⁶

COURT

44'-8"

● A fine contemporary design in two stories, this home also extends its livability to the basement where bonus space could be converted later to an activities or hobby room. On the first floor, living areas revolve around a central kitchen with snack bar in the dining room. The first-floor bedroom could also serve as a study, family room or library. Note the raised-hearth fireplace in the living room. Upstairs are three bedrooms, or two and a lounge, and a sewing or hobby room. Two long balconies here overlook the terrace below.

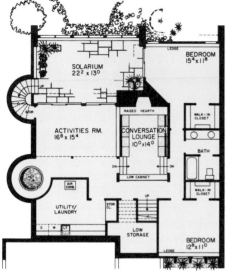

Design W2827

First Floor: 1,458 square feet
Second Floor: 1,618 square feet
Total: 3,076 square feet

L

● The towering, two-story solarium in this bi-level design is its key to energy savings. Study the efficiency of this floor plan. The conversation lounge on the lower level is a unique focal point.

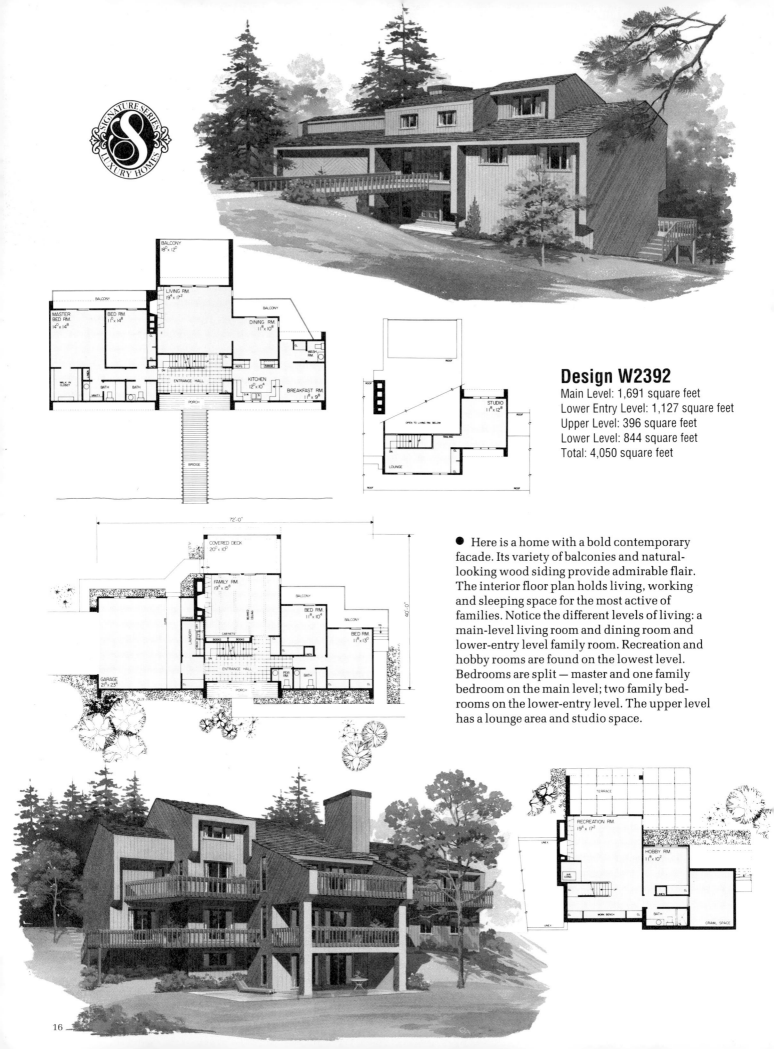

Design W2392

Main Level: 1,691 square feet
Lower Entry Level: 1,127 square feet
Upper Level: 396 square feet
Lower Level: 844 square feet
Total: 4,050 square feet

● Here is a home with a bold contemporary
facade. Its variety of balconies and natural-
looking wood siding provide admirable flair.
The interior floor plan holds living, working
and sleeping space for the most active of
families. Notice the different levels of living: a
main-level living room and dining room and
lower-entry level family room. Recreation and
hobby rooms are found on the lowest level.
Bedrooms are split — master and one family
bedroom on the main level; two family bedrooms on the lower-entry level. The upper level
has a lounge area and studio space.

Design W3368

Square Footage: 2,722

L **D**

● Roof lines are the key to the interesting exterior of this design. Their configuration allow for sloped ceilings in the gathering room and large foyer. The master bedroom suite has a huge walk-in closet, garden whirlpool and separate shower. Two family bedrooms share a full bath. One of these bedrooms could be used as a media room with pass-through wet bar. Note the large kitchen with conversation bay and the wide terrace to the rear.

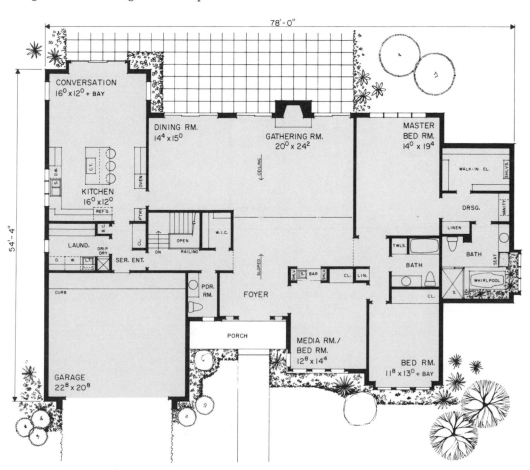

Design W2795

Square Footage: 1,952

● This three-bedroom design leaves no room for improvement. Any size family will find it difficult to surpass the fine qualities that this home offers. Begin with the exterior. This fine contemporary design has open trellis work above the front, covered private court. This area is sheltered by a privacy wall extending from the projecting garage. Inside, the floor plan will be just as breathtaking. Begin at the foyer and choose a direction. To the left is the sleeping wing equipped with three bedrooms and two baths. Straight ahead from the foyer is the gathering room with through-fireplace to the dining room. To the right is the work center. This area includes a breakfast room, a U-shaped kitchen and laundry.

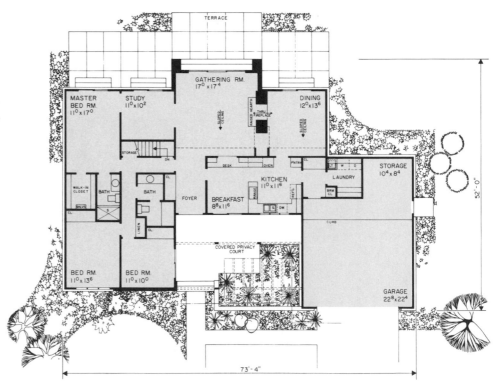

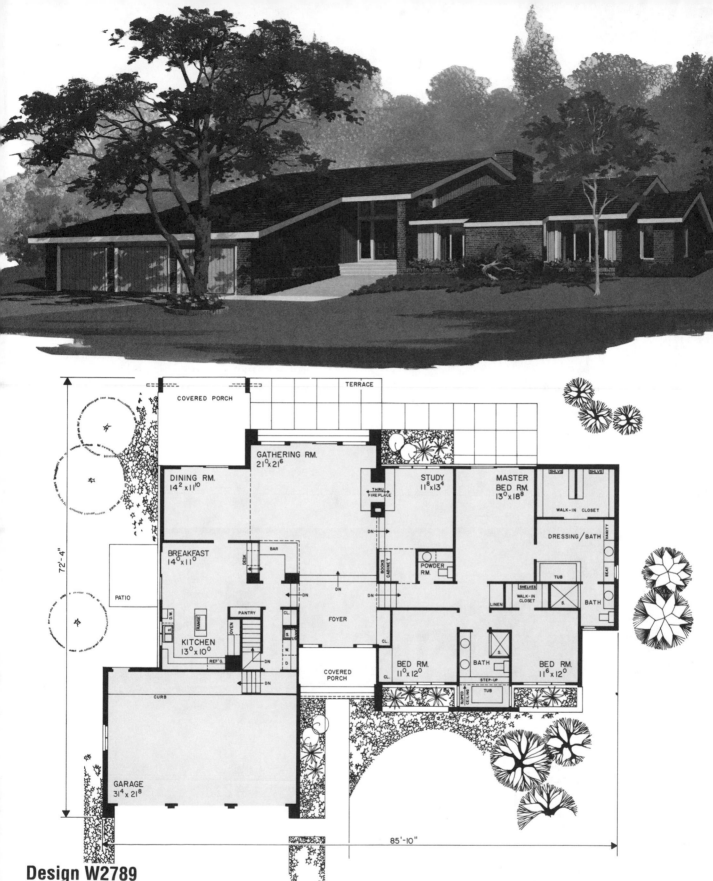

Design W2789
Square Footage: 2,732

L **D**

● An attached three car garage! What a fantastic feature of this three bedroom contemporary design. And there's more. As one walks up the steps to the covered porch and through the double front doors the charm of this design will be overwhelming. Inside, a large foyer greets all visitors and leads them to each of the three areas, each down a few steps. The living area has a large gathering room with fireplace and a study adjacent on one side and the formal dining room on the other. The work center has an efficient kitchen with island range, breakfast room, laundry and built-in desk and bar. Then there is the sleeping area. Note the raised tub with sloped ceiling.

Design W2717
Square Footage: 2,310

● A perfect family plan, this home has a spacious family room in addition to the oversized gathering room. A work-efficient kitchen, featuring a built-in desk and pass-through to the family room, is near to the formal dining room. The three-bedroom sleeping wing contains a master suite and two family bedrooms. Terrace access through sliding glass doors in the master bedroom are a welcome amenity.

Design W2730
Square Footage: 2,490

D

● Here is a basic one-story home loaded with amenities. The central living area of the home includes the gathering room, formal dining room and study. The L-shaped kitchen has an adjacent family room with eating area and an island cooktop. Three bedrooms share space in the sleeping wing of the house. The master has two walk-in closets.

Design W2797

Square Footage: 1,791

● The exterior appeal of this delightful one-story is sure to catch the attention of all who pass by. The overhanging roof adds an extra measure of shading along with the privacy wall which shelters the front court and entry. The floor plan also will be outstanding to include both leisure and formal activities. The gathering room has a sloped ceiling, silding glass door to rear terrace and a through-fireplace to the family room. This room also has access to the terrace and includes the informal eating area. A pass-through from the U-shaped kitchen to the eating area makes serving a breeze. Formal dining can be done in the front dining room. The laundry area is adjacent to the kitchen and garage and houses a washroom. Peace and quiet can be achieved in the study. The sleeping zone consists of three bedrooms and two full back-to-back baths. Additional space will be found in the basement.

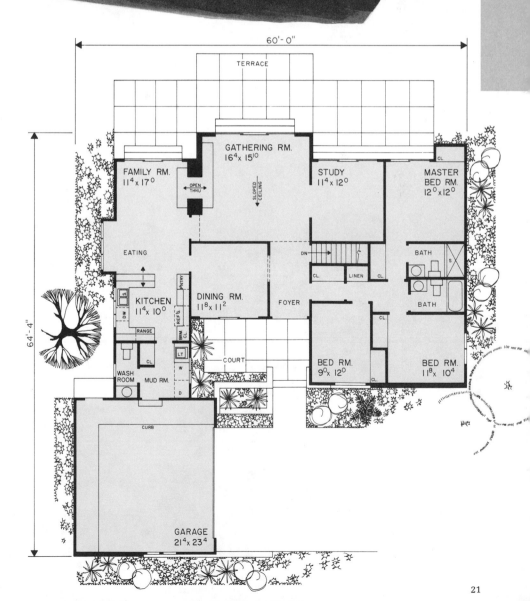

Design W1389

Square Footage: 1,488

D

● Your choice of exterior goes with this outstanding floor plan. If you like French Provincial, Design W1389 is your choice. If you prefer the simple, straightforward lines of contemporary plans, Design W1387 will be your favorite. For the warmth of Colonial adaptations, the charming exterior of design W1388 is perfect. Note the differences in the three plans: window treatment, roof lines and other details.

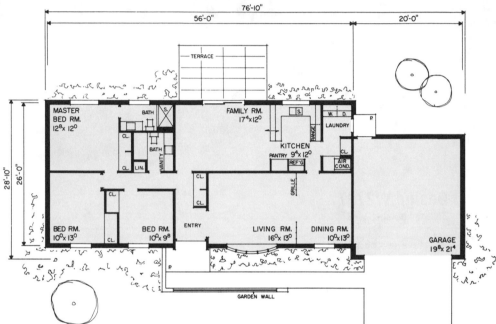

Design W1387

Square Footage: 1,488

D

Design W1388

Square Footage: 1,488

D

Design W2528
Square Footage: 1,754

D

● This inviting, U-shaped western ranch adaptation offers outstanding living potential behind its double front doors. In only 1,754 square feet there are three bedrooms, 2½ baths, a formal living room and an informal family room, a functional kitchen, an adjacent breakfast nook and good storage facilities. Note the raised-hearth fireplace and sloped ceiling.

Design W2753
Square Footage: 1,539

D

● Projecting the attached garage from the front line of the house makes a lot of economic sense and leads to interesting roof lines and plan configurations. Here, a pleasing covered walkway to the front door results. A privacy wall adds an extra measure of design appeal and provides a sheltered terrace for the study/bedroom. It would be difficult to find more livability in 1,539 square feet with three bedrooms, two baths, a spacious living/dining area and a family room.

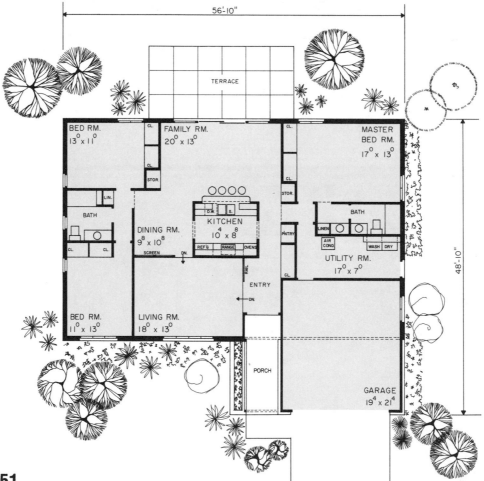

Design W2351
Square Footage: 1,862

D

● The extension of the wide overhanging roof of this distinctive home provides shelter for the walkway to the front door. A raised brick planter adds appeal to the outstanding exterior design. The living patterns offered by this plan are delightfully different, yet extremely practical. Notice the separation of the master bedroom from the other two bedrooms. While assuring an extra measure of quiet privacy for the parents, this master bedroom location may be ideal for a live-in-relative. Locating the kitchen in the middle of the plan frees up valuable outside wall space and leads to interesting planning. The front living room is sunken for dramatic appeal and need not have any cross-room traffic. The utility room houses the laundry and the heating and cooling equipment.

Design W2199
Square Footage: 1,185

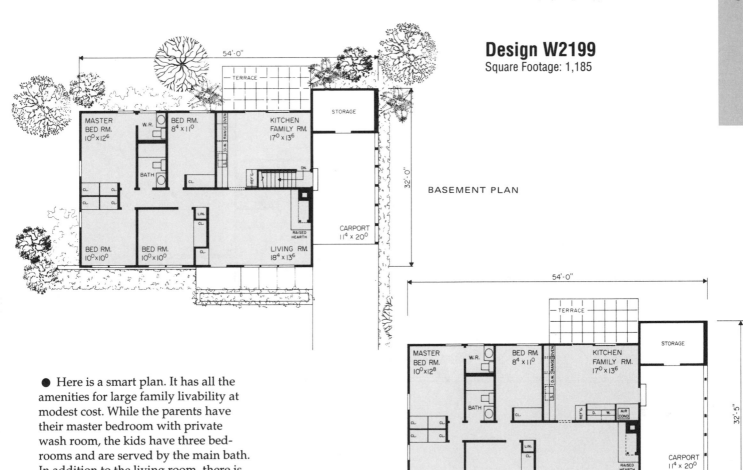

BASEMENT PLAN

NON BASEMENT PLAN

● Here is a smart plan. It has all the amenities for large family livability at modest cost. While the parents have their master bedroom with private wash room, the kids have three bedrooms and are served by the main bath. In addition to the living room, there is extra livability to be enjoyed in the spacious family area which has access to the rear terrace. Don't miss all those closets or the bulk storage room of the carport. Blueprints include optional basement and non-basement details.

Design W2793
Square Footage: 2,065

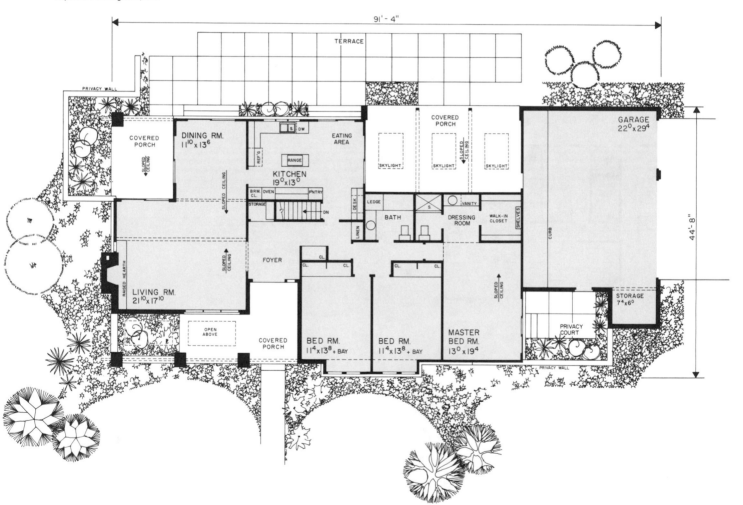

● Privacy will be enjoyed in this home both inside and out. The indoor-outdoor living relationships offered in this plan are outstanding. A covered porch at the entrance. A privacy court off the master bedroom divided from the front yard with a privacy wall. A covered porch serving both the living and dining rooms through sliding glass doors. Also utilizing a privacy wall. Another covered porch off the kitchen eating area. This one is the largest and has skylights above. Also a large rear terrace. The kitchen is efficient with eating space available, an island range and built-in desk. Storage space is abundant. Note storage area in the garage and its overall size. Three front bedrooms. Raised-hearth fireplace in the living room.

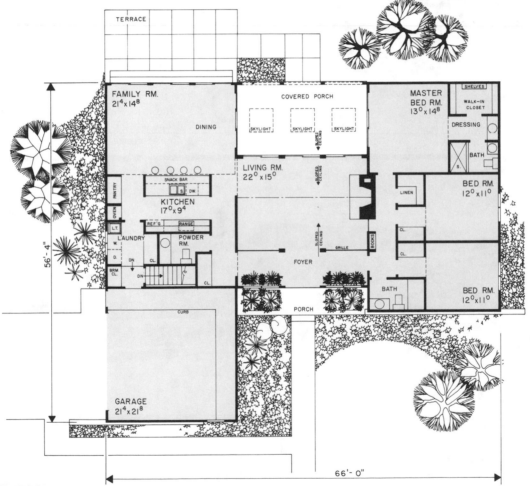

Design W2790
Square Footage: 2,075

● Enter this comtemporary hip-roofed home through the double front doors and immediately view the sloped-ceil-inged living room with fireplace. This room will be a sheer delight when it comes to formal entertaining. It has easy access to the kitchen and also a powder room nearby. The work area will be convenient. The kitchen has an island work center with snack bar. The laundry is adjacent to the service en-trance and stairs leading to the base-ment. This area is planned to be a real "step saver". The sleeping wing con-sists of two family bedrooms, bath and master bedroom suite. Maybe the most attractive feature of this design is the rear covered porch with skylights above. It is accessible by way of slid-ing glass doors in the family/dining area, living room and master bedroom.

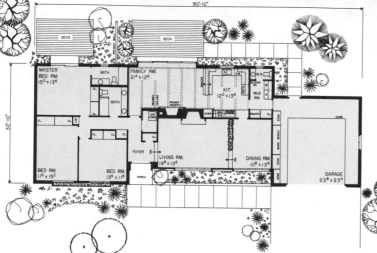

Design W1891
Square Footage: 1,986

● There is much more to a house than just its exterior. And while the appeal of this home would be difficult to beat, it is the living potential of the interior that gives the design such a high ranking. The sunken living room with its adjacent dining room is highlighted by the attractive fireplace, the raised planter and the distinctive glass panels. A raised-hearth fireplace, snack bar and sliding glass doors which open to the outdoor deck are features of the family room. The work center area is efficient. It has plenty of storage space and a laundry area.

Design W1396
Square Footage: 1,664

● Three bedrooms, 2½ baths, a formal dining area, a fine family room and an attached two-car garage are among the highlights of this frame home. The living-dining area is delightfully spacious with the fireplace wall, having book shelves at each end, functioning as a practical area divider. The many storage units found in this home will be a topic of conversion. The cabinets above the strategically located washer and dryer, the family room storage wall and walk-in closet and the garage facilities are particulary noteworthy. Blueprints show how to build this house with and without a basement.

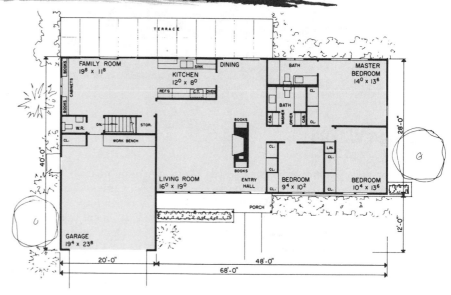

Design W1305

Square Footage: 1,382

D

● Order blueprints for any one of the three exteriors shown on these two pages and you will receive details for building the outstanding floor plan at right. In less than 1,400 square feet there are three bedrooms, two full baths, a separate dining room, a formal living room, a fine kitchen overlooking the rear yard, and an informal family room. In addition, there is the attached two-car garage. Note the location of the stairs when this plan is built with a basement. Each of the exteriors is predominantly brick — the front of Design N1305 features both stone and vertical boards and battens with brick on the other three sides. Design N1382 and Design N1383 both have double front doors.

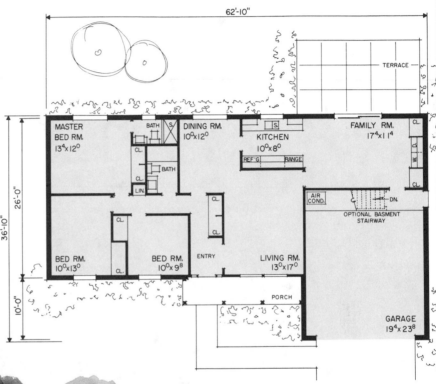

62'-10"

36'-10"

26'-0"

10'-0"

TERRACE

MASTER BED RM. 13⁴x12⁰

BATH

DINING RM. 10⁰x12⁰

KITCHEN 10⁰x8⁰

FAMILY RM. 17⁴x11⁴

BATH

REF'G

RANGE

AIR COND.

DN.

OPTIONAL BASMENT STAIRWAY

BED RM. 10⁰x13⁰

BED RM. 10⁰x9⁸

ENTRY

LIVING RM. 13⁰x17⁰

PORCH

GARAGE 19⁴x23⁸

Design W1382

Square Footage: 1,382

D

Design W1383

Square Footage: 1,382

D

Design W2764
Square Footage: 2,946

● If uniqueness is what you seek, this home will be ideal. Notice the large, gated-in entry court, vertical paned windows and contrasting exterior materials. The entry/dining area has a built-in planter with a skylight above. The living and family rooms both have an attractive sloped ceiling. They share a raised-hearth, through-fireplace and both have access to the large wraparound terrace. The kitchen/nook area also has access to the terrace and features a snack bar, built-in desk and large butler's pantry.

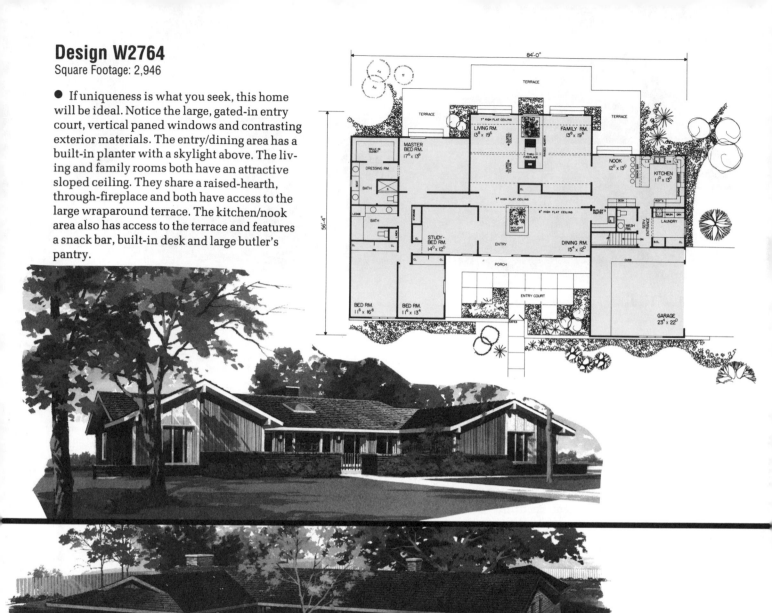

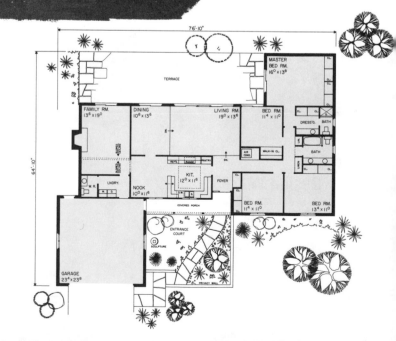

Design W2329
Square Footage: 2,268

● Brick privacy walls create for this design an inviting entrance court. Such an area provides a pleasing view from the kitchen and the nook. Front porch sitting will have its privacy as well as appealing atmosphere. The center entrance is but a few steps from the main areas of the plan. Four bedrooms and two baths will serve the growing family well. Note that two of the bedrooms have direct access to the terrace. Closet space is outstanding. The living and dining rooms encompass a large area with the living room well-defined by being sunken one step. The sloped ceiling family room with its commanding fireplace is off by itself. The laundry and washroom are well situated.

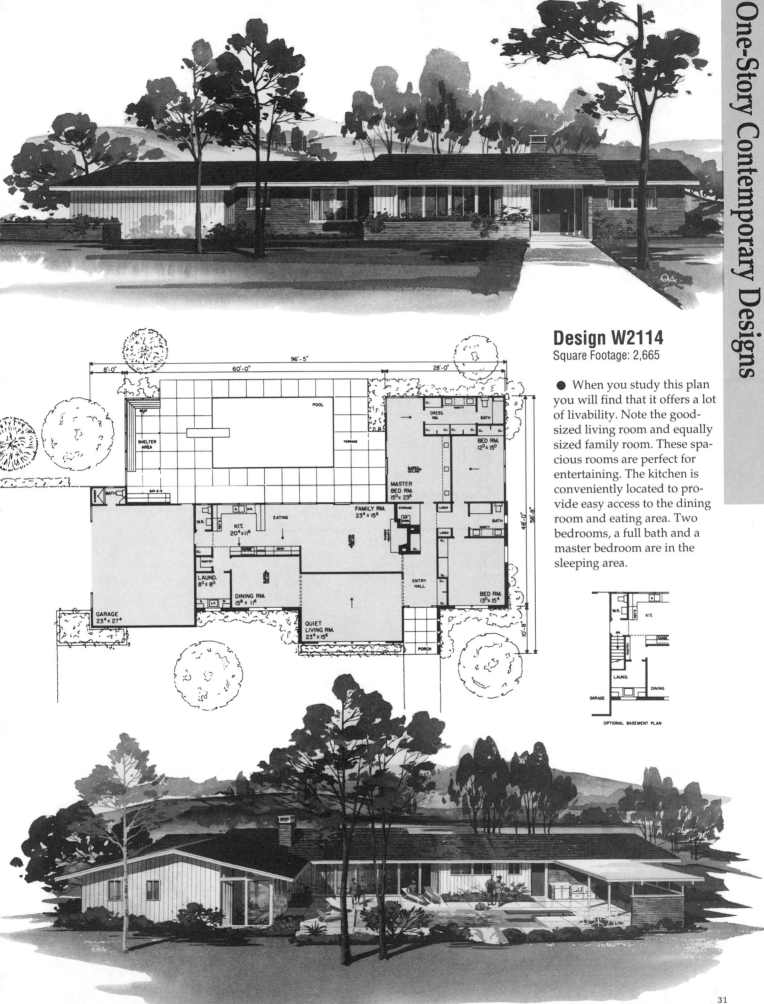

Design W2114
Square Footage: 2,665

● When you study this plan you will find that it offers a lot of livability. Note the good-sized living room and equally sized family room. These spacious rooms are perfect for entertaining. The kitchen is conveniently located to provide easy access to the dining room and eating area. Two bedrooms, a full bath and a master bedroom are in the sleeping area.

OPTIONAL BASEMENT PLAN

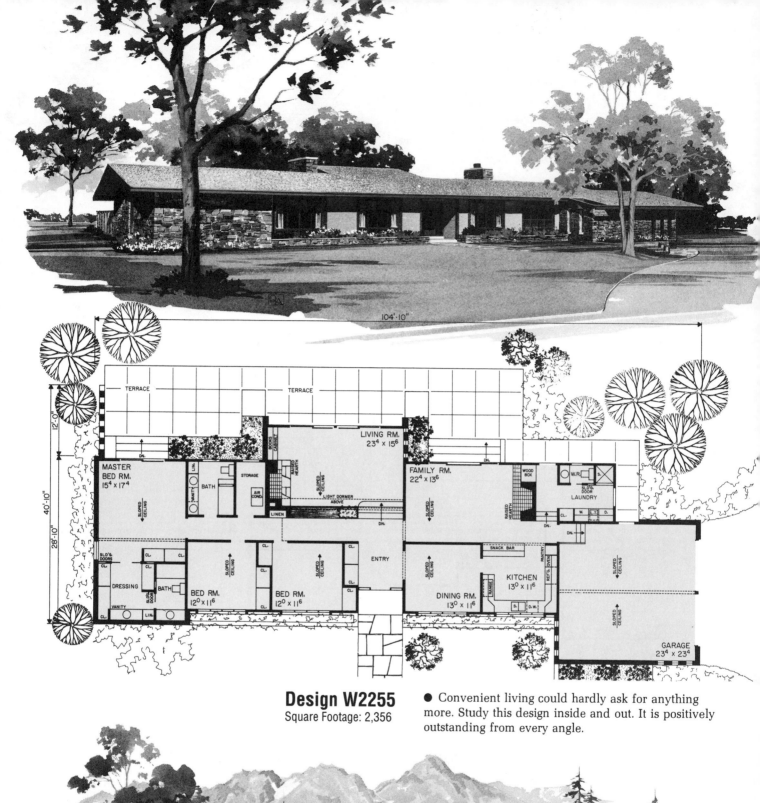

TERRACE

TERRACE

LIVING RM.
23⁴ x 15⁶

MASTER
BED RM.
15⁴ x 17⁴

FAMILY RM.
22⁴ x 13⁶

BATH

STORAGE

AIR COND.

LAUNDRY

LIGHT DORMER ABOVE

LINEN

DRESSING

BATH

BED RM.
12⁰ x 11⁶

BED RM.
12⁰ x 11⁶

ENTRY

SNACK BAR

PANTRY

DINING RM.
13⁰ x 11⁶

KITCHEN
13⁰ x 11⁶

GARAGE
23⁴ x 23⁴

104'-10"

40'-10"

28'-10"

12'-0"

Design W2255
Square Footage: 2,356

● Convenient living could hardly ask for anything more. Study this design inside and out. It is positively outstanding from every angle.

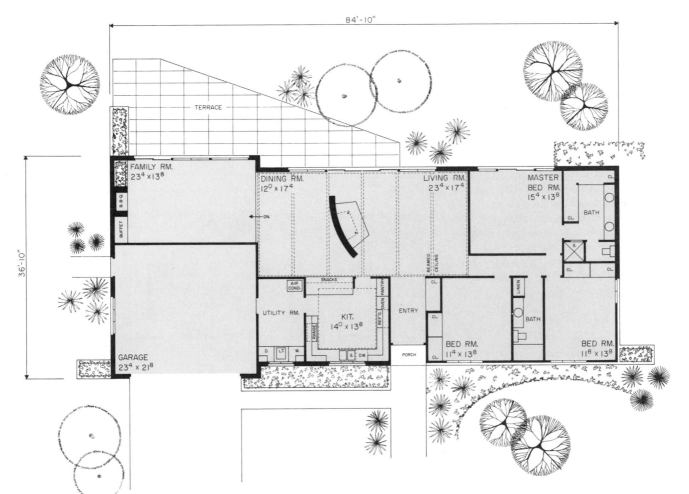

Design W2303

Square Footage: 2,330

● This hip-roof ranch home has a basic floor plan that is the favorite of many. The reasons for its popularity are, of course, easy to detect. The simple rectangular shape means relatively economical construction. The living areas are large and are located to the rear to function through sliding glass doors with the terrace. The front kitchen is popular because of its view of approaching callers and its proximity to the front entry. The big utility room serves as a practical buffer between the garage and the kitchen.

Worthy of particular note is the efficiency of the kitchen, the stylish living room fireplace, the beamed ceiling, the sunken family room with its wall of built-ins (make that a music wall if you wish). Observe the snack bar and the fine master bath.

Design W2892

Square Footage: 1,623

● What a striking contemporary! It houses an efficient floor plan with many outstanding features. The foyer has a sloped ceiling and an open staircase to the basement. To the right of the foyer is the work center. Note the snack bar, laundry and covered dining porch, along with the step-saving kitchen. Both the gathering and dining rooms overlook the backyard. Each of three bedrooms has access to an outdoor area. The second-floor loft could be used as a sewing room, den or lounge.

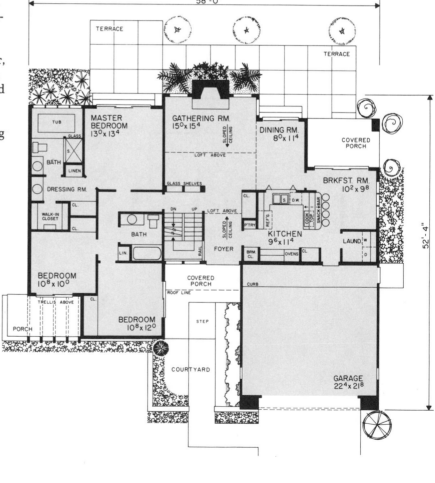

Design W2805
Square Footage: 1,547

L D

● Three completely different exterior facades share one compact, practical and economical floor plan. The major design variations are roof pitch, window placement and garage openings. Each design will hold its own when comparing the three exteriors. The design on the left is a romantic stone-and-shingle cottage design. This design, along with the other two designs presented here, is outstanding.

Design W2806
Square Footage: 1,584

L D

● This Tudor version of the plan is also very appealing. The living/dining room expands across the rear of the plan and has direct access to the covered porch. Notice the built-in planter adjacent to the open staircase leading to the basement.

Design W2807
Square Footage: 1,576

L D

● The contemporary version may be your choice. In addition to living/dining areas, there is a breakfast room that overlooks the covered porch. A desk, snack bar and mud room house laundry facilities and are near the U-shaped kitchen. The master bedroom has a private bath.

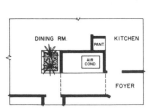

OPTIONAL NON-BASEMENT

DINING RM. KITCHEN
PANT.
AIR COND.
FOYER

58'-0"

50'-4"

COVERED PORCH
SKYLIGHT SKYLIGHT SKYLIGHT

BRKFST. RM.
13⁴ x 11¹⁰

LIVING RM.
13⁴ x 17²

DINING RM.
8⁰ x 9¹⁰

MUD RM.

STORAGE

SNACK BAR
DW S
KITCHEN
13⁴ x 9⁶
OVEN REF'G.
RANGE
LT W D
CURB

FOYER

TV/STUDY
BEDROOM
10⁰ x 10⁴

COVERED
PORCH

GARAGE
19⁸ x 19⁰ + STOR.

BATH

BATH

WALK-IN
CLOSET LIN

MASTER
BEDROOM
13⁶ x 12⁰

BEDROOM
13⁶ x 10⁸ + BAY

Design W2591
Square Footage: 1,428

● Good times and easy work! There's an efficient kitchen with lots of work space and a large storage pantry. Plus a separate breakfast nook to make casual meals convenient and pleasant. This home creates its own peaceful environment! It's especially pleasing to people who love the outdoors.

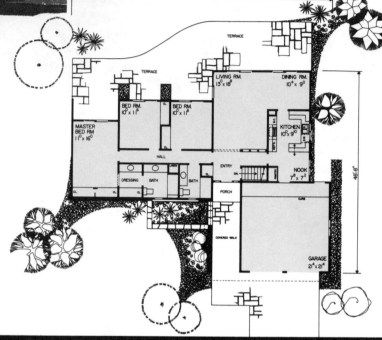

Design W2330
Square Footage: 1,854

● Your family will never tire of the living patterns offered by this appealing home with its low-pitched, wide over-hanging roof. The masonry masses of the exterior are pleasing. While the blueprints call for the use of stone, you may wish to substitute brick veneer. Sloping ceiling and plenty of glass will assure the living area of a fine feeling of spaciousness. The covered porches enhance the enjoyment of outdoor living. Two baths serve the three-bedroom sleeping area.

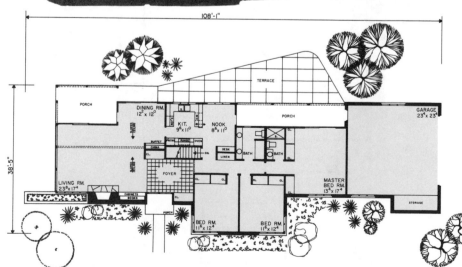

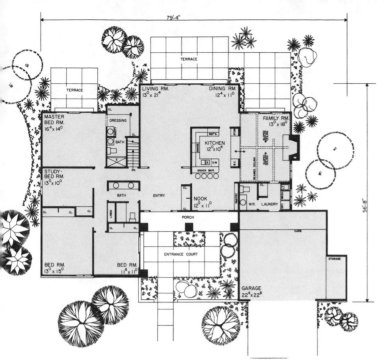

Design W2529
Square Footage: 2,326

● The front entrance court with its plant area and surrounding accents of colorful quarried stone (make it brick, if you prefer), provides a delightful introduction to this interesting contemporary home. The spacious entry hall leads directly to a generous L-shaped living and dining area. Sliding glass doors provide direct access to the outdoor terrace. An efficient, interior kitchen will be fun in which to work. It could hardly be more strategically located—merely a step or two from the formal dining area, the breakfast nook, and the family room. Although this home has a basement, there is a convenient first-floor laundry and an extra washroom. The four-bedroom sleeping wing has two full baths. Two of the rooms have access to the outdoor terrace. Notice garage storage.

Design W2532
Square Footage: 2,112

● Here is a refreshing, modified U-shaped contemporary that is long on both looks and livability. The board-and-batten exterior creates simple lines which are complemented by the low-pitched roof with its wide overhang and exposed rafters. The appeal of the front court is enhanced by the massive stone columns at the edge of the covered porch. A study of the floor plan reveals interestingly different and practical living patterns. The location of the entry hall represents a fine conservation of space for the living areas. The L-shaped formal living-dining zone has access to both front and rear yards. The informal living area is a true family kitchen. Its open planning produces a spacious and cheerful area. Note sloping, beamed ceiling, raised-hearth fireplace and sliding glass doors.

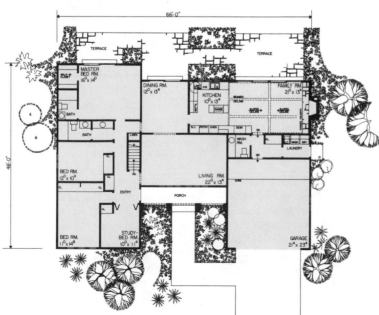

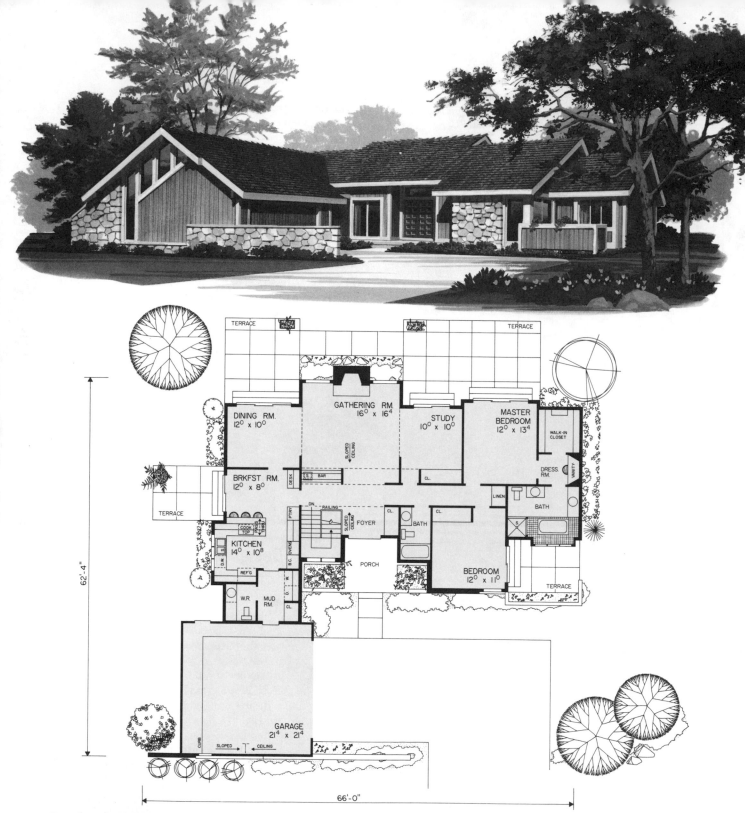

Design W2918
Square Footage: 1,693

D

● An exciting contemporary facade with fieldstone, vertical siding and interesting roof lines. The projecting garage creates a pleasing drive court as the impressive approach to this moderately-sized home. Double front doors open into a spacious foyer. Traffic is efficiently routed to all areas of the interior. Of particular interest is the open staircase to the lower level basement. Sloped ceilings in this area and the gathering room, along with the open planning reinforce the delightful feeling of spaciousness. The U-shaped kitchen is handy to the utility area and works well with the formal and informal dining areas. Like the dining room, the study flanks the gathering room. Open planning makes this 38 foot wide area a cheerful one, indeed. The master bedroom suite features a big walk-in closet, a dressing area with vanity and an outstanding bath. Note the terraces.

Design W2866

Square Footage: 2,371

● An extra living unit has been built into the design of this home. It would make an excellent "mother-in-law" suite. Should you choose not to develop this area as indicated, maybe you might use it as two more bedrooms, a guest suite or even as hobby and game rooms. Whatever its final use, it will complement the rest of this home. The main house also deserves mention. The focal point will be the large gathering room. Its features include a skylight, sloped ceiling, centered fireplace flanked on both sides by sliding glass doors and adjacent is a dining room on one side, study on the other. The work center is clustered together. Three bedrooms and two baths make up the private area. Note the outdoor areas: court with privacy wall, two covered porches and a large terrace.

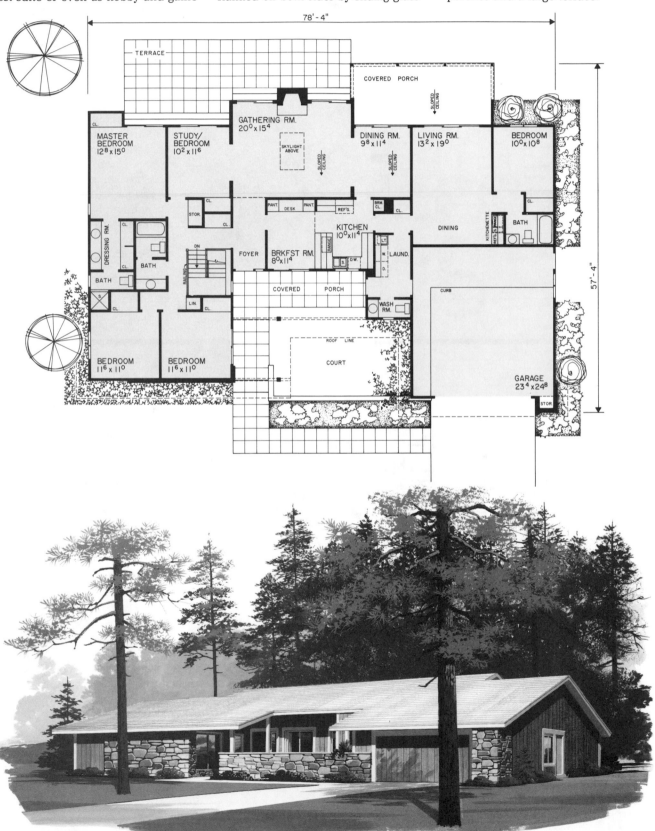

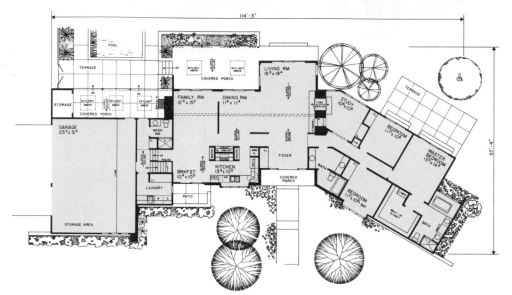

Design W2819
Square Footage: 2,459

● Indoor-outdoor living will be enjoyed to the fullest in this rambling one-story contemporary plan. Each of the rear rooms in this design, excluding the study, has access to a terrace or porch. Even the front breakfast room has access to a private dining patio. The covered porch off the living rooms has a sloped ceiling and skylights. A built-in barbecue unit and a storage room will be found on the second covered porch. Inside, the plan offers exceptional living patterns for various activities. Notice the through-fireplace that the living room shares with the study. A built-in etagere is nearby. The three-car garage has an extra storage area.

Design W2796
Square Footage: 1,828

● This home features a front living room with sloped ceiling and sliding glass doors which lead to a front private court. What a delightful way to introduce this design. This bi-nuclear design has a great deal to offer. First—the children's and parent's sleeping quarters are on opposite ends of this house to assure the utmost in privacy. Each area has its own full bath. The interior kitchen is a great idea. It frees up valuable wall space for the living area's exclusive use. There is a snack bar in the kitchen/family room for those very informal meals. Also, a planning desk is in the family room. The dining room is conveniently located near the kitchen plus it has a built-in china cabinet The laundry area has plenty of storage closets plus the stairs to the basement.

Design W2756

Square Footage: 2,652

L **D**

● This impressive one-story has numerous fine features that will assure the best in contemporary living. The sunken gathering room and dining room with an impressive sloped ceiling are the highlight of this plan; a series of three sliding glass doors provide access to the terrace. The family room, with a cozy fireplace, offers an ideal spot for informal entertaining. The kitchen features an efficient work island, pantry, and built-in desk. The master bedroom opens to the rear terrace, and the bath offers a separate step-up tub and shower. Two additional bedrooms are located at the front of the home.

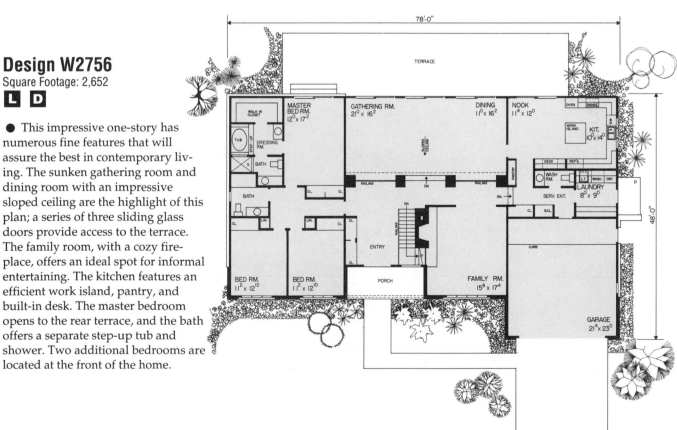

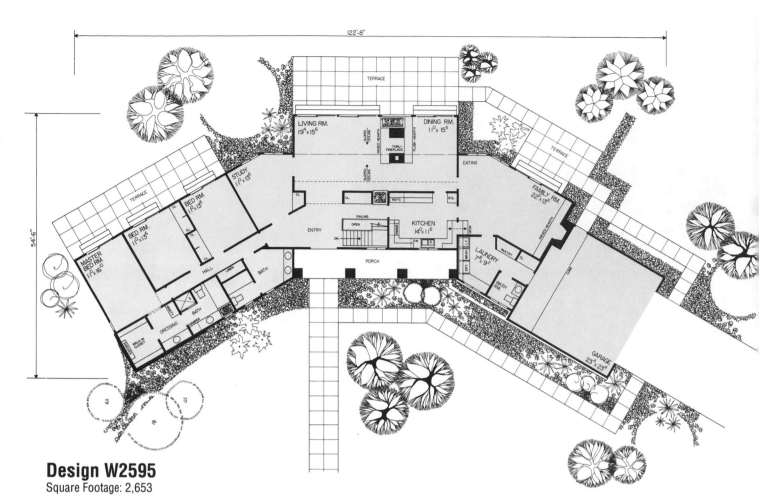

Design W2595
Square Footage: 2,653

● A winged design puts everything in the right place! At the center, formal living and dining rooms with sloped ceiling share one fireplace for added charm. Sliding glass doors in both rooms open onto the main terrace. In the right wing, there is a spacious family room with another raised hearth fireplace, built-in desk, dining area and adjoining smaller terrace. Also, a first floor laundry with pantry and half bath. A study, the master suite and family bedrooms (all bedrooms having access to a third terrace) plus baths are in the left wing. This home has a floor plan that helps you organize your life. Notice the open staircase leading to the basement.

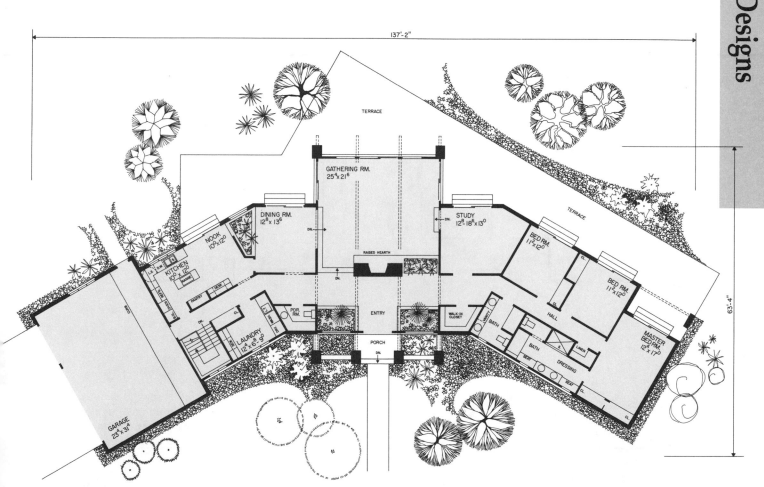

Design W2720
Square Footage: 3,130

● A raised hearth fireplace lights up the sunken gathering room which is exceptionally large and located at the very center of this home! For more living space, a well-located study and formal dining room each having a direct entrance to the gathering room. Plus a kitchen with all the right features . . . an island range, pantry, built-in desk and separate breakfast nook. There's an extended terrace, too . . . accessible from every room! And a master suite with double closets, dressing room and private bath. Plus two family bedrooms, a first-floor laundry and lots of storage space. A basement too, for additional space. This is a liveable home! You can entertain easily or you can hideout with a good book. Study this plan with your family and pick out your favorite features. Don't miss the dramatic front entry planting areas, or the extra curb area in the garage.

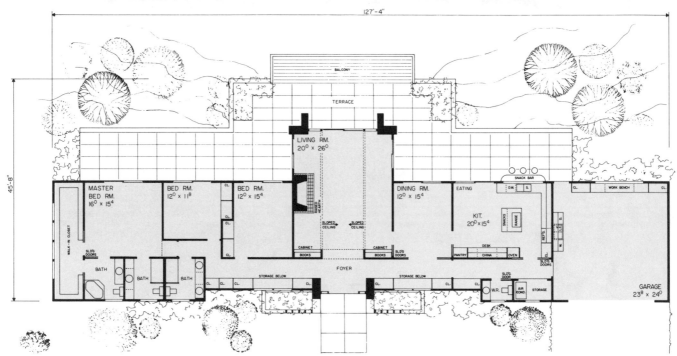

Design W2256
Square Footage: 2,632

● A dream home for those with young ideas. A refreshing, contemporary exterior with a unique, highly individualized interior. What are your favorite features.

Design W2534

Square Footage: 3,262

L

● The angular wings of this ranch home surely contribute to the unique character of the exterior. These wings effectively balance what is truly a dramatic and inviting front entrance. Massive masonry walls support the wide overhanging roof with its exposed wood beams. The patterned double front doors are surrounded by delightful expanses of glass. The raised planters and the masses of quarried stone (make it brick if you prefer) enhance the exterior appeal. Inside, a distinctive and practical floor plan stands ready to shape and serve the living patterns of the active family. The spacious entrance hall highlights sloped ceiling and an attractive open stairway to the lower level recreation area. An impressive fireplace and an abundance of glass are features of the big gathering room. Interestingly shaped dining room and study flank this main living area. The large kitchen offers many of the charming aspects of the family-kitchen of yesteryear. The bedroom wing has a sunken master suite.

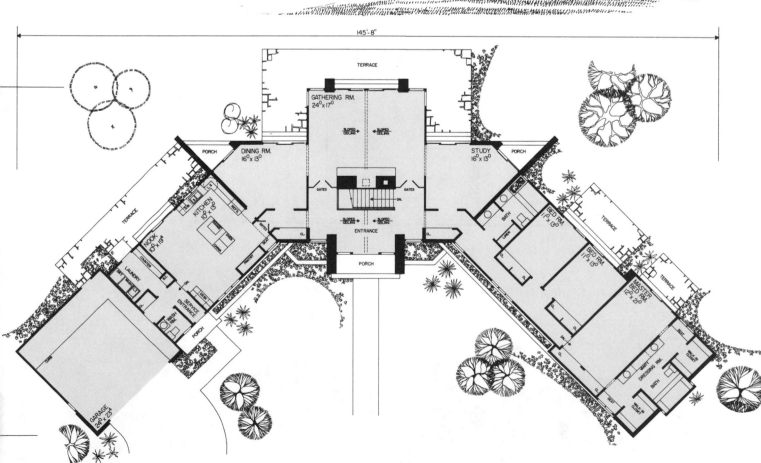

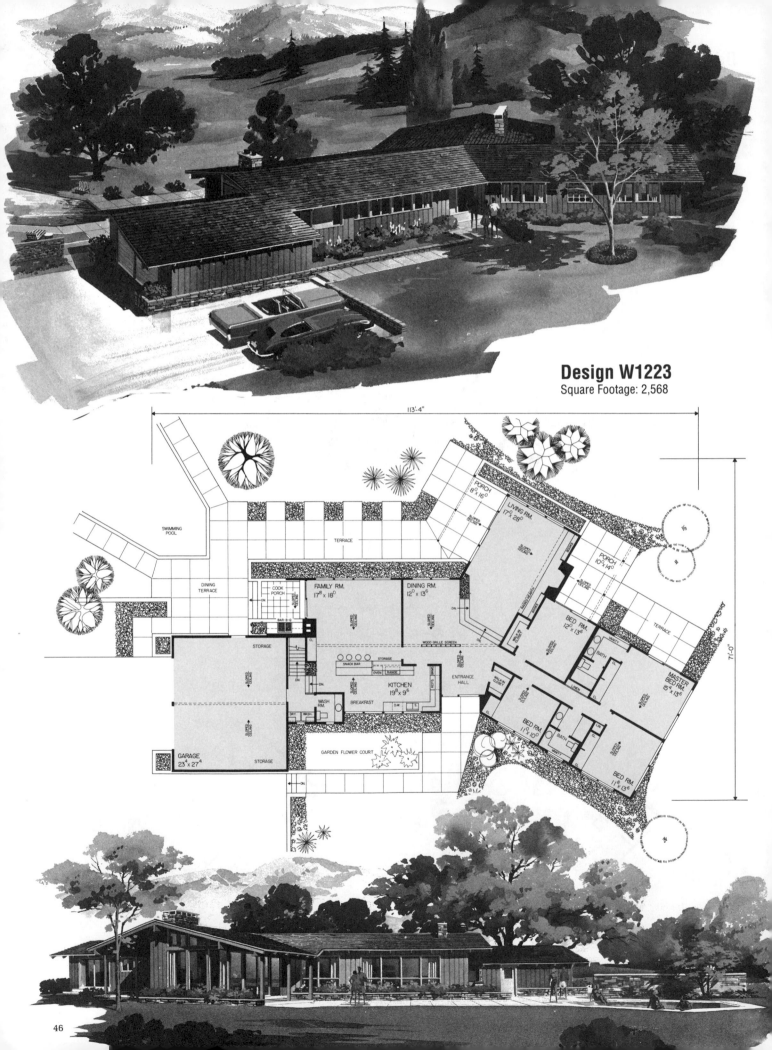

Design W1223
Square Footage: 2,568

Design W2304

Square Footage: 2,313

● What an appealing home! And what a list of reasons why it is so eye-catching. First of all, there is the irregular shape and the low-pitched, wide-overhanging roof. Then, there is the interesting use of exterior materials, including vertical glass window treatment. Further, there are the raised planters flanking the porch of the recessed entrance. Inside, the traffic patterns are excellent. Among the focal points is the 33 foot, beam ceilinged living area. This will surely be fun to plan and furnish for the family's living and dining pursuits. Among other highlights is the layout of the laundry-kitchen-nook area. The extra washroom is strategically located. The sleeping wing has much to offer with its privacy, its convenient bath facilities, and its fine storage.

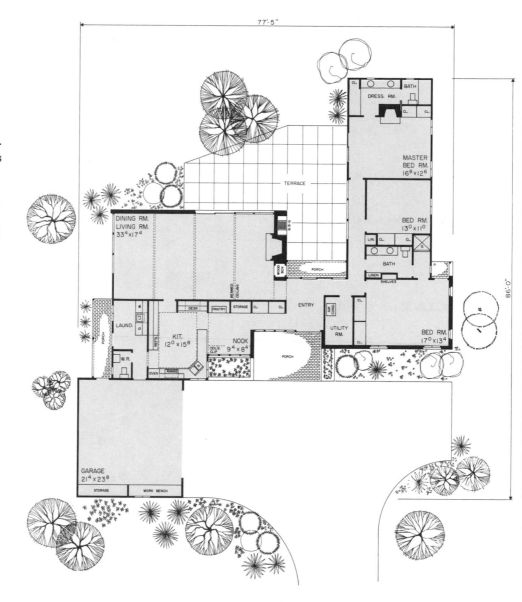

Design W2721

Square Footage: 2,667

● The interior rooms of this home are visually exciting besides being livable. A sunken gathering room with a sloped ceiling, raised-hearth fireplace and corner balcony opens into a formal dining area. Two family rooms allow plenty of room for informal occasions. A lavish master suite and two large bedrooms are found in the left wing of the house. Notice the huge storage area to the right of the garage.

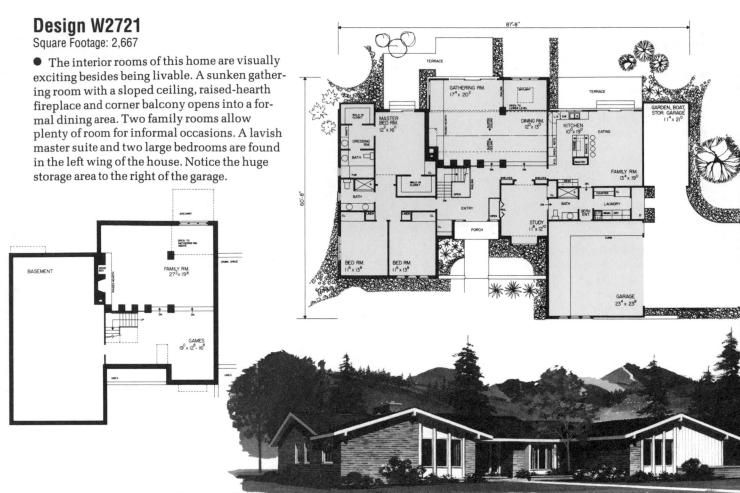

Design W2873

Square Footage: 2,838

● This modern three-bedroom contemporary incorporates many features popular today. A large gathering room with cozy raised-hearth fireplace and sloped ceiling is central focus and centrally located. The dining room has an adjacent bar or butler's pantry. Just off this area is the kitchen with central cooktop island and breakfast room. The master suite is especially luxurious with its own exercise room. There's even a powder room for guests.

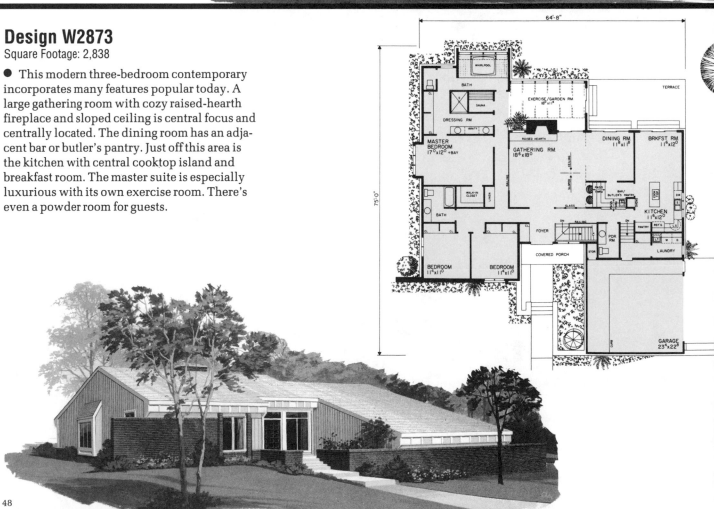

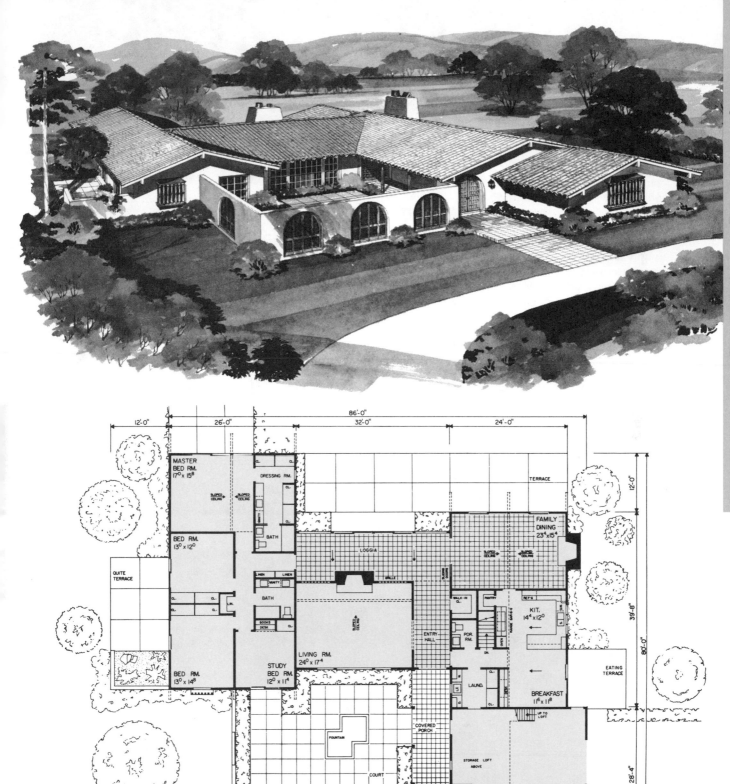

Design W1994 Square Footage: 3,104

● The Spanish flavor of the old Southwest is delightfully captured by this sprawling ranch house. Its L-shape and high privacy wall go together to form a wide open interior court. This will be a great place to hold these formal and/or informal garden parties. The plan itself is wonderfully zoned. The center portion of house is comprised of the big, private living room with sloped ceiling. Traffic patterns will noiselessly skirt this formal area. The two wings—the sleeping and informal living—are connected by the well-lighted and spacious loggia. In the sleeping wing, observe the size of the various rooms and the fine storage. In the informal living wing, note the big family room and breakfast room that family members will enjoy.

Design W2557
Square Footage: 1,955

● This eye-catching design has a flavor of the Spanish Southwest. The character of the exterior is set by the wide, overhanging roof with its exposed beams; the massive arched pillars; the arching of the brick over the windows; the panelled door and the horizontal siding that contrasts with the brick. The master bedroom/study suite is a focal point of the interior. However, if necessary, the study could become the fourth bedroom. The living and dining rooms are large and separated by a massive raised-hearth fireplace.

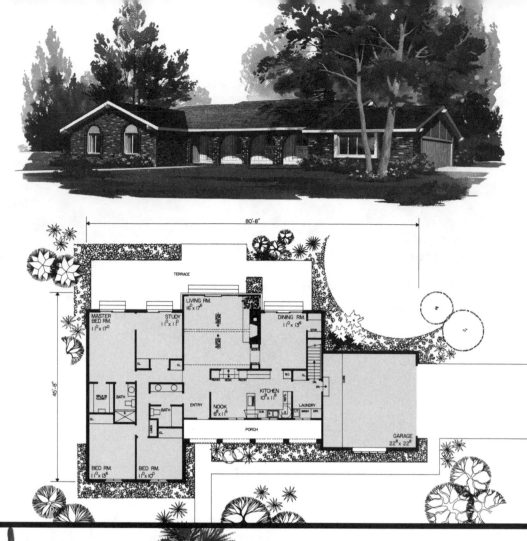

Design W2741
Square Footage: 1,842

● Here is another example of what 1,800 square feet can deliver in comfort and convenience. The setting reminds one of the sun country of Arizona. However, this design would surely be an attractive and refreshing addition to any region. The covered front porch with its adjacent open trellis area shelters the center entry. From here traffic flows efficiently to the sleeping, living and kitchen zones. There is much to recommend each area. The sleeping with its fine bath and closet facilities; the living with its spaciousness, fireplace and adjacent dining room; the kitchen with its handy nook, excellent storage, nearby laundry and extra washroom.

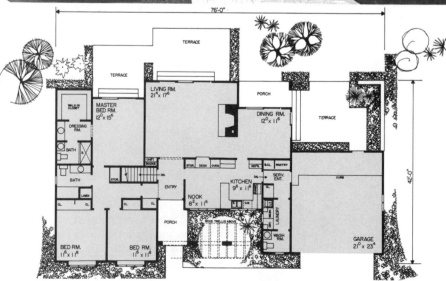

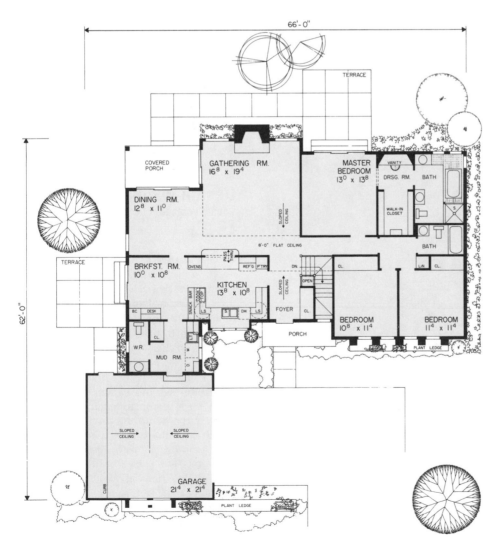

66'-0"

TERRACE

COVERED PORCH

GATHERING RM.
16⁸ x 19⁴

MASTER BEDROOM
13⁰ x 13⁸

VANITY

DRSG. RM.

BATH

DINING RM.
12⁸ x 11⁰

SLOPED CEILING

WALK-IN CLOSET

8'-0" FLAT CEILING

BATH

62'-0"

PASS THRU

TERRACE

BRKFST. RM.
10⁰ x 10⁸

OVENS

REF'G

P'TRY

DN.

SLOPED CEILING

CL.

LIN.

CL.

KITCHEN
13⁸ x 10⁸

SNACK BAR

COOK TOP

OPEN

FOYER

CL.

BC

DESK

LS

S

DW

LS

CL.

BEDROOM
10⁸ x 11⁴

BEDROOM
11⁴ x 11⁴

W.R.

MUD RM.

W

D

PORCH

PLANT LEDGE

SLOPED CEILING

SLOPED CEILING

GARAGE
21⁴ x 21⁴

PLANT LEDGE

Design W2912
Square Footage: 1,864

● This modern design with smart Spanish styling incorporates careful zoning by room functions with lifestyle comfort. All three bedrooms, including a master bedroom suite, are isolated at one end of the one-story home for privacy and out of traffic patterns. Entry to a breakfast room and kitchen is possible through a mud room off the garage. That's good news for people carrying groceries from car to kitchen or people with muddy shoes during inclement weather. The modern kitchen includes a snack bar and cook top with multiple access to breakfast room, side foyer, and pass-thru to hallway. There's also a nearby formal dining room. A large rear gathering room features sloped ceiling and its own fireplace. Note the two-car garage and built-in plant ledge in front. Gabled end window treatment plus varied roof lines further enhance the striking appearance of this efficient design.

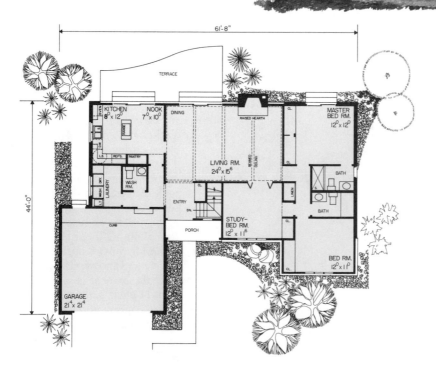

Design W2565

Square Footage: 1,540

L **D**

● This modest sized floor plan has much to offer in the way of livability. It may function as either a two or three bedroom home. The living room is huge and features a fine, raised hearth fireplace. The open stairway to the basement is handy and will lead to what may be developed as the recreation area. In addition to the two full baths, there is an extra wash room. Adjacent is the laundry room and the service entrance from the garage. The blueprints you order for this design will show details for each of the three delightful elevations above. Which is your favorite? The Tudor, the Colonial or the Contemporary?

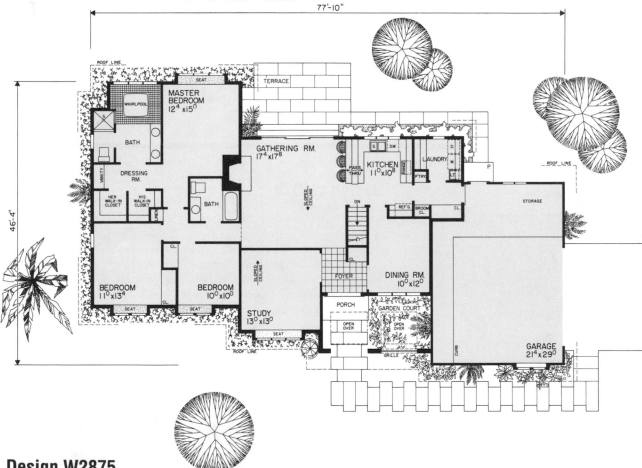

77'-10"

46'-4"

ROOF LINE

SEAT

MASTER
BEDROOM
12⁴ x15⁰

WHIRLPOOL

TERRACE

BATH

VANITY

DRESSING
RM.

GATHERING RM.
17⁴ x17⁸

KITCHEN
11⁰ x10⁸

LAUNDRY

SLOPED CEILING

PASS
THRU

RANGE

P'TRY

HER
WALK-IN
CLOSET

HIS
WALK-IN
CLOSET

BATH

DN

REF'G

BROOM
CL

CL

ROOF LINE

P

STORAGE

BEDROOM
11⁰ x13⁴

CL

SEAT

BEDROOM
10⁰ x10⁰

SLOPED
CEILING

CL

SEAT

FOYER

CL

DINING RM.
10⁰ x12⁰

STUDY
13⁰ x13⁰

PORCH

SEAT

OPEN
OVER

GARDEN COURT

OPEN
OVER

ROOF LINE

GRILLE

CURB

GARAGE
21⁴ x29⁰

Design W2875
Square Footage: 1,913

L **D**

● This elegant Spanish design in-corporates excellent indoor-outdoor living relationships for modern families who enjoy the sun and comforts of a well-planned new home. Note the overhead openings for rain and sun to fall upon a front garden, while a twin arched entry leads to the front porch and foyer. Inside the floor plan features a modern kitchen with pass-thru to a large gathering room with fire-place. Other features include a dining room, laundry room, a study off the foyer, plus three bedrooms including master bedroom with its own whirlpool.

● Here is a relatively low-cost home with a majority of the features found in today's high priced homes. The three-bedroom sleeping area highlights two full baths. The living area is a huge room of approximately 25 feet in depth zoned for both formal living and dining activities. The kitchen is extremely well-planned and includes a built-in desk and pantry. The family room has a snack bar and sliding glass doors to the terrace. Blueprints include optional basement details.

Design W1357
Square Footage: 1,258

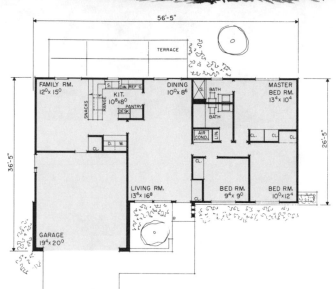

Design W1379
Square Footage: 864

● This low-cost, efficiently-planned, house is custom-designed for a retired person or couple. The compact arrangement of rooms all on one level makes it easy to move from one area to another, inside or out, quickly and without exertion. A large hobby and storage room is ideal for pursuing favorite projects, such as woodworking or gardening. Sliding glass doors across the back of living-dining area make terrace easily accessible from kitchen for outdoor meals and entertaining. Each of the two bedrooms has a built-in chest adjacent to closet.

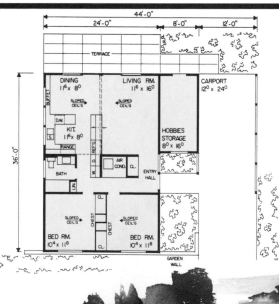

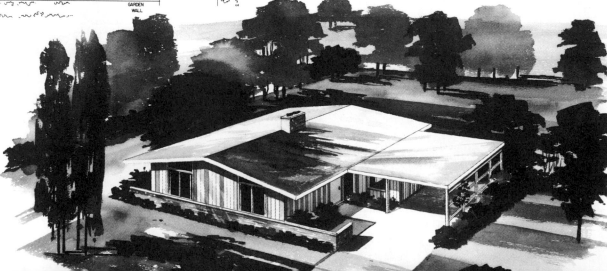

Design W2792
Square Footage: 1,944

● Indoor/outdoor living could hardly be improved upon in this contemporary design. Divide the terrace in three parts and the nook and dining room have access to a dining terrace, the gathering room to a living terrace and two bedrooms to a lounging terrace. Other fine features include the efficient kitchen with plenty of storage space and an island range, a first-floor laundry with stairs to the basement, and a powder room adjacent to the front door.

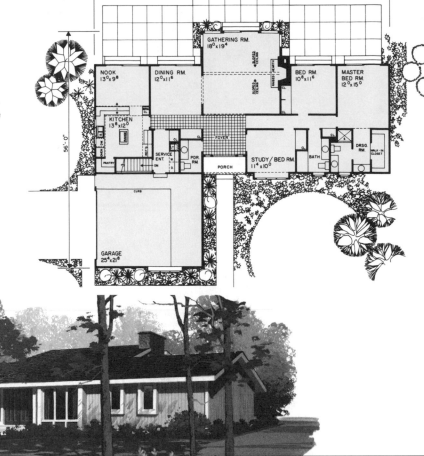

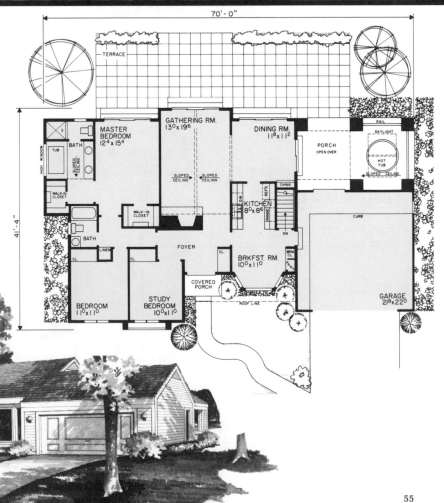

Design W2809
Square Footage: 1,551

● This contemporary home offers the best in indoor/outdoor livability with sliding glass doors in each of the rear rooms leading to the wide terrace. The formal dining room has a second set of doors to the porch with a sloped ceiling, skylights and a hot tub! The interior provides a spacious gathering room with sloped ceiling. The kitchen is conveniently located between the formal and informal dining areas. Two, or optional three, bedrooms are ready to serve the small family.

Design W2802

Square Footage: 1,729

L **D**

● The three exteriors shown at the left house the same, efficiently planned one-story floor plan shown below. Be sure to notice the design variations in the window placement and roof pitch. The Tudor design to the left is delightful. Half-timbered stucco and brick comprise the facade of this English Tudor variation of the plan. Note authentic bay window in the front bedroom.

Design W2803

Square Footage: 1,679

L **D**

● Housed in varying facades, this floor plan is very efficient. The front foyer leads to each of the living areas. The sleeping area of two, or optional three, bedrooms is ready to serve the family. Then there is the gathering room. This room is highlighted by its size, 16 x 20 feet. A contemporary mix of fieldstone and vertical wood siding characterizes this exterior. The absence of columns or posts gives a modern look to the covered porch.

Design W2804

Square Footage: 1,674

L **D**

● Stuccoed arches, multi-paned windows and a gracefully sloped roof accent the exterior of this Spanish-inspired design. Like the other two designs, the interior kitchen will efficiently serve the dining room, covered dining porch and breakfast room with great ease. Blueprints for all three designs include details for an optional non-basement plan.

CUSTOMIZABLE

Custom Alterations? See page 301 for customizing this plan to your specifications.

OPTIONAL NON-BASEMENT

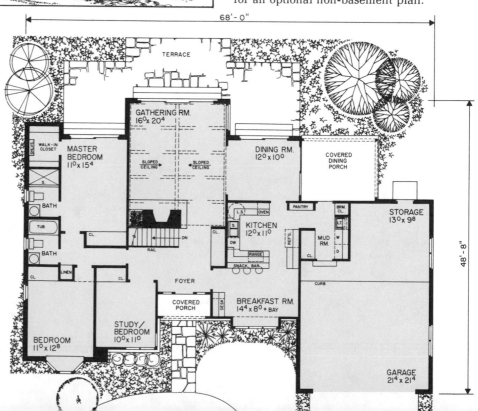

CUSTOMIZABLE

Custom Alterations? See page 301
for customizing this plan to your
specifications.

Design W2505

Square Footage: 1,366

L **D**

● This design offers you a choice of
three distinctively different exteriors.
Which is your favorite? Blueprints
show details for all three optional
elevations. A study of the floor plan
reveals a fine measure of livability. In
less than 1,400 square feet there are
features galore. An excellent return on
your construction dollar. In addition to
the two eating areas and the open
planning of the gathering room, the
indoor-outdoor relationships are of
great interest. The basement may be
developed for recreational activities.
Be sure to note the storage potential,
particularly the linen closet, the pantry,
the china cabinet and the broom closet.

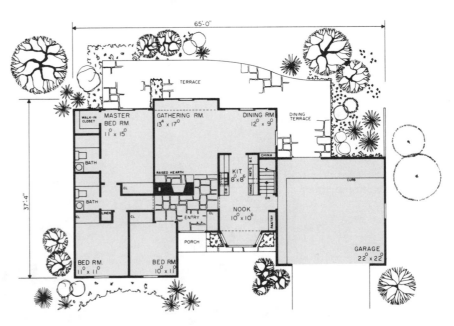

OPTIONAL BASEMENT

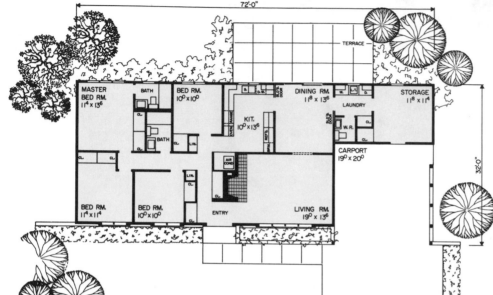

Design W3163
Square Footage: 1,552

● Four bedrooms and two full baths will very adequately serve the growing family occupying this appealing contemporary. Its perfectly rectangular shape means economical construction. Note the attractive built-in planter adjacent to the front door. The large storage area behind the carport will solve any storage problems. Laundry and wash room are strategically located to serve the family.

Design W1884
Square Footage: 1,925

● If you are searching for something with an air of distinction both inside and out then search no more. You could hardly improve upon what this home has to offer. You will forever be proud of the impressive hip-roof and angular facade. As for the interior, your everyday living patterns will be a delight. And little wonder, clever zoning and a fine feeling of spaciousness set the stage. As you stand in the entrance hall, you look across the tip of a four-foot-high planter into the sunken living room. Having an expanse of floor space, the wall of windows and the raised-hearth fireplace, the view will be dramatic. Notice the covered porch, play terrace and quiet terrace which will provide great outdoor enjoyment.

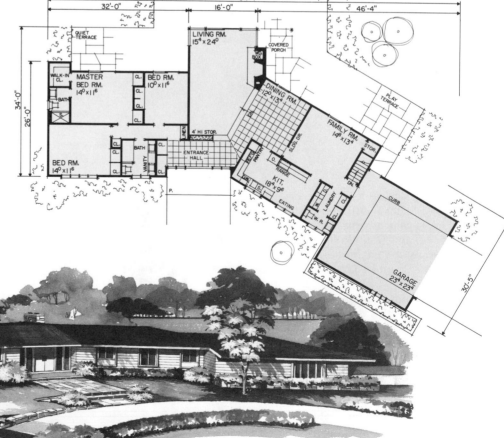

Design W2705
Square Footage: 1,746
L D

Design W2706
Square Footage: 1,746
L D

Design W2704
Square Footage: 1,746
L D

● Three different exteriors, but inside they all have the same livable plan. The gathering room is impressive in size and design with its fireplace flanked by sliding glass doors leading to the terrace. A formal dining room is nearby and leads to an L-shaped kitchen. Three bedrooms include a master suite with private dressing area and bath. For the French adaptation order W2705; for contemporary version order W2706;nd for the Colonial version order W2704.

Design W2930

Square Footage: 2,032

● The clean lines of this L-shaped contemporary are enhanced by the interesting overhanging roof planes. Horizontal and vertical siding complement one another. The floor plan is made to order for the active small family or empty-nesters: sloping ceilings and plenty of glass areas, an outstanding master bedroom with dressing room and whirlpool, guest room with full bath, study with fireplace, open gathering room and dining room. Note the rear covered porch.

CUSTOMIZABLE

Custom Alterations? See page 301 for customizing this plan to your specifications.

Design W2917

Square Footage: 1,813

● Here's an attractive design with many of today's most-asked-for features: gathering room with fireplace, separate formal dining room, roomy kitchen with equally spacious breakfast area, and three bedrooms including a master suite with huge walk-in closet and two private vanities. One other plus: a great-to-stretch-out-on terrace leading to the backyard.

CUSTOMIZABLE

Custom Alterations? See page 301 for customizing this plan to your specifications.

Design W2913

Square Footage: 1,835

D

● This smart design features multi-gabled ends, varied roof lines and vertical windows. A covered porch leads through a foyer to a large central gathering room with fireplace, sloped ceiling and a view of the rear terrace. A modern kitchen with snack bar has a pass-through to a breakfast room; there's also an adjacent dining room. A media room isolated from the rest of the house offers a quiet area. The master bedroom has its own whirlpool.

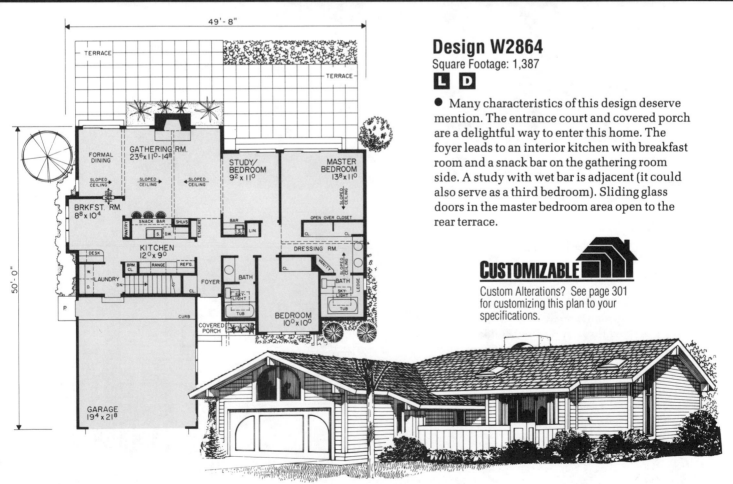

Design W2864

Square Footage: 1,387

L **D**

● Many characteristics of this design deserve mention. The entrance court and covered porch are a delightful way to enter this home. The foyer leads to an interior kitchen with breakfast room and a snack bar on the gathering room side. A study with wet bar is adjacent (it could also serve as a third bedroom). Sliding glass doors in the master bedroom area open to the rear terrace.

CUSTOMIZABLE

Custom Alterations? See page 301 for customizing this plan to your specifications.

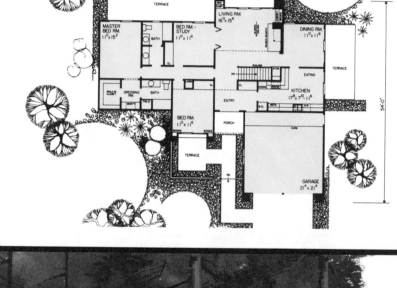

Design W2702
Square Footage: 1,636

● A rear living room with a sloping ceiling, built-in bookcases, a raised-hearth fireplace and sliding glass doors to the rear terrace highlight this design. The kitchen has plenty of cabinet and cupboard space. It features informal eating space and is but a step or two from the separate dining room. Each of the three rooms in the sleeping wing has direct access to outdoor living. The master bedroom has a huge walk-in wardrobe closet, dressing room with built-in vanity and private bath with large towel storage closet.

Design W2754
Square Footage: 1,844

● This really is a most dramatic contemporary home. The U-shaped privacy wall of the front entrance area provides an appealing outdoor living spot accessible from the front bedroom. The rectangular floor plan will be economical to build. Two bedrooms and two full baths comprise the sleeping zone. Note the open planning of the L-shaped living and dining rooms and the through-fireplace to the study. The kitchen and breakfast nook function well together.

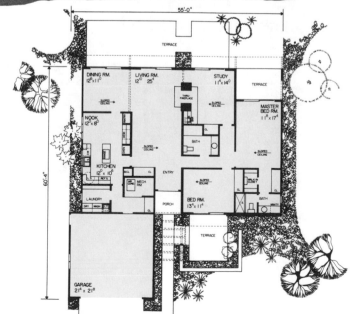

Design W2744

Square Footage: 1,381

● Here is a practical and an attractive contemporary home for that narrow building site. It is designed for efficiency with the small family or retired couple in mind. Sloping ceilings foster an extra measure of spaciousness. In addition to the master bedroom, there is the study that can also serve as the second bedroom or as an occasional guest room. The single bath is compartmented and its dual access allows it to serve living and sleeping areas more than adequately. Note raised-hearth fireplace, snack bar, U-shaped kitchen, laundry, two terraces, etc.

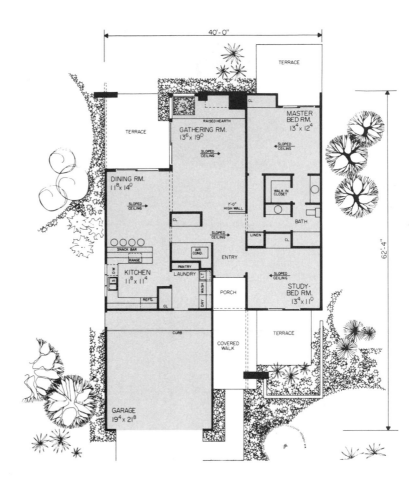

Design W1820

Square Footage: 2,730

D

● Whatever the location, snugly tucked in among the hills or impressively oriented on the flatlands - this trim hip-roof ranch home will be fun to own. Here is a gracious exterior whose floor plan has "everything". Traffic patterns are excellent. The zoning of the sleeping wing, as well as the formal and informal living areas, is outstanding. Indoor-outdoor living relationships are most practical and convenient.

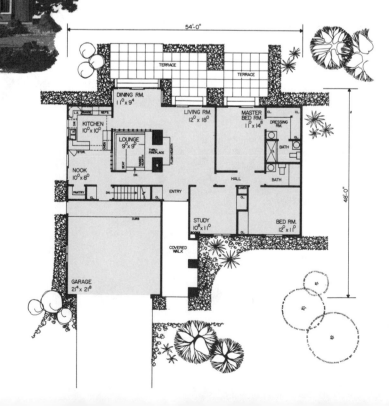

Design W2703

Square Footage: 1,445

D

● This modified, hip-roofed contemporary design will be the answer for those who want something both practical, yet different, inside and out. The covered front walk sets the stage for entering a modest-sized home with tremendous livability. The focal point will be the pleasant conversation lounge. It is sunken, partially open to the other living areas and shares the enjoyment of the through-fireplace with the living room. There are two bedrooms, two full baths and a study. The kitchen is outstanding.

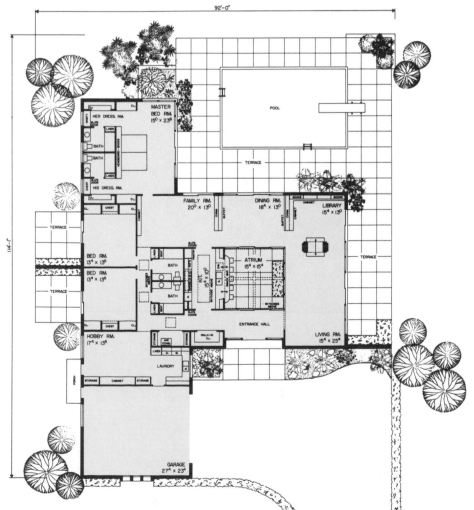

Design W2226
Square Footage: 3,340

● If anything has been left out of this home it would certainly be difficult to determine just what it is that is missing. Containing over 3,300 square feet, space for living is abundant. Each of the various rooms is large. Further, each major room has access to the outdoors. The efficient inside kitchen is strategically located in relation to the family and dining rooms. Observe how it functions with the enclosed atrium to provide a snack bar. Functional room dividers separate various areas. Study closely the living area. A two-way fireplace divides the spacious living room and the cozy library highlighted by built-in cabinets and bookshelves. A hobby room with laundry adjacent will be a favorite family activities spot.

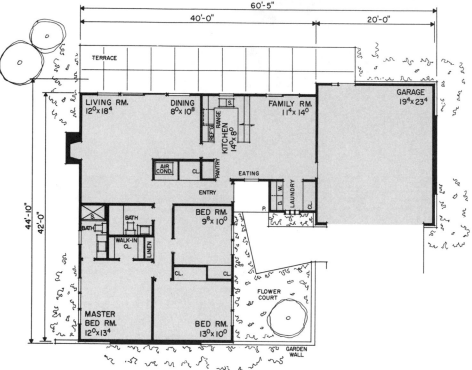

Design W1307

Square Footage: 1,357

L **D**

● The exterior of this stylish home has many features to recommend it. It features a low-pitched, wide-over-hanging roof, a pleasing use of horizontal siding and brick and an enclosed front flower court. Inside, there is an abundance of livability. The formal living and dining area is spacious, and the U-shaped kitchen is efficient. There is informal eating space, a separate laundry and a fine family room. Note the sliding glass doors to the terrace. The blueprints include details for building either with or without a basement. Observe the pantry to the non-basement plan.

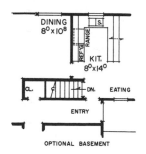

58' - 0"

TERRACE

| MASTER BED RM. 14⁴ x 11⁴ | | PDR. RM. VANITY | BATH | LIVING RM. 18⁰ x 13⁸ | FAMILY RM. 13⁴ x 17⁰ |

SLOPED CEILING

WALK-IN CL.

BATH

AIR COND.

HEARTH RAISED

3'-6" HI STORAGE

| BED RM. 11⁰ x 13⁶ | BED RM. 11⁸ x 10⁰ | ENTRY | DINING RM. 11⁸ x 13⁶ | KIT. 13⁴ x 10⁴ |

GLASS GABLE

SLOPED CEILING

GLASS GRILLE

SLOPED CEILING

RANGE BAR-B-Q

BR'M

SINK

REF'G

LAUND. TRAY

PANTRY

MUD RM. 10⁰ x 10⁰

W.R.

CL.

26' - 0"

60' - 0"

CURB

GARAGE 21⁴ x 21⁴

Design W1947
Square Footage: 1,764

● When it comes to housing your family, if you are among the contemporary-minded, you'll want to give this L-shaped design a second, then even a third, or fourth, look. Its available as either three or fur bedroom home. If you desire the three bedroom, 58 foot wide design order blueprints for W1947; for the four bedroom, 62 foot wide design, order W1948. Inside, you will note a continuation of the contemporary theme with sloping ceilings, exposed beams and a practical 42 inch high storage divider between the living and dining rooms. Don't miss the mud rooms.

62' - 0"

TERRACE

| MASTER BED RM. 14⁴ x 11⁴ | | BED RM. 10⁰ x 11⁴ | LIVING RM. 18⁰ x 13⁶ | FAMILY RM. 13⁴ x 17⁰ |

SHOWER

BATH

VANITY

AIR COND.

RAISED HEARTH

3'-6" HI STORAGE

| BED RM. 11⁰ x 13⁶ | PDR. RM. BATH | STUDY- BED RM. 10⁴ x 10⁰ | ENTRY | DINING RM. 11⁸ x 13⁶ | KIT. 13⁴ x 10⁴ |

GLASS GABLE

SLOPED CEILING

SLOPED CEILING

LIN.

GLASS GRILLE

SLOPED CEILING

RANGE BAR-B-Q

BR'M

WASH. DRY.

REF'G

LAUND. TRAY

PANTRY

MUD RM. 10⁰ x 10⁰

W.R.

CL.

28' - 0"

60' - 0"

CURB

GARAGE 21⁴ x 21⁴

Design W1948
Square Footage: 1,876

Design W4186

Square Footage: 1,775

● A symmetrically pleasing exterior leads to a most functional interior plan in this one-story design. An entry bridge leads to a lovely front entry with dual coat closets for convenience. The great room is open and large enough for all sorts of entertaining. Sliding glass doors to the rear deck and a fireplace are highlights in this room. The country kitchen is nearby and allows plenty of room for a table and chairs and access to the rear deck. Sleeping areas are to the right of the plan. The master bedroom has a great dressing area and large walk-in closet. The rear deck can also be accessed from the master bedroom. Two family bedrooms share a full bath with dressing area.

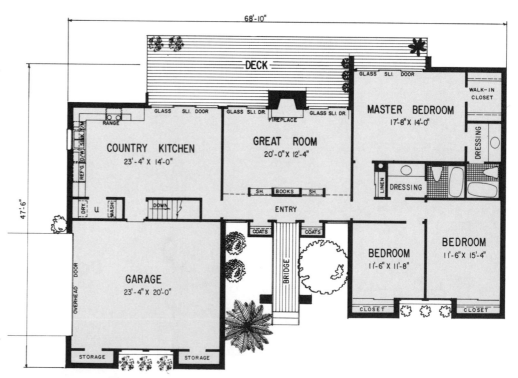

LIFESTYLE
HOME PLANS

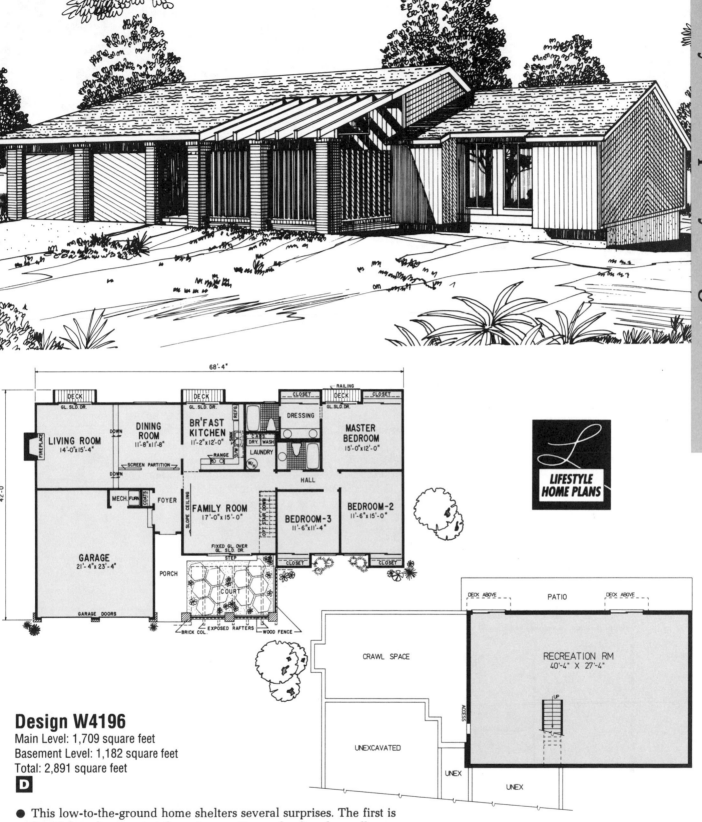

Design W4196

Main Level: 1,709 square feet
Basement Level: 1,182 square feet
Total: 2,891 square feet

D

● This low-to-the-ground home shelters several surprises. The first is a cheerful garden court at the entrance. Exposed rafters here allow just the right combination of sun and shade. Inside are more delights, like the three decks off the living room, breakfast room, and master bedroom. And note that the living room is sunken a step down from the main house. The real secret, however, to this home's hillside nature is its optional basement, which, if developed, allows walk-out potential on a lower level.

Design W4155

Square Footage: 1,326

L **D**

● A traditional family favorite, the country kitchen comes home to light up this contemporary design. Though modest in size, this home provides a wealth of livability. Notice the abundance of special amenities: entryway coat closet, two rear decks, open staircase to the basement, laundry area near bedrooms, large storage area in the garage. The master suite has two levels, one of which could function as a sitting room area.

LIFESTYLE HOME PLANS

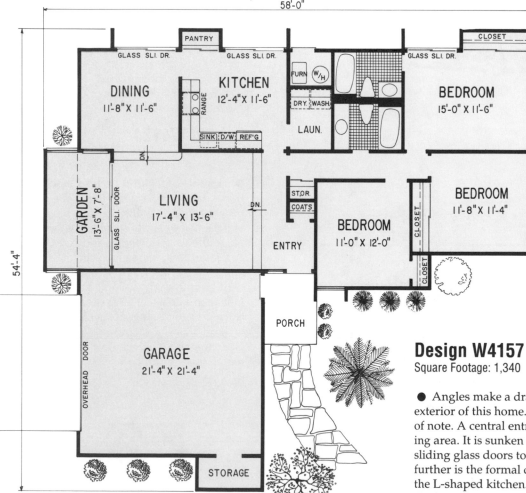

DINING
11'-8" X 11'-6"

KITCHEN
12'-4" X 11'-6"

PANTRY

GLASS SLI. DR.

GLASS SLI. DR.

GLASS SLI. DR.

CLOSET

BEDROOM
15'-0" X 11'-6"

FURN

W/H

DRY. WASH

LAUN.

RANGE

SINK | D/W | REF'G

DN.

GARDEN
13'-6" X 7'-8"

GLASS SLI. DOOR

LIVING
17'-4" X 13'-6"

DN.

ST. OR.

COATS

ENTRY

BEDROOM
11'-0" X 12'-0"

CLOSET

CLOSET

BEDROOM
11'-8" X 11'-4"

OVERHEAD DOOR

GARAGE
21'-4" X 21'-4"

PORCH

STORAGE

58'-0"

54'-4"

LIFESTYLE
HOME PLANS

Design W4157
Square Footage: 1,340

● Angles make a dramatic design statement on the exterior of this home. The interior plan is also worthy of note. A central entry opens directly to the large living area. It is sunken down two steps and also has sliding glass doors to a garden room. Sunken even further is the formal dining room which connects to the L-shaped kitchen. A nearby laundry handles washday problems with ease. Three bedrooms include a master with yard access and full bath. Two family bedrooms share a full bath.

Design W4124
Square Footage: 1,772

● From the delightful bridged entry to the expansive rear deck, this home will provide great livability in limited square footage. An open staircase to the basement allows the potential for expansion at a later time. Living areas include a great room with fireplace, dining room with built-in shelves, and a spacious L-shaped kitchen. The master bedroom is truly fit for a king: notice the huge walk-in closet, dressing area and sliding glass doors to the deck. Two family bedrooms share a full bath.

Floor Plan

56'-0"

RAILING

DECK

STEP

GLASS SLI. DOOR

GLASS SLI. DOOR

BOOKS
DESK

GLASS SLI. DR.

SLOPED CLG.

WALK-IN CLOSET

GLASS SLI. DOOR

LINE OF FLAT CLG.

DRESSING

MASTER BEDROOM
17'-8" X 14'-0"

DINING
11'-4" X 11'-8"

GREAT ROOM
20'-0" X 16'-0"

DOWN

LINEN

DRESSING

OPEN RAILING

38'-4"

DRY | UTI. | WASH

ENTRY

COATS | COATS

KITCHEN
11'-4" X 14'-0"

RANGE | PANTRY

BRIDGE

BEDROOM
11'-6" X 11'-8"

BEDROOM
11'-6" X 15'-4"

REF'G. | D/W | SINK | T/M

STEPS

CLOSET

CLOSET

CLOSET

LIFESTYLE HOME PLANS

Design W4317

Square Footage: 1,792

D

● There's a lot going on in this clever design that's not immediately evident from its facade. Beyond the side entry are four bedrooms, two full baths, and formal and informal living areas. Outdoor livability is a major focus with deck extensions from the family room, living room, master bedroom, kitchen, and entry. Note the garden atrium just off the dining room.

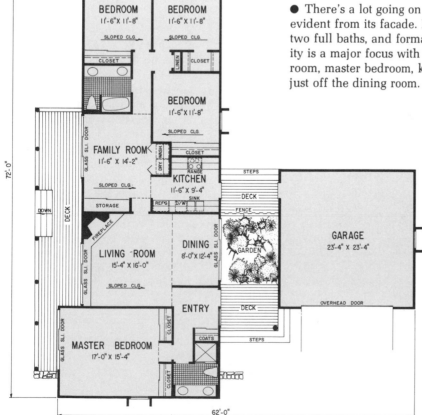

LIFESTYLE
HOME PLANS

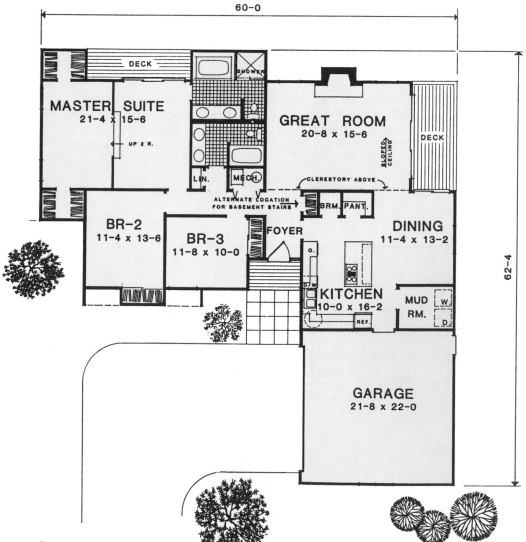

Floor plan labels:

DECK

MASTER SUITE
21-4 x 15-6

UP 2 R.

SHOWER

LIN.   MECH.

BR-2
11-4 x 13-6

BR-3
11-8 x 10-0

FOYER

ALTERNATE LOCATION
FOR BASEMENT STAIRS

GREAT ROOM
20-8 x 15-6

SLOPED CEILING

DECK

CLERESTORY ABOVE

BRM. PANT.

DINING
11-4 x 13-2

KITCHEN
10-0 x 16-2

MUD
RM.

W.

D.

REF.

GARAGE
21-8 x 22-0

60-0

62-4

Design W4340

Square Footage: 1,842

 L

● Diagonal siding accents provide a touch of interest to the facade of this home. Inside the living areas are to the rear, away from traffic flow and street noise. The great room has a warming fireplace and sliding glass doors to a side deck. It is day lighted by clerestory windows. The formal dining room also has deck access and connects to the L-shaped island kitchen. The bedroom wing is to the left and provides three bedrooms. The master suite has two closets, a private deck and bath with separate shower and tub. Two family bedrooms share a full bath with twin vanity.

Design W4203

Square Footage: 1,470
Optional Walk-Out Basement: 455 square feet

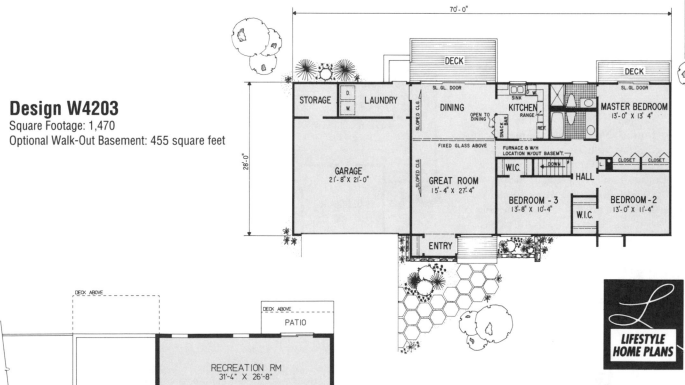

LIFESTYLE HOME PLANS

● Though most of the living in this house takes place on one level, if built on a hillside lot, the plan could have a lower-level recreation room with outdoor access. Decks off the dining room and master bedroom would serve as covers for the lower level patios. Living and sleeping zones inside are well placed and harbor plenty of storage and closet space.

Design W4323

Square Footage: 1,459

● Dramatic style pervades the facade of this comfortable one-story home. Its interior configuration, though small, is convenient and thoughtful. The living areas are found to the right side of the plan and are graced with sliding glass doors to a side deck. The great room has a fireplace; the kitchen leads handily to the two-car garage. Two family bedrooms and a master suite are found to the left of the plan. The master has its own deck, two closets and a railed-off sitting area. Note the hall linen closet and entry coat closet.

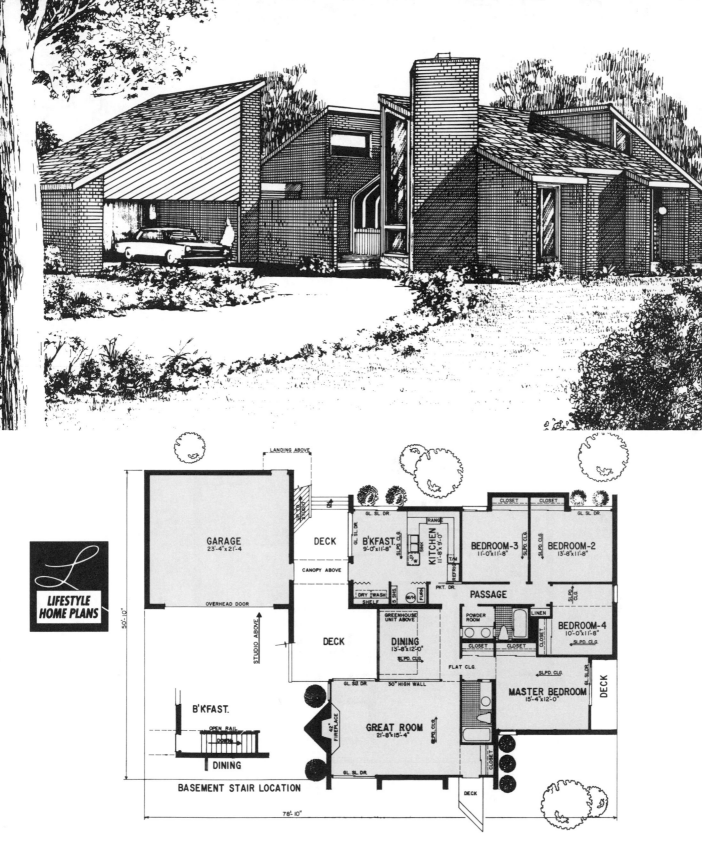

Design W4183

Square Footage: 1,885

 L

● Nothing is excluded in this delightful contemporary one-story. Enter the home from a deck entry to the oversized great room. A fireplace and sliding glass doors are nice accents here. The dining room is separated from this area by a divider wall. It is embellished with a greenhouse unit and sloped ceiling. The breakfast area and kitchen have access to the rear yard as well as to a side deck. Four bedrooms include three family bedrooms (two with sliding glass doors) and a master suite with private deck. This plan can be built with a basement included with blueprints.

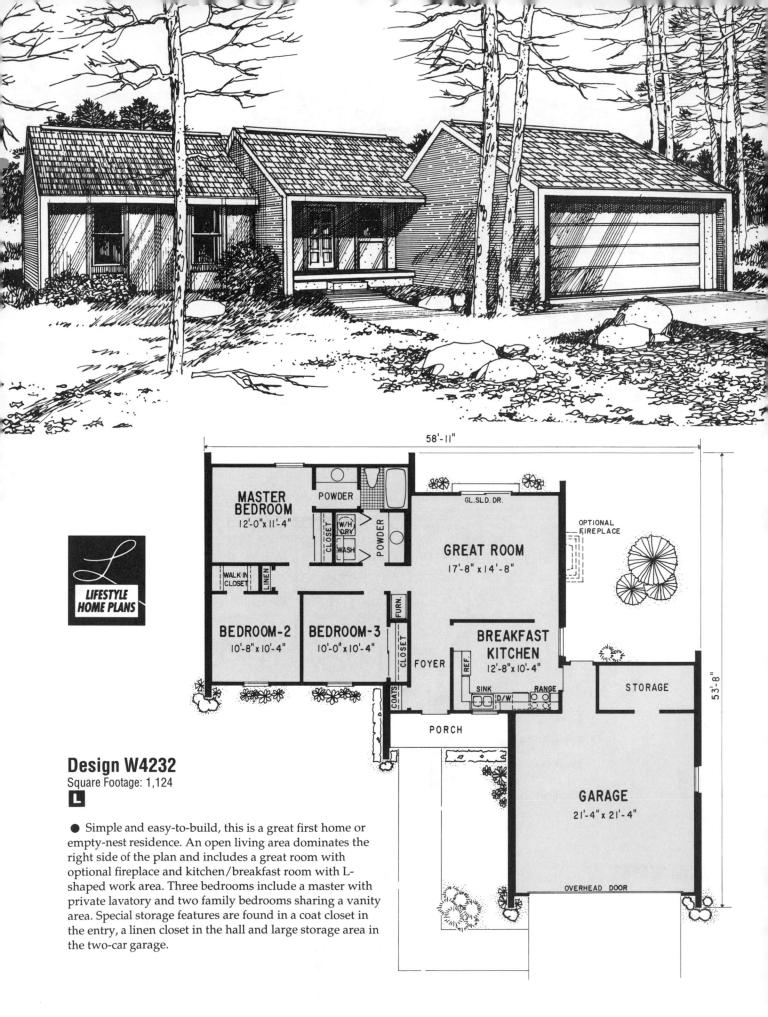

MASTER BEDROOM
12'-0" x 11'-4"

POWDER

CLOSET

W/H DRY

WASH

POWDER

WALK-IN CLOSET

LINEN

GL. SL D. DR.

OPTIONAL FIREPLACE

GREAT ROOM
17'-8" x 14'-8"

BEDROOM-2
10'-8" x 10'-4"

BEDROOM-3
10'-0" x 10'-4"

FURN.

CLOSET

FOYER

BREAKFAST KITCHEN
12'-8" x 10'-4"

REF.

SINK   D/W   RANGE

STORAGE

COATS

PORCH

GARAGE
21'-4" x 21'-4"

OVERHEAD DOOR

58'-11"

53'-8"

LIFESTYLE HOME PLANS

Design W4232

Square Footage: 1,124

L

● Simple and easy-to-build, this is a great first home or empty-nest residence. An open living area dominates the right side of the plan and includes a great room with optional fireplace and kitchen/breakfast room with L-shaped work area. Three bedrooms include a master with private lavatory and two family bedrooms sharing a vanity area. Special storage features are found in a coat closet in the entry, a linen closet in the hall and large storage area in the two-car garage.

MASTER BEDROOM
14'-0"x11'-4"

DRESS

WALK-IN CLOSET

LINEN

BEDROOM-2
11'-8"x10'-4"

BEDROOM-3
11'-0"x10'-4"

CLOSET

W/H DRY WASH

POWDER

SHVS WASH

PANTRY

WOOD DECK

SLD. GL. DR.

SLD. GL. DR.

KITCHEN BREAKFAST
13'-4"x11'-4"

D/W

REFG.

STORAGE

HVAC

SLOPE CLG.

GREAT ROOM
15'-4"x17'-4"

FOYER

SLOPE CLG.

COAT

STOOP

GARAGE
21'-4"x21'-4"

33'-8"

OVERHEAD GARAGE DOORS

70'-0"

Design W4242
Square Footage: 1,178

● Private outdoor living takes center stage to the rear of this home with a wood deck accessed from the great room and the kitchen. The foyer and great room both feature sloped ceilings and special storage space is contained in a coat closet, garage storage and hall linen storage. The bedrooms have ample closet space and share a full bath with Hollywood lavatories. A warm fireplace keeps living areas cozy in the winter.

LIFESTYLE HOME PLANS

Design W4293
Square Footage: 1,873

D

● This spacious layout has a big, big advantage—a country kitchen with all the trimmings: 300 square feet, a large island counter and breakfast bar, plenty of space for more formal dining, and a laundry room close at hand. The great room is also a center of attention, showing off clerestory windows and a large fireplace. What's more, the entrance is grand indeed, with a raised bridge leading into a large foyer. The master bedroom is long on living and storage space, and the rear deck ties everything together, connecting with the kitchen, great room, and master bedroom.

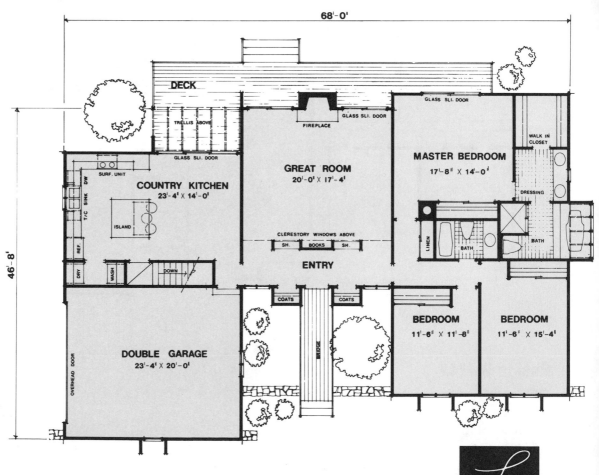

68'-0"

46'-8"

DECK

TRELLIS ABOVE

GLASS SLI. DOOR

FIREPLACE

GLASS SLI. DOOR

GLASS SLI. DOOR

GLASS SLI. DOOR

WALK IN CLOSET

SURF. UNIT

COUNTRY KITCHEN
23'-4" X 14'-0"

ISLAND

GREAT ROOM
20'-0" X 17'-4"

MASTER BEDROOM
17'-8" X 14'-0"

DRESSING

T/C SINK DW

REF.

DRY

WASH

DOWN

CLERESTORY WINDOWS ABOVE

SH. BOOKS SH.

ENTRY

LINEN

BATH

BATH

COATS COATS

BEDROOM
11'-6" X 11'-8"

BEDROOM
11'-6" X 15'-4"

DOUBLE GARAGE
23'-4" X 20'-0"

OVERHEAD DOOR

BRIDGE

L
LIFESTYLE
HOME PLANS

Design W3556

First Floor: 1,828 square feet
Second Floor: 1,344 square feet
Total: 3,172 square feet

L **D**

● Two-story living takes a lovely turn in contemporary living. The rounded stairwell works as an accent on the exterior and the interior. The gathering room has a fireplace and attached formal dining room. The smaller media room is sunken a few steps and contains a greenhouse. The U-shaped kitchen has a pass-through snack bar to a conversation area with another fireplace. Upstairs there are four bedrooms including a master suite with a grand bath and two walk-in closets.

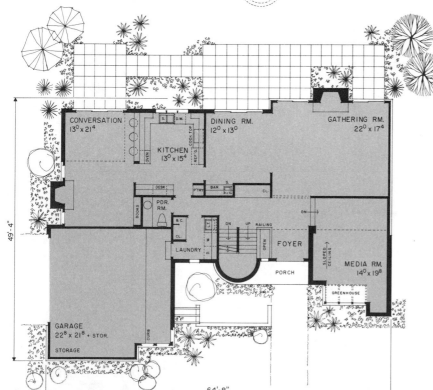

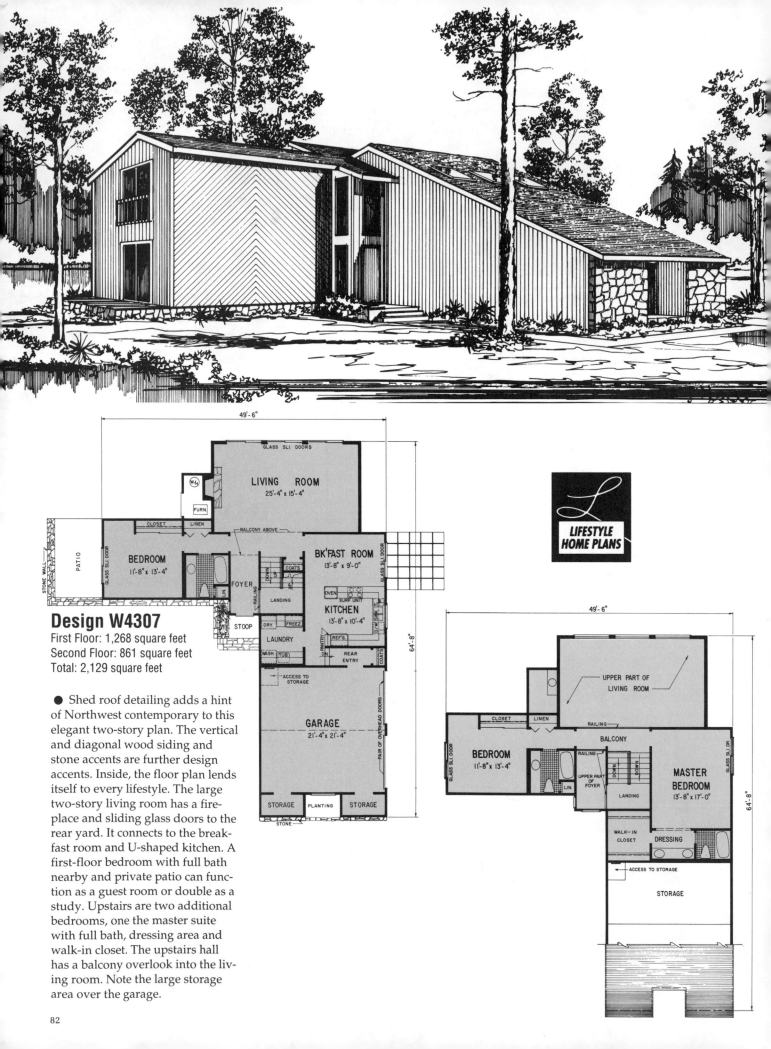

LIFESTYLE HOME PLANS

First floor plan labels:

49'-6"

GLASS SLI. DOORS

LIVING ROOM
25'-4" x 15'-4"

CLOSET | LINEN

BALCONY ABOVE

BK'FAST ROOM
13'-8" x 9'-0"

PATIO

STONE WALL

BEDROOM
11'-8" x 13'-4"

GLASS SLI. DOOR

FOYER

LIN

DOWN | UP

COATS

LANDING

RAILING

KITCHEN
13'-8" x 10'-4"

OVEN | SURF UNIT

GLASS SLI. DOOR

STOOP

DRY | FREEZ

LAUNDRY

PANTRY

D/W | SINK | REF'G

WASH | TUB

REAR ENTRY

COATS

ACCESS TO STORAGE

64'-8"

GARAGE
21'-4" x 21'-4"

PAIR OF OVERHEAD DOORS

STORAGE | PLANTING | STORAGE

STONE

Design W4307

First Floor: 1,268 square feet
Second Floor: 861 square feet
Total: 2,129 square feet

● Shed roof detailing adds a hint of Northwest contemporary to this elegant two-story plan. The vertical and diagonal wood siding and stone accents are further design accents. Inside, the floor plan lends itself to every lifestyle. The large two-story living room has a fireplace and sliding glass doors to the rear yard. It connects to the breakfast room and U-shaped kitchen. A first-floor bedroom with full bath nearby and private patio can function as a guest room or double as a study. Upstairs are two additional bedrooms, one the master suite with full bath, dressing area and walk-in closet. The upstairs hall has a balcony overlook into the living room. Note the large storage area over the garage.

Second floor plan labels:

49'-6"

UPPER PART OF LIVING ROOM

CLOSET | LINEN

RAILING

BALCONY

GLASS SLI. DOOR

BEDROOM
11'-8" x 13'-4"

RAILING

UPPER PART OF FOYER

LIN

DOWN | DOWN

LANDING

MASTER BEDROOM
13'-8" x 17'-0"

GLASS SLI. DR

WALK-IN CLOSET

DRESSING

ACCESS TO STORAGE

STORAGE

64'-8"

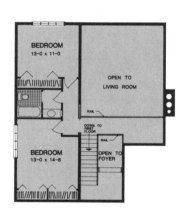

BEDROOM
13-0 x 11-0

OPEN TO
LIVING ROOM

RAIL

DOWN TO
FIRST
FLOOR

RAIL

BEDROOM
13-0 x 14-8

OPEN TO
FOYER

58'-0"

RAIL

DECK

GREENHOUSE
WINDOW

DINING
13-0 x 11-8

SLIDING GL. DOOR

RAIL

SLIDING GL. DOOR

SUN SPACE

SLOPED CEILING

SLIDING GL. DOOR

BREAKFAST
DECK

KITCHEN
13-0 x 12-0

LIVING ROOM
17-6 x 23-0

MASTER BEDROOM
15-8 x 15-2

SLOPED

BALCONY ABOVE

SOLAR
GREENHOUSE

BREAKFAST
11-4 x 9-8

DOWN TO
BASEMENT

64'-8"

PANTRY

SLOPED CEILING

DRESSING

WALK-IN
CLOSET

STORAGE

LAUNDRY

D W S

DOWN

UP TO
SECOND
FLOOR

FOYER

AIR LOCK
ENTRY

DOWN

GARAGE
21-4 x 21-8

Design W4334

First Floor: 1,838 square feet
Second Floor: 640 square feet
Total: 2,478 square feet

L

● Grand sloping rooflines and a design
created for southern orientation are the
unique features of this contemporary
home. Outdoor living is enhanced by a
solar greenhouse off the breakfast room,
a sun space off the master bedroom, a
greenhouse window in the dining room,
a casual breakfast deck, and full-width
deck to the rear. The split-bedroom plan
allows for the master suite (with fireplace, and huge walk-in closet) to be situated on the first floor and two family
bedrooms and a full bath to find space
on the second floor. Be sure to notice
the balcony overlook to the sloped-
ceiling living room below.

LIFESTYLE
HOME PLANS

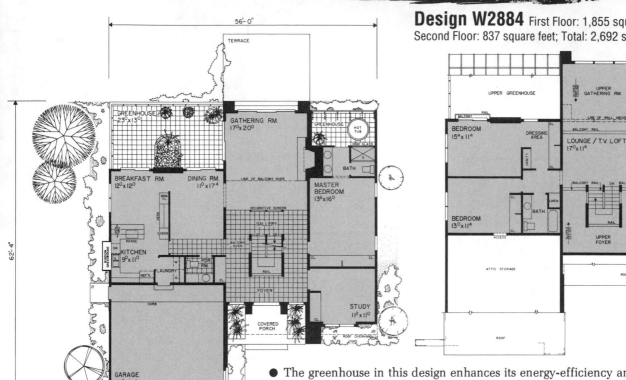

Design W2884 First Floor: 1,855 square feet
Second Floor: 837 square feet; Total: 2,692 square feet

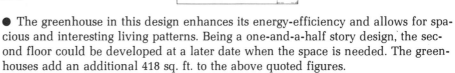

● The greenhouse in this design enhances its energy-efficiency and allows for spacious and interesting living patterns. Being a one-and-a-half story design, the second floor could be developed at a later date when the space is needed. The greenhouses add an additional 418 sq. ft. to the above quoted figures.

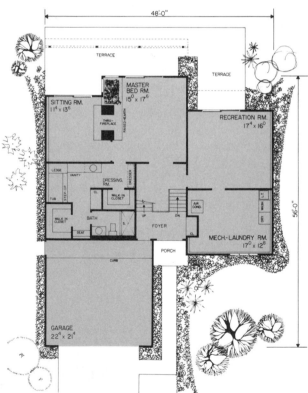

Design W2759

Upper Level: 1,747 square feet
Lower Level: 1,513 square feet; Total: 3,260 square feet

● A contemporary bi-level with a large bonus room on a third level over the garage. This studio will serve as a great room to be creative in or just to sit back in. The design also provides great indoor/outdoor living relationships with terraces and decks. The formal living/dining area has a sloped ceiling and built-in wet bar. The dramatic beauty of a raised hearth fireplace and built-in planter will be enjoyed by those in the living room. Both have sliding glass doors to the rear deck. The breakfast area will serve as a pleasant eating room with ample space for a table plus the built-in snack bar. The lower level houses the recreation room, laundry and an outstanding master suite. This master suite includes a thru-fireplace, sitting room, tub and shower and more.

Design W2780

First Floor: 2,006 square feet
Second Floor: 718 square feet
Total: 2,724 square feet

● This 1½-story contemporary has more fine features than one can imagine. The livability is outstanding and can be appreciated by the whole family. Note the fine indoor-outdoor living relationships.

● This exciting contemporary has dramatic roof lines and glass areas. The spaciousness of the dining/family room will make entertaining a memorable occasion. Note the privacy of the master bedroom. The second floor is devoted to the activities of the younger generation. The lounge looks down into the gathering room.

Design W2530

First Floor: 1,616 square feet
Second Floor: 997 square feet; Total: 2,613 square feet

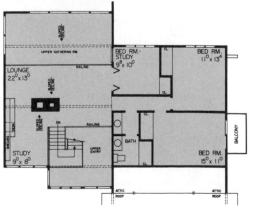

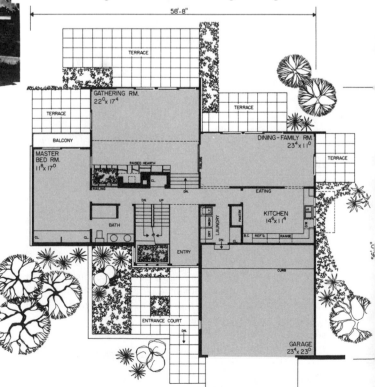

Design W2904

First Floor: 2,724 square feet
Second Floor: 1,019 square feet
Total: 3,743 square feet

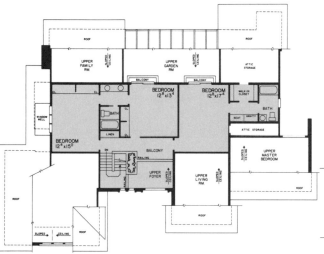

● This four-bedroom contemporary Trend Home is loaded with extras that include a spacious garden room with its own whirlpool, snack bar off the kitchen, and deluxe master bedroom suite. The master bedroom has access to an exercise room with its own bath and view of a back-yard terrace. Adjacent to the master bedroom is a spacious living room with sloped ceiling. Three other bedrooms are isolated upstairs. Two upstairs rooms have their own balconies.

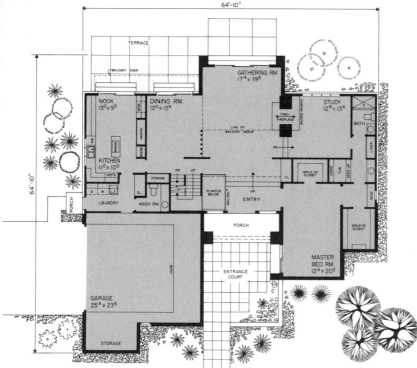

Design W2771

First Floor: 2,087 square feet
Second Floor: 816 square feet
Total: 2,903 square feet

● This design will provide an abundance of livability for your family. The second floor is highlighted by an open lounge which overlooks both the entry and the gathering room below.

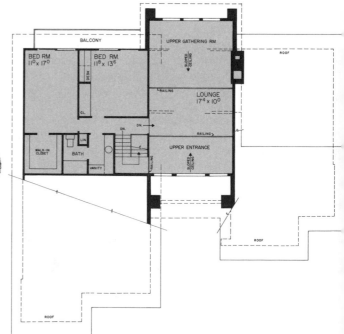

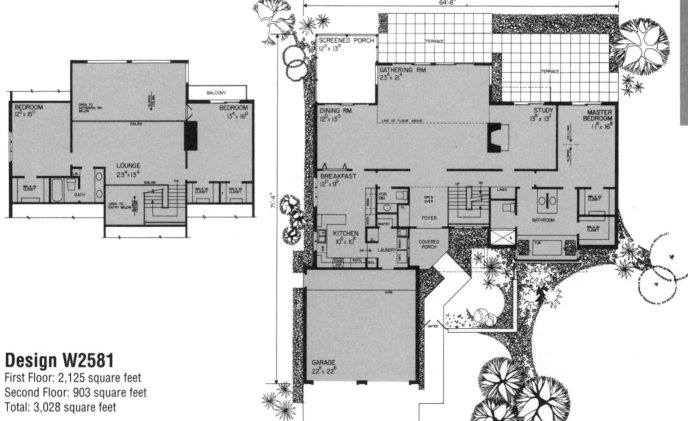

Design W2581

First Floor: 2,125 square feet
Second Floor: 903 square feet
Total: 3,028 square feet

● A study with a fireplace! What a fine attraction to find in this lovely three-bedroom home. And the fine features certainly do not stop there. The gathering room has a sloped ceiling and two sliding glass doors to the rear terrace. The study and master bedroom (which has first floor privacy and convenience) also have glass doors to the wrap-around terrace. Adjacent to the gathering room is a formal dining room and screened-in porch. The efficient kitchen with its many built-ins has easy access to the first floor laundry. The separate breakfast nook has a built-in desk. The second floor has two bedrooms each having at least one walk-in closet. Also, a lounge overlooking the gathering room below and a balcony. Note the oversized two-car garage for storing bikes and lawn mowers. The front courtyard adds a measure of privacy to the covered porch entrance.

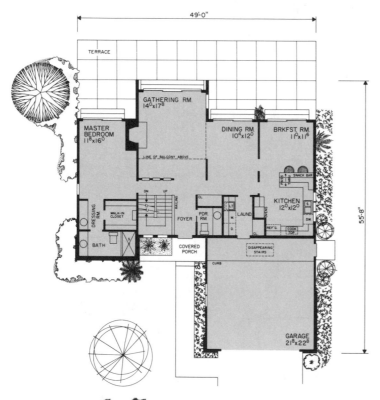

Design W2905

First Floor: 1,342 square feet
Second Floor: 619 square feet
Total: 1,961 square feet

L

● All of the livability in this plan is in the back! Each first floor room, except the kitchen, has access to the rear terrace via sliding glass doors. A great way to capture an excellent view. This plan is also ideal for a narrow lot seeing that its width is less than 50 feet. Two bedrooms and a lounge, overlooking the gathering room, are on the second floor.

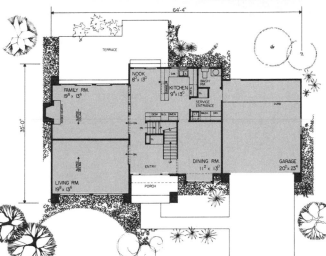

Design W2748

First Floor: 1,232 square feet
Second Floor: 720 square feet
Total: 1,952 square feet

● This four-bedroom contemporary will definitely have appeal for the entire family. The U-shaped kitchen/nook area with its built-in desk, adjacent laundry/wash room and service entrance will be very efficient for the busy kitchen activities. The living and family rooms are both sunken one step.

● Here is another contemporary, two-story design which offers fine contemporary living patterns. There are four bedrooms, 2½ baths and formal and informal living and dining areas. The fireplace with its raised hearth in the family room is flanked with bookshelves. Blueprints for this design include details for an optional non-basement.

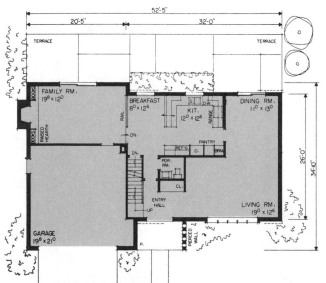

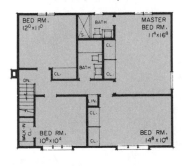

Design W1908

First Floor: 1,122 square feet
Second Floor: 896 square feet
Total: 2,018 square feet

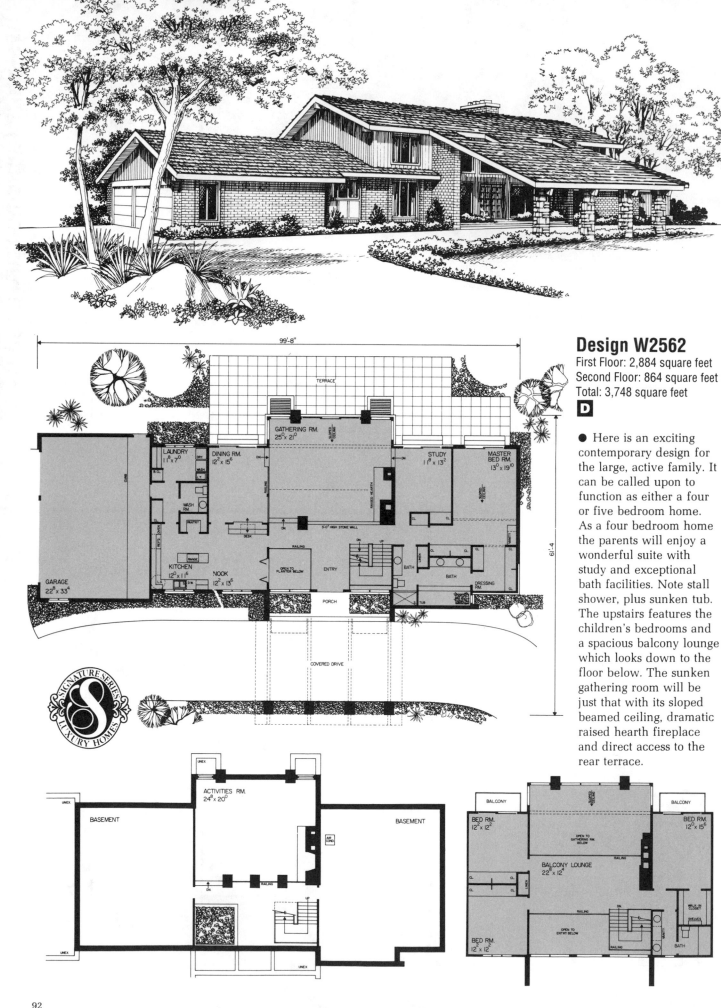

Design W2562

First Floor: 2,884 square feet
Second Floor: 864 square feet
Total: 3,748 square feet

D

● Here is an exciting contemporary design for the large, active family. It can be called upon to function as either a four or five bedroom home. As a four bedroom home the parents will enjoy a wonderful suite with study and exceptional bath facilities. Note stall shower, plus sunken tub. The upstairs features the children's bedrooms and a spacious balcony lounge which looks down to the floor below. The sunken gathering room will be just that with its sloped beamed ceiling, dramatic raised hearth fireplace and direct access to the rear terrace.

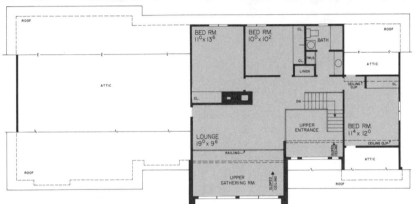

Design W2782

First Floor: 2,060 square feet
Second Floor: 897 square feet
Total: 2,957 square feet

D

● What makes this such a distinctive four-bedroom design? This plan includes great formal and informal living for the family at home or when entertaining guests. The formal gathering room and informal family room share a dramatic raised-hearth fireplace. Other features of the sunken gathering room include: high, sloped ceilings, built-in planter and sliding glass doors to the front entrance court. The kitchen has a snack bar, many built-ins, a pass-through to dining room and easy access to the large laundry/washroom. The master bedroom suite is located on the main level for added privacy and convenience. There's even a study with a built-in bar. The upper level has three more bedrooms, a bath and a lounge looking down into the gathering room.

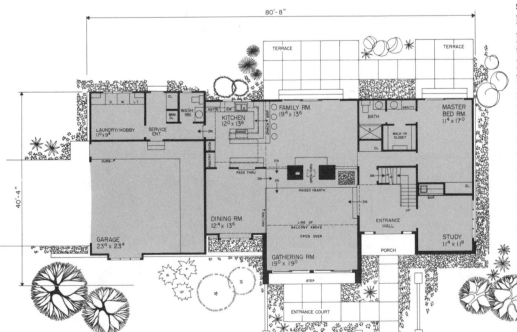

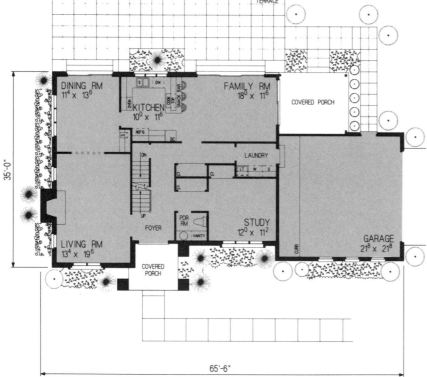

TERRACE

DINING RM
11⁴ x 13⁶

KITCHEN
10⁰ x 11⁶

FAMILY RM
18⁰ x 11⁶

COVERED PORCH

LAUNDRY

LIVING RM
13⁴ x 19⁶

UP

FOYER

PDR RM

vanity

STUDY
12⁰ x 11²

GARAGE
21⁸ x 21⁸

COVERED PORCH

35'-0"

65'-6"

Design W3338

First Floor: 1,314 square feet
Second Floor: 970 square feet
Total: 2,284 square feet

● For the new parents or empty-nesters, this plan's master suite has an attached nursery or sitting room. Downstairs there's a formal living room and dining room and the more casual family room with snack-bar eating area. A front study is near the powder room.

ROOF

DRESS RM

SITTING/ NURSERY
10⁰ x 9⁰

BEDROOM
12⁰ x 10⁰

LINEN

RAILING

MASTER BEDROOM
13⁴ x 15⁴

DN

WHIRLPOOL

BATH

BEDROOM
10⁰ x 11⁰

LINEN

BATH

ROOF

ROOF

ROOF

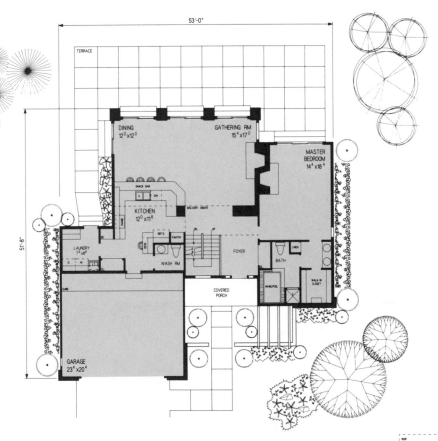

Design W2490

First Floor: 1,414 square feet
Second Floor: 620 square feet
Total: 2,034 square feet

● Split-bedroom planning makes the most of this contemporary plan. The master suite pampers with a lavish bath and a fireplace. The living areas are open and have easy access to the rear terrace.

CUSTOMIZABLE

Custom Alterations? See page 301 for customizing this plan to your specifications.

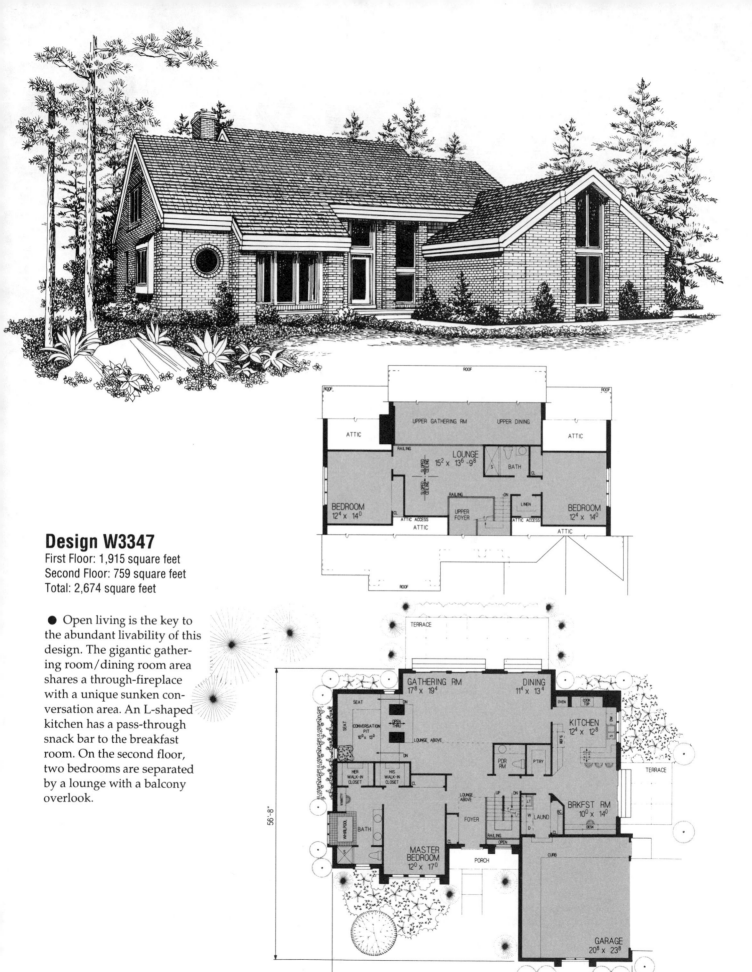

Design W3347

First Floor: 1,915 square feet
Second Floor: 759 square feet
Total: 2,674 square feet

● Open living is the key to the abundant livability of this design. The gigantic gathering room/dining room area shares a through-fireplace with a unique sunken conversation area. An L-shaped kitchen has a pass-through snack bar to the breakfast room. On the second floor, two bedrooms are separated by a lounge with a balcony overlook.

Design W2772 First Floor: 1,579 square feet
Second Floor: 1,240 square feet; Total: 2,819 square feet

● This four-bedroom two-story contemporary design is sure to suit your growing family needs. The rear U-shaped kitchen, flanked by the family and dining rooms, will be very efficient to the busy homemaker. Parents will enjoy all the convenience of the master bedroom suite.

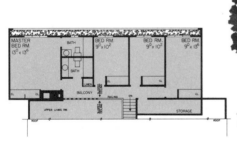

Design W2377 First Floor: 1,170 square feet
Second Floor: 815 square feet; Total: 1,985 square feet

● What an impressive, up-to-date home. Its refreshing configuration will command a full measure of attention. Note that all of the back rooms on the first floor are a couple steps lower than the entry and living room area. Separating the living room and the slightly lower level is a through-fireplace, which has a raised hearth in the family room. Four bedrooms, serviced by two full baths, comprise the second floor which looks down into the living room.

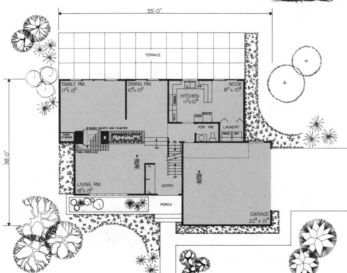

Design W2831 First Floor: 1,758 square feet
Second Floor: 1,247 square feet; Total: 3,005 square feet

D

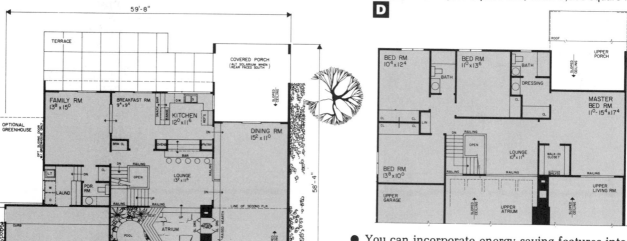

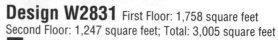

● You can incorporate energy-saving features into the elevation of this passive solar design to enable you to receive the most sunlight on your particular site. Multiple plot plans (included with the blueprints) illustrate which elevations should be solarized for different sites and which extra features can be incorporated. The features can include a greenhouse added to the family room, the back porch turned into a solarium or skylights installed over the entry.

Design W4313

First Floor: 1,685 square feet
Second Floor: 818 square feet
Total: 2,503 square feet

● There are five decks to enjoy in this home, each strategically placed to accept full use. Begin with the front entry deck that leads to grand double doors. From the entry hall step down into the great room with corner fireplace. Dining takes place to either side of the galley kitchen in the formal dining room or casual breakfast room. The master bedroom is found on this floor also and has its own full bath. Upstairs there are three more bedrooms, one with a deck; the other two have walk-in closets.

LIFESTYLE HOME PLANS

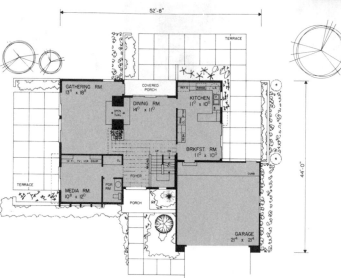

Design W2925 First Floor: 1,128 square feet
Second Floor: 844 square feet; Total: 1,972 square feet

● Living areas for every kind of activity are found in this Northwest contemporary home. A gathering room with through fireplace to the formal dining room handles both formal and informal occasions. The nearby kitchen and attached breakfast room have access to the outdoor terrace and also attach to the front entry hall. A quiet media room has an attached powder room and can double as a guest room. Upstairs there are two bedrooms and two full baths. The master suite has a fireplace, whirlpool tub and His and Hers walk-in closets.

Design W2823

First Floor: 1,370 square feet
Second Floor: 927 square feet
Total: 2,297 square feet

L **D**

● The street view of this contemporary design features a small courtyard entrance as well as a private terrace off the study. Inside the livability will be outstanding. This design features spacious first-floor activity areas that flow smoothly into one another. In the gathering room a raised-hearth fireplace creates a dramatic focal point. An adjacent covered terrace, featuring a skylight, is ideal for outdoor dining and could be screened in later for an additional room.

Design W2729

First Floor: 1,590 square feet
Second Floor: 756 square feet
Total: 2,346 square feet

L

● A sheltered walkway and double front doors make a welcome entrance to this remarkable contemporary home. The two-story entry and sunken gathering room (with a raised-hearth fireplace) add dimension. Indoor/outdoor living relationships are incorporated into the design; each of the first-floor living areas opens to a terrace. The first-floor master suite, which includes a large walk-in closet, dressing room, and separate shower and tub, offers much privacy. Two additional second-floor bedrooms feature private baths and dressing rooms.

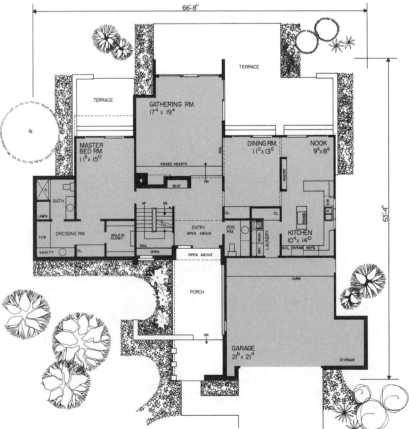

Design W2708

First Floor: 2,108 square feet
Second Floor: 824 square feet
Total: 2,932 square feet

D

● If you like your contemporary design with a touch of traditional styling, this plan, with its exact proportions and fine features, may be the one you're looking for. Inside is a plan with lots of extras. Notables include a master suite with dressing room, twin vanities, huge walk-in closet and access to a private terrace out back. It also features a roomy study that leads to a small patio in front, combo dining room and gathering room with a raised-hearth fireplace, and loads of pantry storage. On the second floor is a spacious lounge that's open to the gathering room below.

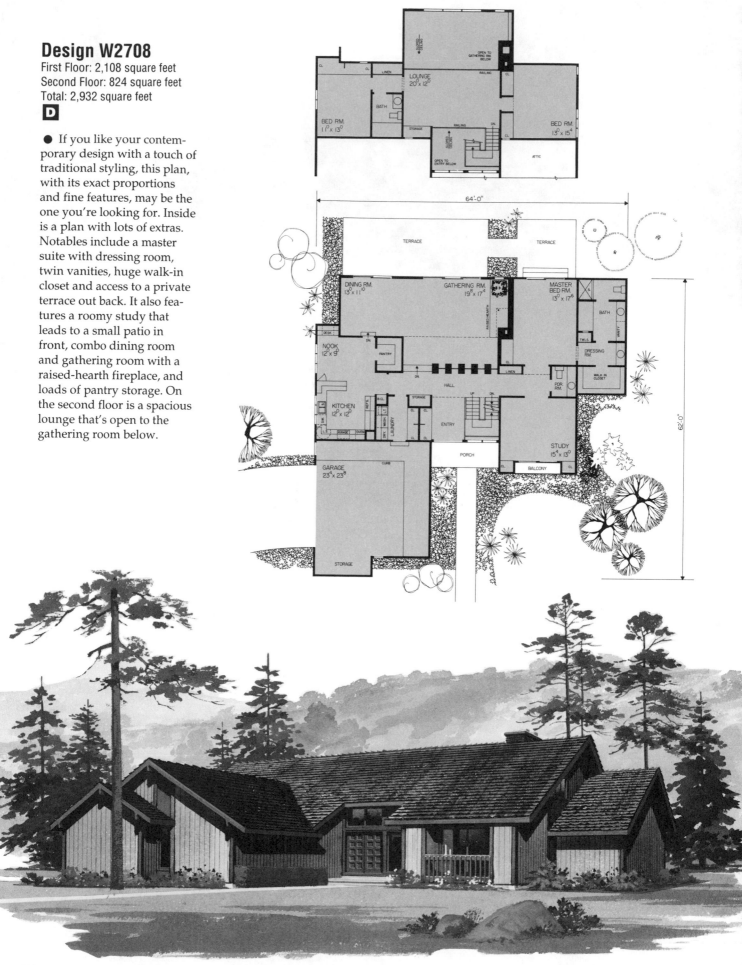

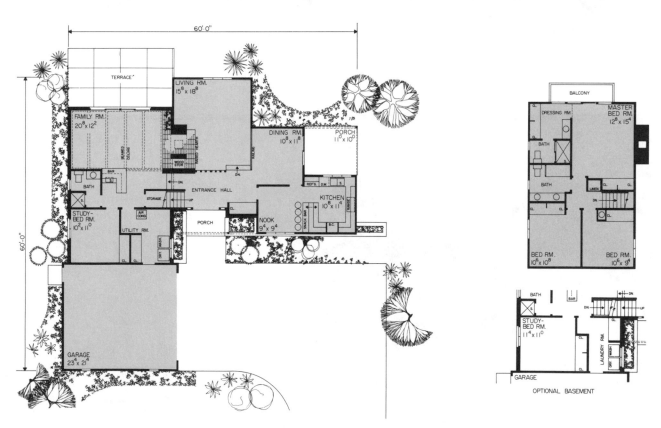

Design W2379 First Floor: 1,525 square feet; Second Floor: 748 square feet; Total: 2,273 square feet

L **D**

● A house that has "everything" may very well look just like this design. Its exterior is well-proportioned and impressive. Inside the inviting double front doors there are features galore. The living room and family room level is sunken. Separating these two rooms is a dramatic thru fireplace. A built-in bar, planter, and beamed ceiling highlight the family room. Nearby is a full bath and a study which could be utilized as a fourth bedroom. A fine functioning kitchen has a pass-thru to the snack bar of the breakfast nook. The adjacent dining room overlooks the living room and has sliding doors to the covered porch. Upstairs three bedrooms, two baths, and an outdoor balcony. Blueprints for this design include optional basement details. Laundry still remains on first floor.

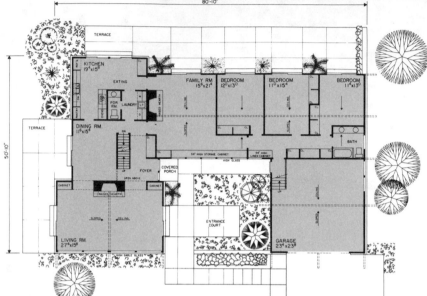

Design W1783

First Floor: 2,412 square feet
Second Floor: 640 square feet
Total: 3,052 square feet

● Solid and lasting, the look of a stone house is appealing. This one works well on a lot that slopes slightly to the front. Living areas are abundant and spacious: Large sloped ceiling living room with fireplace, formal dining room with sliding glass doors, family room with fireplace and sloped ceiling. Family bedrooms are on the first floor and share a full bath. The master suite dominates the second floor and has a private balcony.

● Varying roof planes, wide overhangs, interestingly shaped blank wall areas and patterned, double front doors provide the distinguishing characteristics of this contemporary design. The extension of the front wall results in a private, outdoor patio area accessible from the living room. There is a fine feeling of spaciousness inside this plan. The living area features open planning. Upstairs, four good-sized bedrooms and two baths.

Design W2602 First Floor: 1,154 square feet
Second Floor: 1,120 square feet; Total: 2,274 square feet

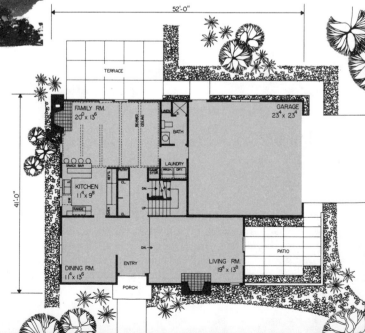

104

● This seemingly low-slung ranch home holds some delightful surprises on the inside. There's an open staircase to a second floor! The main living area on the first floor is highlighted with a large living room and dining room, both with beamed ceilings. The L-shaped kitchen is found nearby and connects conveniently to the family room (notice the corner fireplace here). Three bedrooms and two full baths occupy the right wing of the home. Upstairs is space for expansion to another bedroom and full bath. A study area here is skylit and has a balcony overlook to the living room.

Design W4036
First Floor: 1,833 square feet
Second Floor: 409 square feet
Total: 2,242 square feet

D

**LIFESTYLE
HOME PLANS**

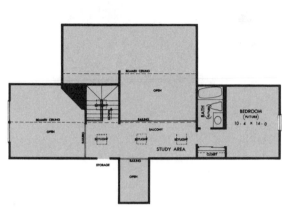

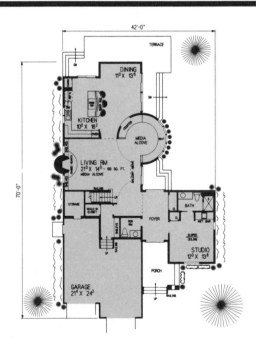

Design W3410
First Floor: 2,061 square feet
Second Floor: 997 square feet
Total: 3,058 square feet

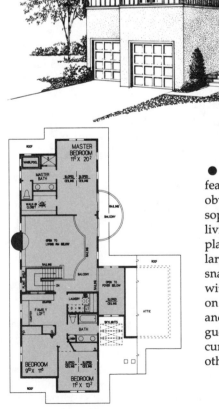

● Designed for a narrow lot, this home features a surprising amount of space. An obvious highlight on the first floor is the sophisticated circular media alcove. The living room features a raised-hearth fireplace with shelves on either side. The large kitchen with central cook top and a snack bar is adjacent to the dining room with sliding glass doors to a terrace. Also on the first floor is a studio with a wet bar and full bath, a perfect place for overnight guests. Upstairs, the master suite and curved balcony are separated from the other two family bedrooms.

Design W2339 First Floor: 2,068 square feet; Second Floor: 589 square feet; Total: 2,657 square feet

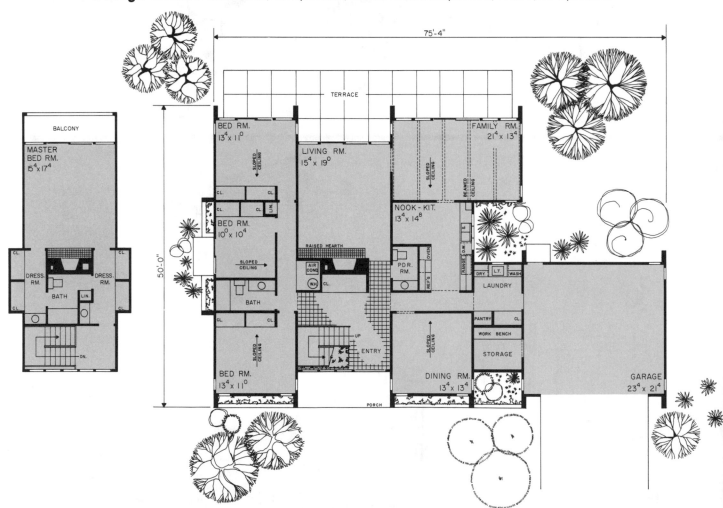

● Here, the influence of the Spanish Southwest comes into clear view. The smooth texture of the stucco exterior contrasts pleasingly with the roughness of the tile roofs. Contributing to the appeal of this contemporary design are the varying roof planes, the interesting angles and the blank wall masses punctuated by the glass areas. Whether called upon to function as a two-story home, or a one-story ranch with an attic studio, this design will deliver interesting and enjoyable living patterns. Sloping ceilings and generous glass areas foster a feeling of spaciousness. Traffic patterns are excellent and the numerous storage facilities are outstanding. Fireplaces are the focal point of the living room and the second floor master bedroom. Three more bedrooms are on the first floor.

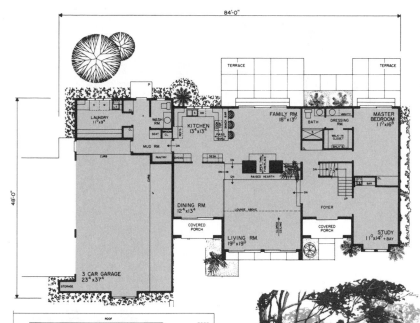

Design W2906

First Floor: 2,121 square feet
Second Floor: 913 square feet
Total: 3,034 square feet

D

● This striking contemporary with Spanish good looks offers outstanding livability. An efficient, spacious kitchen opens to a spacious dining room, with pass-through also leading to a family room. The family room and adjoining master bedroom suite overlook a backyard terrace. Just off the master bedroom is a sizable study that opens to a foyer. The center point is a living room that faces a front courtyard and a lounge above the living room. Three second-story bedrooms join the upstairs lounge.

Design W2390 First Floor: 1,368 square feet

Second Floor: 1,428 square feet; Total: 2,796 square feet

D

● If yours is a large family and you like the architecture of the Far West, don't look further. Particularly if you envision building on a modest sized lot. Projecting the garage to the front contributes to the drama of this two-story. Its stucco exterior is beautifully enhanced by the clay tiles of the varying roof surfaces. The focal point, of course, is the five bedroom, three bath second floor. Four bedrooms have access to the outdoor balcony.

Design W3418

First Floor: 1,283 square feet
Second Floor: 552 square feet
Total: 1,835 square feet

● This home is ideal for the economically minded who don't want to sacrifice livability. The entry foyer opens directly into the two-story living room with fireplace. To the right, the kitchen with peninsula cooktop and snack bar conveniently serves both the breakfast room and the formal dining room. Also on this level, the master bedroom boasts an enormous bath with a whirlpool and His and Hers walk-in-closets. Three other bedrooms are located upstairs to ensure peace and quiet. Also notice the abundant storage space in the attic.

Custom Alterations? See page 301 for customizing this plan to your specifications.

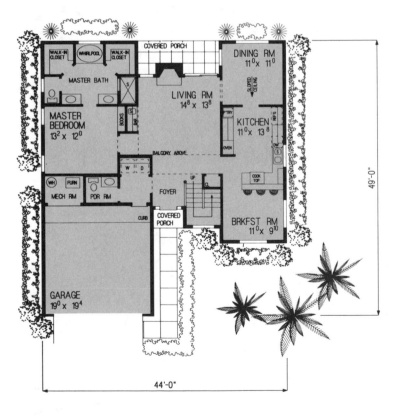

108

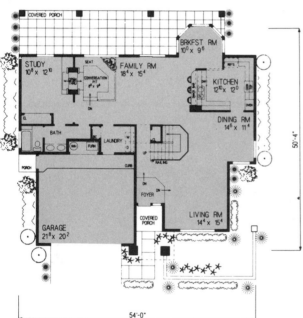

CUSTOMIZABLE

Custom Alterations? See page 301 for customizing this plan to your specifications.

Design W3424
First Floor: 1,625 square feet
Second Floor: 982 square feet
Total: 2,607 square feet

● You'll find plenty about this Spanish design that will convince you that this is the home for your family. Enjoy indoor/outdoor living in the gigantic family room with covered patio access and a sunken conversation area sharing a through-fireplace with the study. An L-shaped kitchen has an attached, glass-surrounded breakfast room and is conveniently located next to the formal dining room/living room combination. Besides the opulent master suite on the second floor, there are two family bedrooms and a full bath.

Design W1877

First Floor: 1,162 square feet
Second Floor: 883 square feet
Total: 2,045 square feet

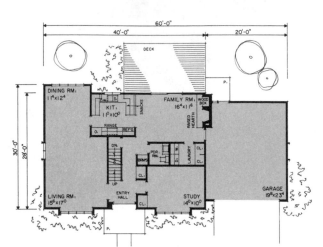

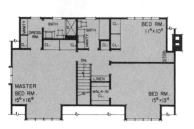

● This simple, straightforward plan has much to offer in the way of livability and economical construction costs. Worthy of particular note are the excellent traffic patterns and the outstanding use of space. Notice the cozy family room with its raised-hearth fireplace, wood box and sliding glass doors to the sweeping outdoor deck. The efficient kitchen is flanked by the informal snack bar and the formal dining area. Open planning between the living and dining areas promotes a fine feeling of spaciousness. The study is a great feature. It may function as just that or become the sewing or TV room, the guest room or even the fourth bedroom.

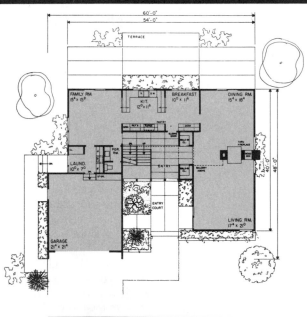

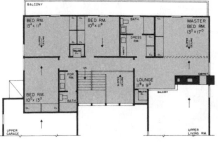

Design W2123

First Floor: 1,624 square feet
Second Floor: 1,335 square feet
Total: 2,959 square feet

● Inside there is close to 3,000 square feet of uniquely planned floor area. The spacious, well-lighted entry has, of course, a high sloping ceiling. The second floor ceiling also slopes and, consequently, adds to the feeling of spaciousness.

Design W2887 First Floor: 1,338 square feet; Second Floor: 661 square feet; Total: 1,999 square feet

● This attractive, contemporary 1½-story will be the envy of many. First, examine the efficient kitchen. Not only does it offer a snack bar for those quick meals but also a large dining room. Notice the adjacent dining porch. The laundry and garage access are also adjacent to the kitchen. An exciting feature is the gathering room with fireplace. The first floor also offers a study with a wet bar and sliding glass doors that open to a private porch. This will make those quiet times cherishable. Adjacent to the study is a full bath followed by a bedroom. Upstairs a large master bedroom suite occupies the entire floor. It features a bath with an oversized tub and shower, a large walk-in closet with built-ins and an open lounge with fireplace. Both the lounge and master bedroom, along with the gathering room, have sloped ceilings. Develop the lower level for additional space.

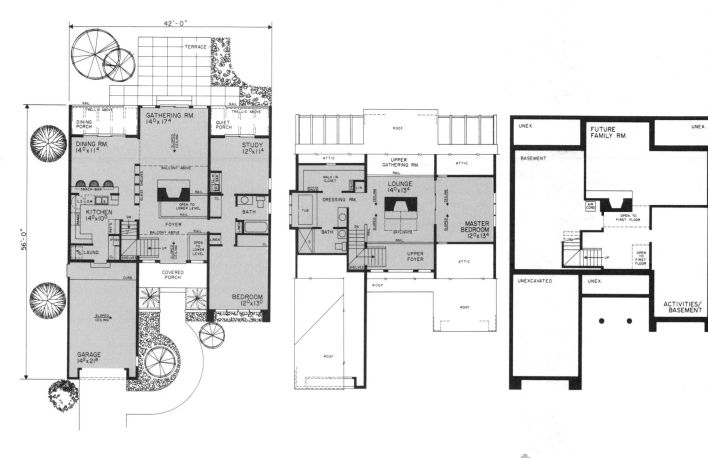

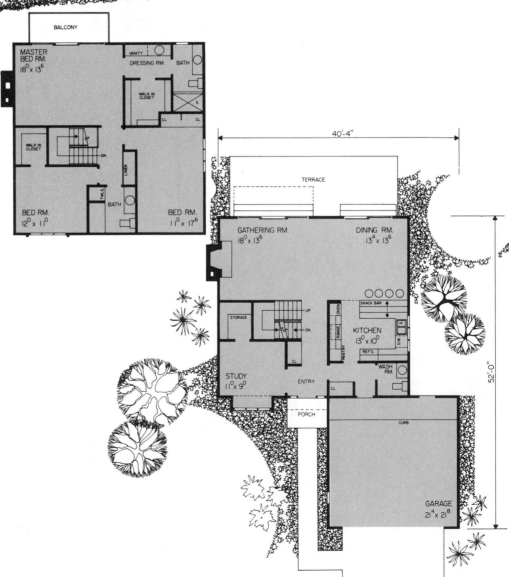

CUSTOMIZABLE

Custom Alterations? See page 301 for customizing this plan to your specifications.

Design W2711

First Floor: 975 square feet
Second Floor: 1,024 square feet
Total: 1,999 square feet

L D

● Sleek, affordable style. Large dining area, kitchen, mudroom off the garage, and spacious bedroom are key selling points for a young family. Also, note: private balcony off the master suite, cozy study with lots of storage space, terrace to the rear of the house, and a sizable snack bar for the kids—and adults.

Design W3352

First Floor: 1,148 square feet
Second Floor: 1,010 square feet
Total: 2,158 square feet

L **D**

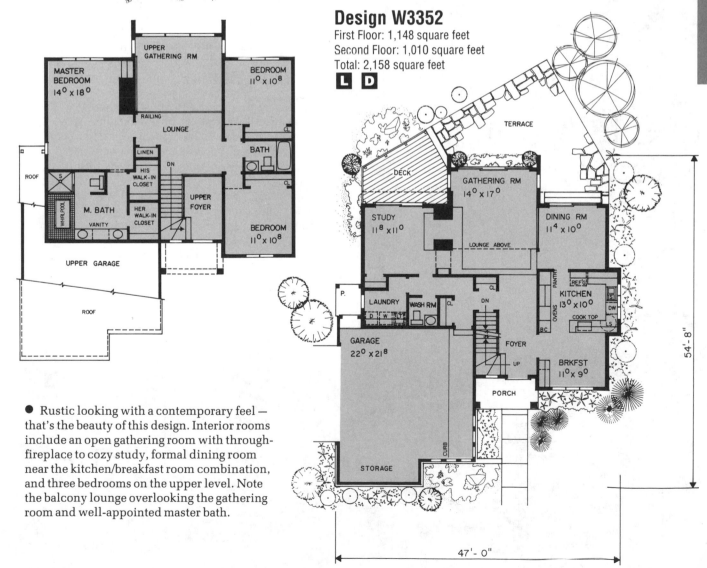

● Rustic looking with a contemporary feel —
that's the beauty of this design. Interior rooms
include an open gathering room with through-
fireplace to cozy study, formal dining room
near the kitchen/breakfast room combination,
and three bedrooms on the upper level. Note
the balcony lounge overlooking the gathering
room and well-appointed master bath.

11

TERRACE

DECK
HOT TUB
SKYLITE

STUDY / BED RM
11⁰ x 11⁰

GREAT RM.
16⁰ x 14²

COVERED PORCH

LOUNGE ABOVE

RAISED HEARTH

MASTER BED RM
12⁰ x 14⁶

CL

LINEN

DINING
14⁰ x 9⁴

GL. SHLVS

PANTRY

BATH

LINEN

UP

DN

BRM

BRM

OVENS

KITCHEN
13⁰ x 8⁰

DRESSING RM

TUB

VANITY

SEAT

WALK-IN CLOSET

FOYER

LAUND.

CL

D.W.

RANGE

REF'G

PORCH OPEN ABOVE

CURB

ROOF LINE

GARAGE
21⁴ x 21⁸

54'-8"

52'-0"

UPPER GREAT RM

CL

LOUNGE / HOBBIES
16⁰ x 9²

SKYLITE

CL

DN

UPPER FOYER

STOR. / BATH

RAILING

RAILING

RAILING

Design W2822

First Floor: 1,363 square feet
Second Floor: 351 square feet
Total: 1,714 square feet

L

● Here is a truly unique house whose interior was designed with the current decade's economies, life-styles and demographics in mind. While function-ing as a one-story home, the second floor provides an extra measure of livability when required. In addition, this two-story section adds to the dramatic appeal of both the exterior and the interior. Within only 1,363 square feet, this contemporary delivers refreshing and outstanding living patterns for those who are buying their first home, those who have raised their family and are looking for a smaller home and those in search of a retirement home.

BALCONY

LOUNGE / GUEST RM. / GRANDCHILDREN'S RM.
16⁰ x 19²

CL

CL

DN

RAILING

UPPER FOYER

BATH

RAILING

ALTERNATE SECOND FLOOR

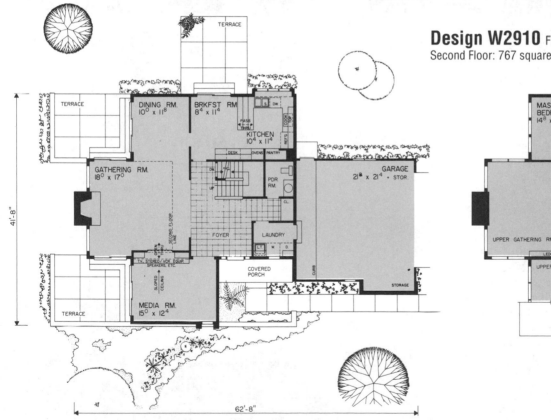

Design W2910 First Floor: 1,221 square feet
Second Floor: 767 square feet; Total: 1,988 square feet

● This two-story home offers excellent zoning by room functions and modern amenities for comfort. A two-story gathering room, with attached dining room, serves the needs of any get-together, both formal and informal.

Sliding glass doors on either side of this room lead to two separate terrace areas. A third terrace can be reached via sliding glass doors in the breakfast room. Be sure to note the special features of this home: dramatic ceiling

heights, built-in storage areas, and pass-throughs. Notice also the media room for stereos/VCRs, plush master bedroom with a whirlpool, modern kitchen, and balcony.

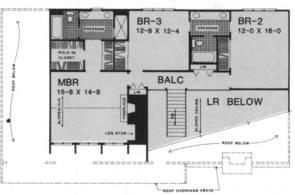

Design W4264

First Floor: 1,406 square feet
Second Floor: 1,067 square feet
Total: 2,473 square feet

D

● Contemporary configuration makes a dramatic statement in this lovely two-story home. The list of special features is quite impressive: two fireplaces (one in the living room, one in the master suite), large storage room and tool room off the garage, walk-in pantry and island cook top in the kitchen, dressing areas in both full baths. The second floor has a balcony overlook to the living room below.

LIFESTYLE HOME PLANS

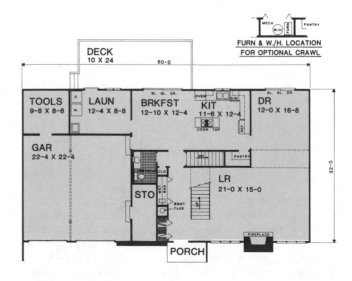

Design W4214

First Floor: 1,152 square feet
Second Floor: 1,144 square feet
Total: 2,296 square feet

● Combining some of the best features of both contemporary and traditional design, this home is comfortable as either a country or city dweller. Beyond its rustic covered front porch is a classic of a floor plan. Because the open staircase to the second floor is located in the entry foyer, it contributes to the feeling of space and height throughout the home. A grand-sized family room blends in with the U-shaped kitchen, sharing a pass-through snack bar with it. Formal entertaining is handled easily in the living room and dining room on the right side of the home. Upstairs there's plenty of sleeping room in four bedrooms. Two full baths here serve the family's needs.

LIFESTYLE
HOME PLANS

OPTION OMITTING BASEMENT

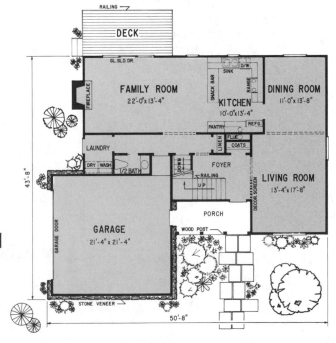

LIFESTYLE HOME PLANS

Design W4226

First Floor: 784 square feet
Second Floor: 845 square feet
Total: 1,629 square feet

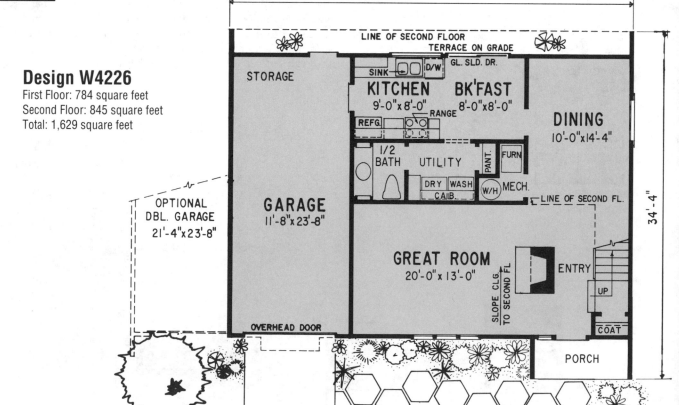

40'-0"

LINE OF SECOND FLOOR
TERRACE ON GRADE

STORAGE

SINK | D/W | GL. SLD. DR.

KITCHEN
9'-0" x 8'-0"

BK'FAST
8'-0" x 8'-0"

RANGE

REFG.

DINING
10'-0" x 14'-4"

1/2 BATH

UTILITY

PANT.

FURN

DRY | WASH
CAIB.

W/H | MECH.

LINE OF SECOND FL.

GARAGE
11'-8" x 23'-8"

OPTIONAL
DBL. GARAGE
21'-4" x 23'-8"

GREAT ROOM
20'-0" x 13'-0"

SLOPE CLG.
TO SECOND FL.

ENTRY

UP

34'-4"

OVERHEAD DOOR

COAT

PORCH

LIFESTYLE HOME PLANS

Design W4225

First Floor: 784 square feet
Second Floor: 845 square feet
Total: 1,629 square feet

● Simple styling is the element that makes this home so attractive. The front entry opens to a great room to the left and formal dining room to the rear. The great room is separated from the entry by a fireplace and its ceiling slopes up to the second floor. Upstairs, an open-railed balcony overlooks the great room below. Two family bedrooms share a full bath with dual lavatories. The master bedroom has a private bath and walk-in closet. Two different exteriors from which you can choose are offered on this page and on the opposite page.

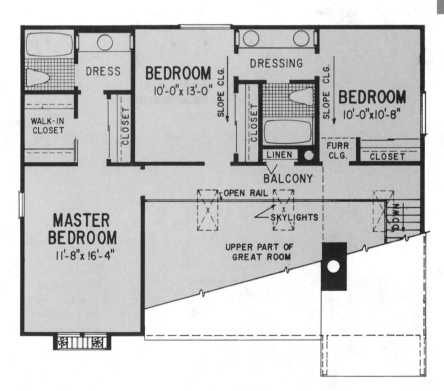

Design W4019

First Floor: 676 square feet
Second Floor: 969 square feet
Total: 1,645 square feet

L

BEDROOM-3
12'-0"x11'-8"

WALK-IN CLOSET

CLOSET

DRY.

WASH

LINEN

DISAP. STAIR

WALK-IN CLOSET

BEDROOM-2
13'-0"x11'-4"

CLOSET

DOWN

RAIL

OPEN TO FIRST FL.

MASTER BEDROOM
15'-4"x15'-0"

OPT. FIREPLACE

LIFESTYLE HOME PLANS

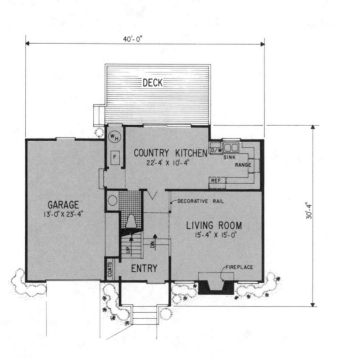

40'-0"

DECK

W H

F

COUNTRY KITCHEN
22'-4" X 10'-4"

D/W

SINK

RANGE

REF.

DECORATIVE RAIL

30'-4"

GARAGE
13'-0" X 23'-4"

UP

DN

COATS

ENTRY

LIVING ROOM
15'-4" X 15'-0"

FIREPLACE

● Those looking for an economical, easy-to-build home, look no further. The rectangular shape of this design will help hold down construction costs. The first level features a spacious living room with fireplace and a large country kitchen. The kitchen work area is contained to one side, leaving room for both eating and sitting areas. A wood deck is just a few steps away. An open stair leads up to the second level which contains three good-sized bedrooms; the master boasts a huge walk-in closet, a bath with double vanity, and an optional fireplace. The washer and dryer are conveniently near the source of dirty laundry.

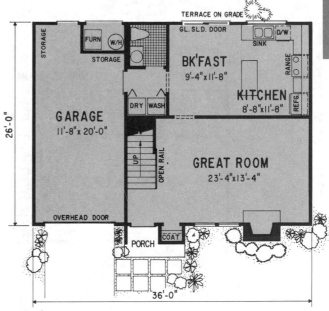

LIFESTYLE HOME PLANS

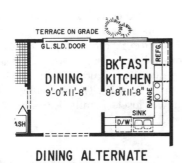

TERRACE ON GRADE
GL.SLD. DOOR

DINING
9'-0"x11'-8"

BK'FAST
KITCHEN
8'-8"x11'-8"

REFG.

RANGE

SINK

D/W

WASH

DINING ALTERNATE

CLOSET

DRESSING

LINEN

BEDROOM-2
15'-0"x 11'-8"

MASTER
BEDROOM
11'-8"x 17'-0"

DOWN

BEDROOM-3
13'-0"x 13'-4"

WALK-IN
CLOSET

WALK-IN
CLOSET

WALK-IN
CLOSET

Design W4224

First Floor: 641 square feet
Second Floor: 936 square feet
Total: 1,577 square feet

L

● Magnificent diagonal wood siding adds interest to this two-story plan. Its interior simplicity appeals to first-time builders or empty-nesters. The first floor contains a large great room with fireplace and open rail to the second floor. An island kitchen complements this area and has an attached breakfast room. A laundry area has a powder room for quick clean ups. Upstairs are three bedrooms, each with walk-in closet and two full baths. An alternative plan for a formal dining room is included with the blueprints.

Design W4216

First Floor: 784 square feet
Second Floor: 784 square feet
Total: 1,568 square feet

L

● A covered entry leads the way to this simple two-story home. The front-facing great room has a fireplace and leads back to a formal dining room. The kitchen/breakfast room features sliding glass doors to the rear yard and has access to a pantry and laundry room with ½-bath. Three bedrooms are found upstairs. The master bedroom has a full bath with two closets. Family bedrooms share a full compartmented bath.

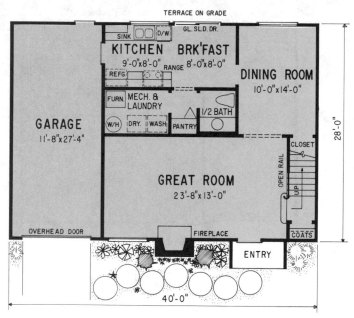

TERRACE ON GRADE

GL. SL'D. DR.

SINK | D/W

KITCHEN | **BRK'FAST**
9'-0"x8'-0" | RANGE | 8'-0"x8'-0"

REFG

DINING ROOM
10'-0"x14'-0"

FURN. | MECH. &
LAUNDRY

W/H | DRY. | WASH | 1/2 BATH

PANTRY

GARAGE
11'-8"x27'-4"

CLOSET

OPEN RAIL

UP

GREAT ROOM
23'-8"x13'-0"

28'-0"

OVERHEAD DOOR

FIREPLACE

COATS

ENTRY

40'-0"

LIFESTYLE HOME PLANS

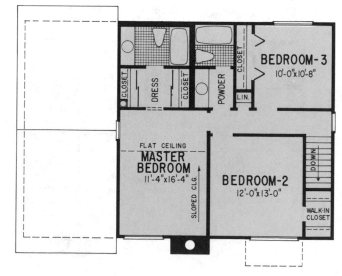

CLOSET

DRESS

CLOSET

POWDER

LIN.

CLOSET

BEDROOM-3
10'-0"x10'-8"

FLAT CEILING
MASTER BEDROOM
11'-4"x16'-4"

SLOPED CLG.

DOWN

BEDROOM-2
12'-0"x13'-0"

WALK-IN CLOSET

Design W4227

First Floor: 784 square feet
Second Floor: 845 square feet
Total: 1,629 square feet

● Sloped ceilings are a great touch in the great room and two bedrooms of this home. Other interior features that add to its appeal include a fireplace in the great room, a ½-bath in the utility area, sliding glass doors leading outdoors from the breakfast room, and a balcony overlook on the second floor. Sleeping accommodations are handled in a master suite with full bath and walk-in closet plus two family bedrooms with shared bath. The one-car garage can be expanded to a two-car garage if needed.

LIFESTYLE
HOME PLANS

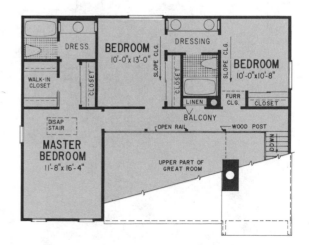

Design W4247

First Floor: 1,096 square feet
Second Floor: 1,157 square feet
Total: 2,253 square feet

● This design features a first-floor plan near-ly identical to W4248. A raised-hearth fire-place placed at one end of the great room cre-ates a living-area focus. The difference between the two plans lies upstairs. This design boasts four nice-sized bedrooms and two full baths. This additional space makes this plan ideal for larger families.

LIFESTYLE
HOME PLANS

Design W4248

First Floor: 1,157 square feet
Second Floor: 841 square feet
Total: 1,998 square feet

L D

● This appealing contemporary packs lots of livability into a moderate amount of space. Downstairs
from the entry is the enormous great room. This
multi-purpose room features a living area with a
sloped ceiling and fireplace and dining area with a
sliding glass door to the patio. Conveniently adjacent is the kitchen with L-shaped work area. A
small window greenhouse provides a cheerful back-
drop for the breakfast nook. Also on this level, the
master bedroom includes a walk-in closet, bathroom
with double vanities, and patio access. Two more
bedrooms and a shared bath are located upstairs as
well as a large study balcony overlooking the great
room.

LIFESTYLE
HOME PLANS

125

Design W4261

First Floor: 2,012 square feet
Second Floor: 1,577 square feet
Total: 3,589 square feet

 L

● This house says, We've arrived!
Features include: five bedrooms, 3½
baths, a large family room, a spacious
foyer separating living space on the
first floor, a long kitchen with snack
bar, a light-filled studio on the second
floor, window greenhouse, deck, lots
of storage and closet space, and a
large fireplace in the beam-ceilinged
living room. Without a doubt, this is a
plan that could well become the talk
of the town.

LIFESTYLE
HOME PLANS

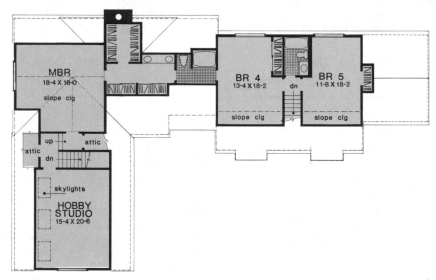

MBR
18-4 X 18-0
slope clg

BR 4
13-4 X 18-2
slope clg

BR 5
11-8 X 18-2
slope clg

up   attic
attic   dn

skylights

HOBBY
STUDIO
15-4 X 20-6

86-0

deck

furn mech wh

window greenhouse

DINING
11-6 X 14-8

beam clg

LIVING
19-6 X 14-8

dn   dn

foyer

laun
w
d
tub

lin

BR 2
11-2 X 17-0

clg

52-0

snack bar

ref

KIT
17-6 X 8-0

dw

B'FAST
11-6 X 8-0

range
pant
pant

FAMILY
13-4 X 23-0

up

BR 3
11-8 X 11-0

slope

tool
storage

up

GARAGE
23-4 X 20-8

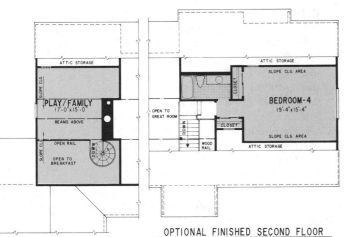

ATTIC STORAGE

SLOPE CLG.

PLAY/FAMILY
17'-0"x15'-0"

BEAMS ABOVE

OPEN RAIL

SLOPE CLG

OPEN TO BREAKFAST

ATTIC STORAGE

SLOPE CLG. AREA

BEDROOM-4
19'-4"x15'-4"

SLOPE CLG. AREA

ATTIC STORAGE

OPEN TO GREAT ROOM

CLOSET

WOOD RAIL

OPTIONAL FINISHED SECOND FLOOR

Design W4330

First Floor: 2,292 square feet
Second Floor: 714 square feet
Total: 3,006 square feet

LIFESTYLE
HOME PLANS

● There's bonus space in this home that might easily be missed from a cursory glance at its wood-sided exterior. The first floor houses complete livability with the centralized great room, formal dining room, kitchen with island range and attached breakfast nook, three bedrooms and two full baths. Three decks (two partially covered) complement these rooms. But upstairs is the real treat — an optional fourth bedroom and full bath and playroom or family room with spiral staircase down to the first floor. Two storage areas in the garage and attic storage add to this home's practicality.

54'-0"

KITCHEN
10'-4" X 10'-0"
S. UNIT
REF
SINK
OVEN

DINING
11'-0" X 11'-4"

LIVING
15'-0" X 22'-0"

SLOPED CLG.

MASTER BEDROOM
16'-0" X 12'-0"

SLOPED CLG.

BKFAST

PANTRY
UP

LINE OF BALCONY ABOVE

CLOSET

DRESSING

DECK

64'-0"

LINE OF FLAT CLG.

FAMILY ROOM
15'-0" X 18'-0"

SLOPED CLG.

CLOSET

ENTRY

BEDROOM - 2
11'-4" X 12'-8"

BEDROOM - 3
13'-8" X 11'-0"

CLOSET

COATS

BAR

DOUBLE GARAGE
21'-8" X 25'-8"

OPEN TO LIVING AND DINING BELOW

BEDROOM-4
12'-8" X 14'-4"

CLOSET

DN

BALCONY

RAIL

SKY LIGHTS ABOVE

DRESS.

CLOSET

BEDROOM-5
10'-4" X 13'-6"

LINEN

ATTIC STORAGE

OPEN TO ENTRY

ATTIC STORAGE

FAMILY ROOM BELOW

LINE OF WALL BELOW

● It's hard to believe that this compact-looking plan houses five bedrooms, three baths, and room for casual and formal entertaining. Its unique design moves from front entry to living and dining rooms and U-shaped kitchen with breakfast room to the rear. The family room is oriented to the front and has a wet bar, a fireplace and sliding glass doors to the deck. Three bedrooms are found in the right wing of the first floor. One is the master suite. Upstairs are two more bedrooms and a full bath. The skylit balcony here overlooks the living and dining rooms.

Design W4328

First Floor: 2,035 square feet
Second Floor: 700 square feet
Total: 2,735 square feet

L **D**

LIFESTYLE HOME PLANS

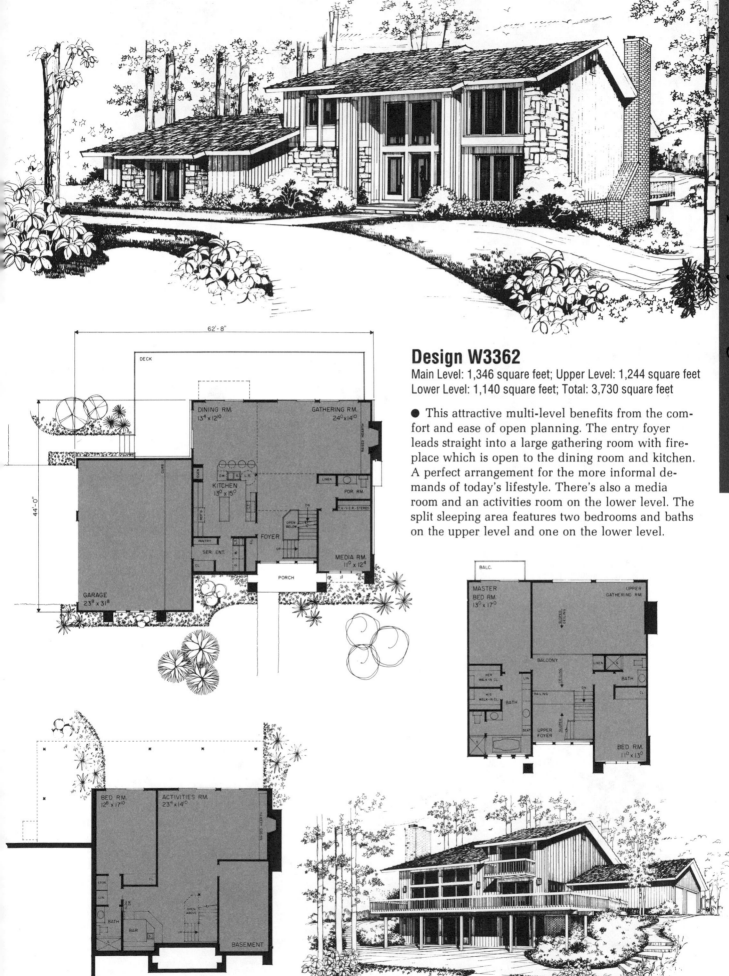

Design W3362

Main Level: 1,346 square feet; Upper Level: 1,244 square feet
Lower Level: 1,140 square feet; Total: 3,730 square feet

● This attractive multi-level benefits from the comfort and ease of open planning. The entry foyer leads straight into a large gathering room with fireplace which is open to the dining room and kitchen. A perfect arrangement for the more informal demands of today's lifestyle. There's also a media room and an activities room on the lower level. The split sleeping area features two bedrooms and baths on the upper level and one on the lower level.

129

Design W2679 Main Level: 1,179 square feet
Upper Level: 681 square feet; Lower Level: 680 square feet
Family Room Level: 643 square feet; Total: 3,183 square feet

● This spacious modern Contemporary home offers plenty of livability on many levels. Main level includes a breakfast room in addition to a dining room. Adjacent is a sloped-ceiling living room with raised hearth. The upper level features isolated master bedroom suite with adjoining study or sitting room and balcony. Family room level includes a long rectangular family room with adjoining terrace on one end and adjoining bar with washroom at the other end. A spacious basement is included. Two other bedrooms are positioned in the lower level with their own view of the terrace and quiet privacy. Note the rear deck.

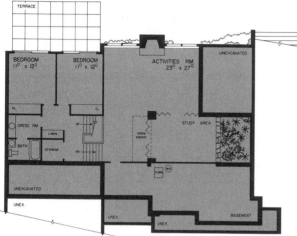

Design W2936

Main Level: 1,357 square feet; Master Bedroom Level: 623 square feet
Lower Level: 623 square feet; Activity Room: 852 square feet
Total: 3,455 square feet

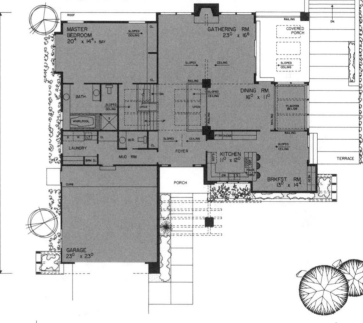

● This dramatic contemporary multi-level will offer the active family exciting new living patterns. The main level is spacious. Sloping ceilings and easy access to the outdoor living areas contribute to that feeling of openness. Imagine the enjoyment to be experienced when passing through the dining area and looking down upon the planting area of the activities level. Observe that the parents and the children each have a separate sleeping level. Don't miss the laundry, covered porch, and basement utility area.

131

Design W4199

Middle Level: 926 square feet
Upper Level: 874 square feet
Study: 152 square feet
Total: 2,047 square feet

LIFESTYLE HOME PLANS

● Two decks adorn this plan — one reached from the great room and breakfast nook on the entry level, and one from the master bedroom on the upper-level. Other welcome features include a fireplace, an upper-level study, washer/dryer area close to bedrooms, and a large storage area sharing lower-level space with garages for two cars.

Design W4327

Middle Level: 1,122 square feet
Upper Level: 1,152 square feet
Lower Level: 985 square feet
Total: 3,259 square feet

D

● This spacious contemporary will meet all the demands of today's active family. There's a sunken living room and adjoining dining room for entertaining and formal occasions. The enormous family room with its sloped ceiling and fireplace will be a favorite spot to gather and relax. Next door is a large kitchen with breakfast room. Upstairs are four good-sized bedrooms and two baths. The lower level features a sizable playroom. Sliding glass doors open onto a covered terrace. Also downstairs is an extra bedroom and bath. Don't miss the deck off the family room.

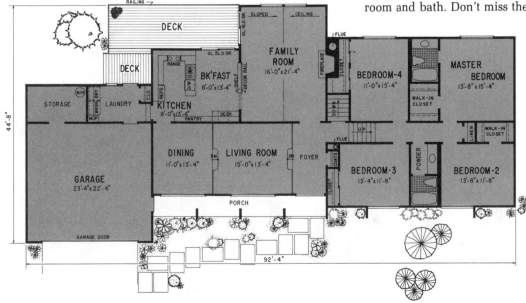

LIFESTYLE HOME PLANS

● There's a lot to love in this wood-and-stone contemporary. From three wood decks to the second-floor balcony overlook, the planning is just right. The split-bedroom design puts the master bedroom on the first floor. It is luxuriously appointed with a sloped ceiling, fireplace, walk-in closet, and deck access. A U-shaped kitchen serves both breakfast room and dining room. On the basement level is a large playroom, a washroom, and shop area that could be converted to a fourth bedroom with full bath.

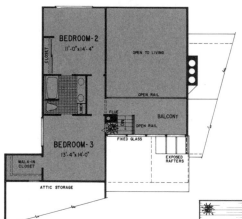

Design W4331

First Floor: 1,580 square feet
Second Floor: 730 square feet
Basement Level: 1,323 square feet
Total: 3,633 square feet

L

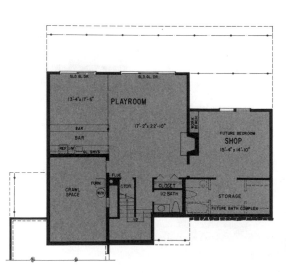

LIFESTYLE HOME PLANS

134

BEDROOM-2
11'-0"x14'-4"

OPEN TO LIVING

OPEN RAIL

BALCONY

FIXED GLASS

BEDROOM-3
13'-4"x14'-0"

CLOSET

Design W4241

First Floor: 1,580 square feet
Second Floor: 702 square feet
Basement Level: 967 square feet
Total: 3,249 square feet

L

● Similar to Design W4331, this home introduces some differences that may make it better suited to some lifestyles or building situations. Note, for instance, that the garage is placed at the basement level, alongside the playroom. An outside storage area is created just off the garage. The first floor has remained essentially the same, but there are subtle changes in the second-floor layout.

WOOD RAIL

WOOD DECK

WOOD DECK

DINING
13'-4"x12'-4"

SLD. GL. DR.   SLD. GL. DR.

LIVING
17'-4"x23'-0"

SLD. GL. DR.

MASTER
BEDROOM
15'-8"x15'-0"

CEILING

SLOPE CLG TO 2ND. FL.

KITCHEN
12'-10"x10'-0"

LINE OF BALCONY

SLOPE

REFG.

38'-0"

WOOD
DECK

BREAKFAST
13'-4"x11'-0"

POWDER RM.   BATH   DRESSING   WALK-IN
CLOSET

DRY   WASH   PANTRY   FOYER   ENTRY
DECK

STONE
VENEER

50'-0"

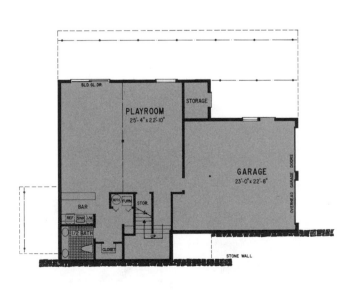

SLD. GL. DR.

PLAYROOM
25'-4" x 22'-10"

STORAGE

GARAGE
23'-0" x 22'-8"

OVERHEAD GARAGE DOORS

BAR

W/H FURN   STOR.

REF SINK W/M

1/2 BATH

CLOSET   UP

STONE WALL

Design W2580

Upper Level: 1,852 square feet
Lower Level: 1,297 square feet
Total: 3,149 square feet

● Indoor-outdoor living hardly could ask for more and here's why. Imagine, five balconies and three terraces! These unique balconies add great beauty to the exterior while adding pleasure to those who utilize them from the interior. And there's more. This home has enough space for all to appreciate. Take note of the size of the gathering room, family room and activity room. There's also a large dining room and four bedrooms for the large or growing family. Or three plus a study. Two fireplaces, one to service each of the two levels in this bi-level design. The rear ter-

race is accessible through sliding glass doors from the lower level bedroom and activity room. The master suite has two walk-in closets and a private bath.

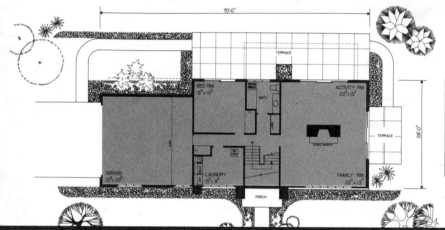

Design W2536 Main Level: 1,077 square feet

Upper Level: 1,319 square feet
Lower Level: 914 square feet
Total: 3,310 square feet

● Here are three levels of outstanding livability all packed in a delightfully contemporary exterior. The low-pitched roof has a wide overhang with exposed rafter tails. The stone masses contrast effectively with the vertical siding and the glass areas. The extension of the sloping roof provides the recessed feature of the front entrance with the patterned double doors. The homemaker's favorite highlight will be the layout of the kitchen.

No crossroom traffic here. Only a few steps from formal and informal eating areas, it is the epitome of efficiency. A sloping beamed ceiling, sliding glass doors and a raised-hearth fireplace enhance the appeal of the living room. The upper level offers the option of a fourth bedroom or a sitting room functioning with the master bedroom. On the lower level, the big family room, quiet study, laundry and extra washroom are present.

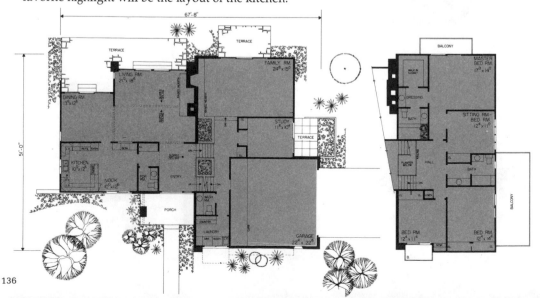

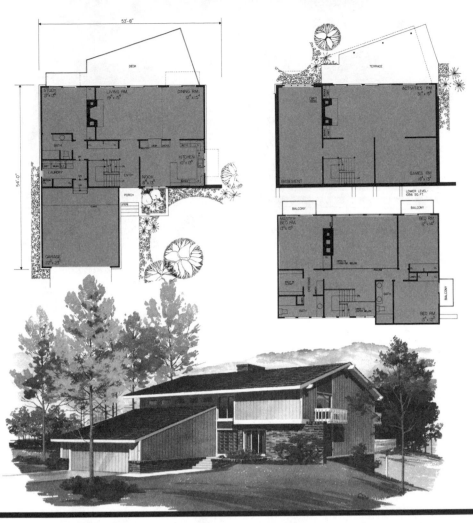

Design W2552

First Floor: 1,437 square feet
Second Floor: 1,158 square feet;
Total: 2,595 square feet

● This is a flexible, two-story design. By having the exposed basement to the rear, this home has an additional level of livability. After the development of this area, your family will enjoy an additional 1,056 square feet of informal living space. The second floor hall and master bedroom look down into the living room.

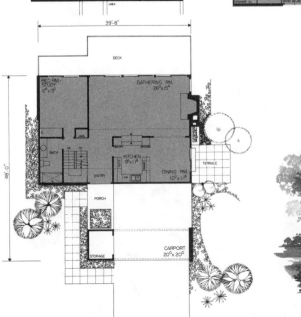

Design W2548

Main Level: 1,109 square feet
Upper Level: 739 square feet
Lower Level: 869 square feet
Total: 2,717 square feet

● Three levels of living take place in this hillside home. The gathering room and formal dining area along with the kitchen are found on the main level. A bedroom that could double as a study has a full bath nearby. The upper level has another bedroom with full bath plus a sleeping loft with balcony overlook. On the lower level is a giant activities room, another bedroom with full bath and a huge laundry area.

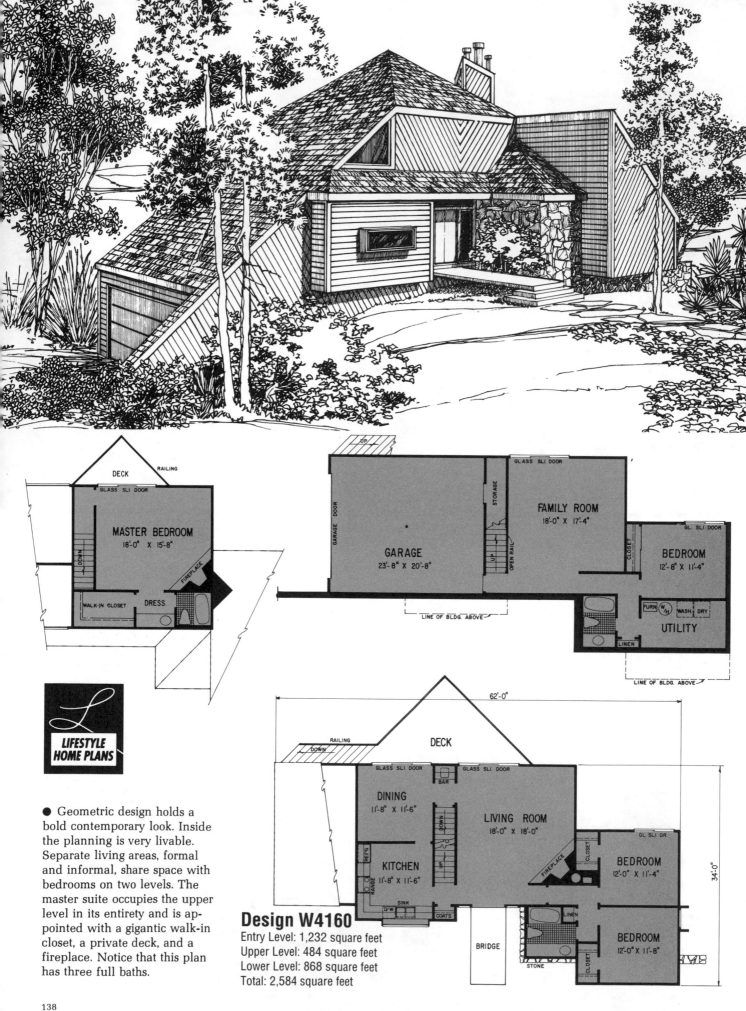

DECK

RAILING

GLASS SLI DOOR

MASTER BEDROOM
18'-0" X 15'-8"

DOWN

FIREPLACE

WALK-IN CLOSET

DRESS.

UP

GARAGE DOOR

GLASS SLI. DOOR

STORAGE

FAMILY ROOM
18'-0" X 17'-4"

GARAGE
23'-8" X 20'-8"

OPEN RAIL

UP

CLOSET

GL. SLI. DOOR

BEDROOM
12'-8" X 11'-4"

LINE OF BLDG. ABOVE

FURN

W H

WASH

DRY

LINEN

UTILITY

LINE OF BLDG. ABOVE

LIFESTYLE HOME PLANS

● Geometric design holds a bold contemporary look. Inside the planning is very livable. Separate living areas, formal and informal, share space with bedrooms on two levels. The master suite occupies the upper level in its entirety and is appointed with a gigantic walk-in closet, a private deck, and a fireplace. Notice that this plan has three full baths.

62'-0"

RAILING

DOWN

DECK

GLASS SLI. DOOR

GLASS SLI. DOOR

DINING
11'-8" X 11'-6"

BAR

LIVING ROOM
18'-0" X 18'-0"

DOWN

UP

REFG

KITCHEN
11'-8" X 11'-6"

RANGE

SINK

D/W

COATS

FIREPLACE

CLOSET

GL. SLI. DR.

BEDROOM
12'-0" X 11'-4"

34'-0"

LINEN

BEDROOM
12'-0" X 11'-8"

BRIDGE

STONE

CLOSET

Design W4160
Entry Level: 1,232 square feet
Upper Level: 484 square feet
Lower Level: 868 square feet
Total: 2,584 square feet

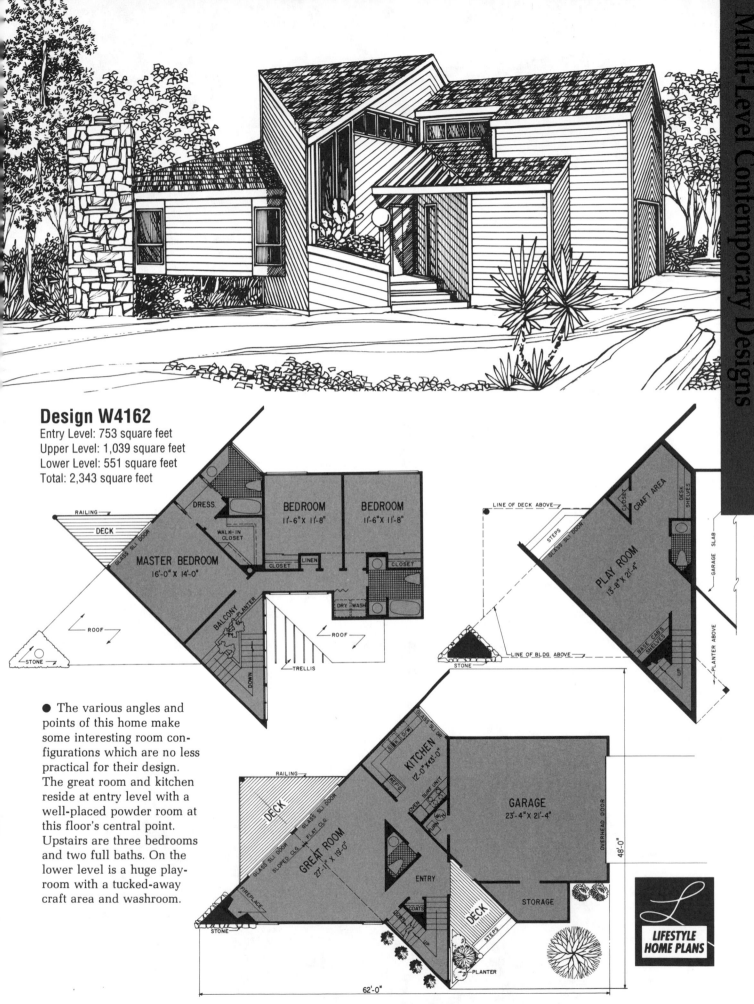

Design W4162

Entry Level: 753 square feet
Upper Level: 1,039 square feet
Lower Level: 551 square feet
Total: 2,343 square feet

● The various angles and points of this home make some interesting room configurations which are no less practical for their design. The great room and kitchen reside at entry level with a well-placed powder room at this floor's central point. Upstairs are three bedrooms and two full baths. On the lower level is a huge playroom with a tucked-away craft area and washroom.

LIFESTYLE
HOME PLANS

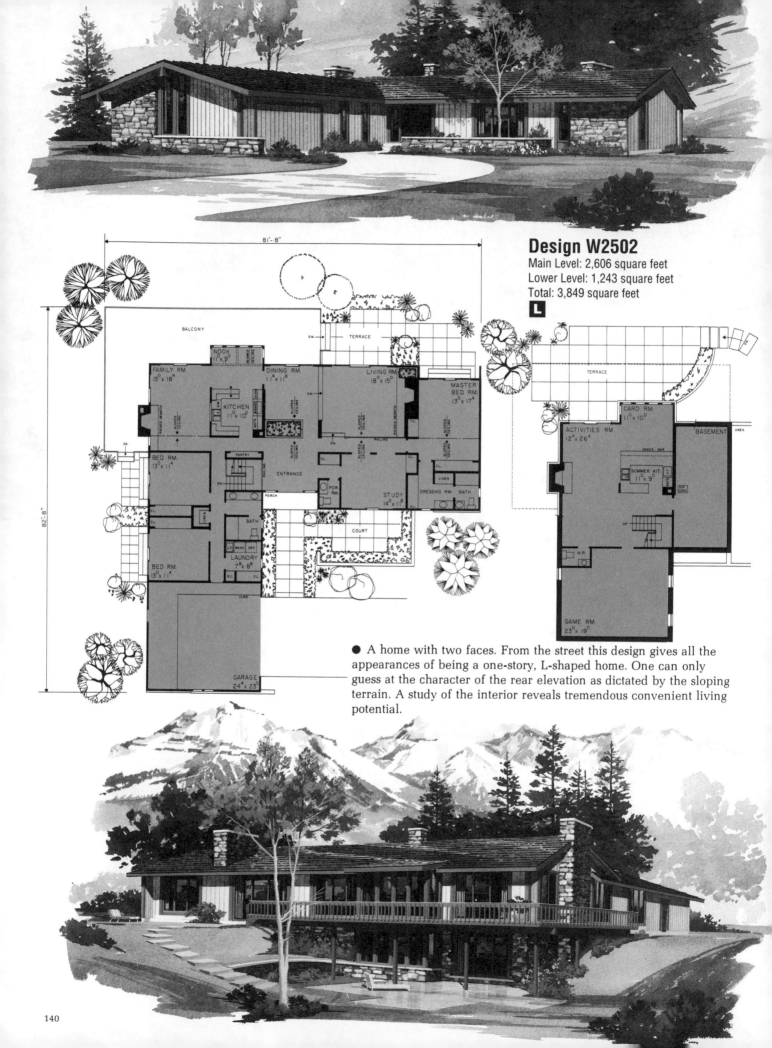

Design W2502

Main Level: 2,606 square feet
Lower Level: 1,243 square feet
Total: 3,849 square feet

L

● A home with two faces. From the street this design gives all the appearances of being a one-story, L-shaped home. One can only guess at the character of the rear elevation as dictated by the sloping terrain. A study of the interior reveals tremendous convenient living potential.

● The rustic nature of this split-level design is captured by the rough-textured stone, natural-toned wood siding and wide, overhanging roof with exposed beams. Indoor-outdoor living relationships are outstanding. The foyer will be dramatic, indeed.

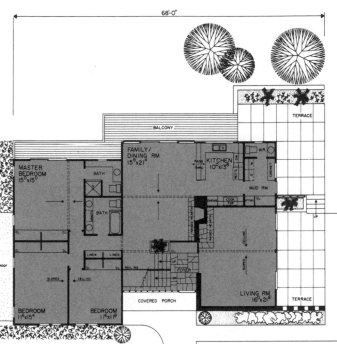

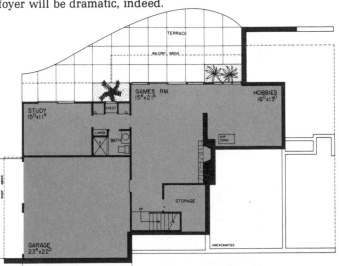

Design W2248

Upper Level: 1,501 square feet; Living Room Level: 511 square feet
Lower Level: 1,095 square feet; Total: 3,107 square feet

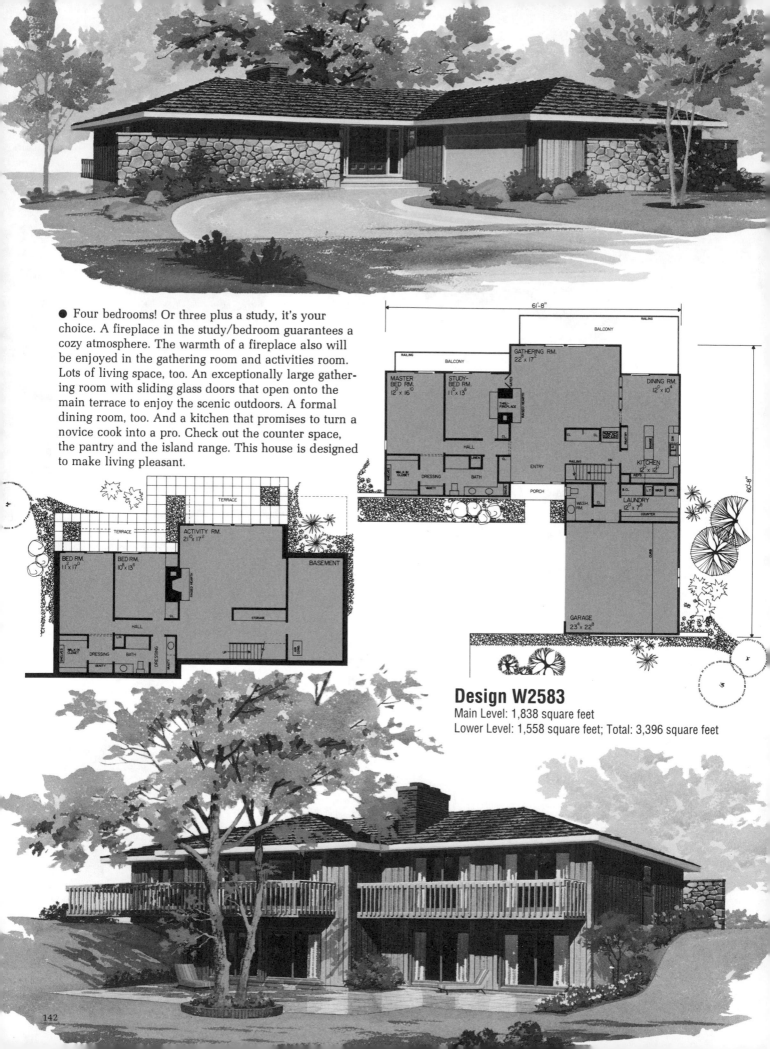

● Four bedrooms! Or three plus a study, it's your choice. A fireplace in the study/bedroom guarantees a cozy atmosphere. The warmth of a fireplace also will be enjoyed in the gathering room and activities room. Lots of living space, too. An exceptionally large gathering room with sliding glass doors that open onto the main terrace to enjoy the scenic outdoors. A formal dining room, too. And a kitchen that promises to turn a novice cook into a pro. Check out the counter space, the pantry and the island range. This house is designed to make living pleasant.

Design W2583
Main Level: 1,838 square feet
Lower Level: 1,558 square feet; Total: 3,396 square feet

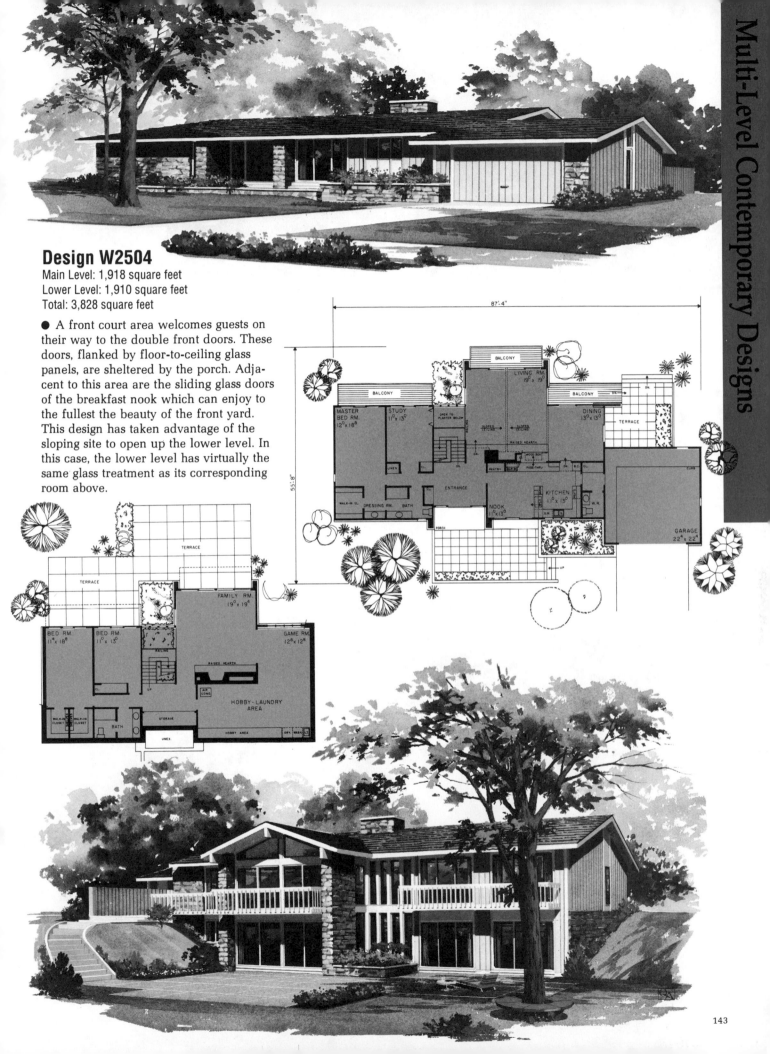

Design W2504

Main Level: 1,918 square feet
Lower Level: 1,910 square feet
Total: 3,828 square feet

● A front court area welcomes guests on their way to the double front doors. These doors, flanked by floor-to-ceiling glass panels, are sheltered by the porch. Adjacent to this area are the sliding glass doors of the breakfast nook which can enjoy to the fullest the beauty of the front yard. This design has taken advantage of the sloping site to open up the lower level. In this case, the lower level has virtually the same glass treatment as its corresponding room above.

143

Design W2715

Upper Level: 2,299 square feet
Lower Level: 1,524 square feet; Total: 3,823 square feet

● A lounge with built-in seating and a thru-fireplace to the gathering room highlights this upper level. A delightful attraction to view upon entrance of this home. A formal dining room, study and U-shaped kitchen with breakfast nook are present, too. That is a lot of room. There's more! A huge activities room has a fireplace, snack bar and adjacent summer kitchen. This is the perfect set-up for teenage parties or family cook-outs on the terrace. The entire family certainly will enjoy the convenience of this area. All this, plus three bedrooms (optional four without the study), including a luxury master suite with its own outdoor balcony. The upper level, outdoor deck provides partial cover for the lower level ter-race. This home offers outdoor living potential on both levels.

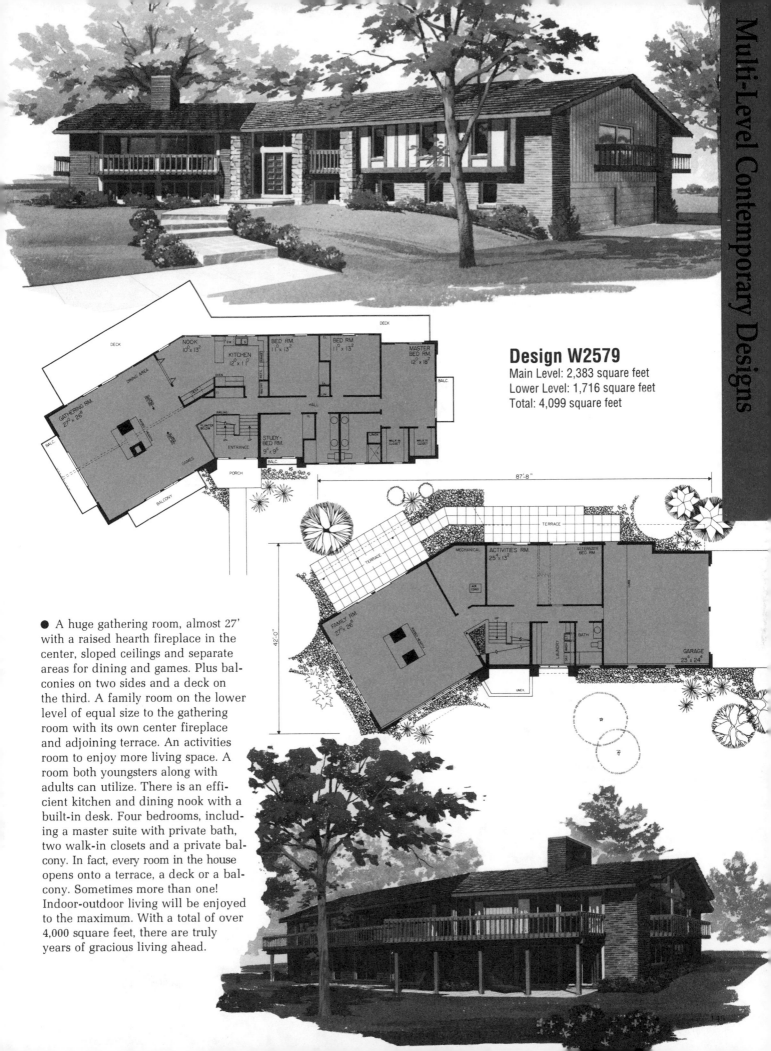

Design W2579

Main Level: 2,383 square feet
Lower Level: 1,716 square feet
Total: 4,099 square feet

● A huge gathering room, almost 27' with a raised hearth fireplace in the center, sloped ceilings and separate areas for dining and games. Plus balconies on two sides and a deck on the third. A family room on the lower level of equal size to the gathering room with its own center fireplace and adjoining terrace. An activities room to enjoy more living space. A room both youngsters along with adults can utilize. There is an efficient kitchen and dining nook with a built-in desk. Four bedrooms, including a master suite with private bath, two walk-in closets and a private balcony. In fact, every room in the house opens onto a terrace, a deck or a balcony. Sometimes more than one! Indoor-outdoor living will be enjoyed to the maximum. With a total of over 4,000 square feet, there are truly years of gracious living ahead.

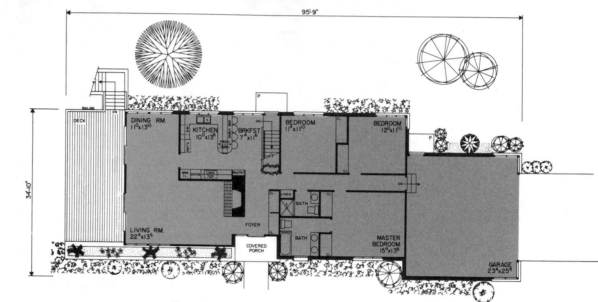

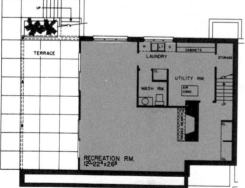

Design W2272

Main Level: 1,731 square feet

Lower Level: 672 square feet; Total: 2,403 square feet

● Certainly not a huge house. But one, nevertheless, that is long on livability and one that surely will be fun to live in. With its wide-overhanging hip roof, this unadorned facade is the picture of simplicity. As such, it has a quiet appeal all its own. The living-dining area is one of the focal points of the plan. It is wonderfully spacious. The large glass areas and the accessibility, through sliding glass doors, of the outdoor balcony are fine features. For recreation, there is the lower-level area which opens onto a large terrace covered by the balcony above.

54'-0"

BALCONY

FAMILY RM.
12'⁸ x 19'⁴

DINING RM.
11'⁰ x 13'⁶

LIVING RM.
13'⁰ x 23'⁴

KIT.
10' x 16'

PLAY
DECK

REFS.

ENTRY

PDR.
RM.

WASH DRY
LAUNDRY

PORCH

CURB

GARAGE
23'⁴ x 23'⁰

TERRACE

MASTER
BED. RM.
12'⁰ x 15'⁸

BED. RM.
10'⁰ x 11'⁶

BED. RM.
11'⁶ x 11'⁶

BED. RM.
11'⁶ x 11'⁶

DRESS.
RM.

WALK-IN
CL.

VANITY
SLOP.
CLOOR

BATH

STOR.

LIN.

STOR.

PDR.
RM.

BATH

STOR.

AIR
COND.

Design W2205

Upper Level: 1,229 square feet
Lower Level: 1,229 square feet
Total: 2,458 square feet

● Whether your sloping site be near the lakeshore or not, this L-shaped hillside design offers the best in gracious living. What fine indoor-outdoor relationships.

Design W2719

Main Level: 2,363 square feet
Lower Level: 1,523 square feet; Total: 3,886 square feet

● If you have a flair for something different and useful at the same time, then expose the basement for hillside living. This design offers three large living areas: gathering room, family room and all-purpose activity room. Note the features in each of the three: balcony, sloping ceiling and through-fireplace in the gathering room; deck and eating area in the family room; terrace and raised-hearth fireplace in the activities room. The staircase to the lower level is delightfully open which adds to the spacious appeal of the entry hall. Cabinets and shelves are also a delightful feature of this area. There are three bedrooms with the master bedroom suite on the main level and two family bedrooms on the lower level. An efficient U-shaped kitchen easily serves the eating areas of the family room and the formal dining room. The laundry is just a step away. The front projection of the two-car garage reduces the size of the lot required to build this exciting contemporary home.

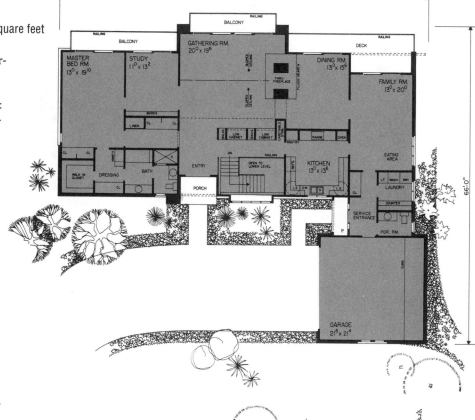

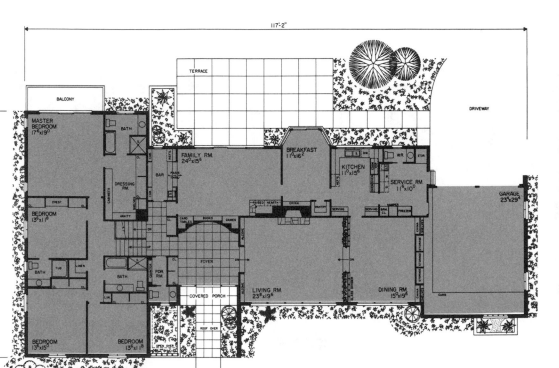

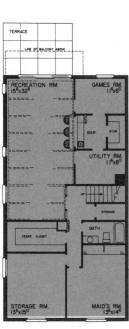

Design W2173

Main Level: 2,290 square feet; Upper Level: 1,621 square feet
Lower Level: 1,638 square feet; Total: 5,549 square feet

● This hillside home gives all the appearances of being a one-story ranch home; and what a delightful one at that! Should the contours of your property slope to the rear, this plan permits the exposing of the lower level. This results in the activities room and bedroom/study gaining direct access to outdoor living. Certainly a most desirable aspect for active, outdoor family living. The large and growing family will be admirably served with five bedrooms and three baths. An extra washroom and separate laundry add to the convenient living potential.

Design W2549

Main Level: 2,260 square feet
Lower Level: 1,406 square feet
Total: 3,666 square feet

Design W2895 Upper Level: 2,700 square feet
Lower Level: 1,503 square feet; Total: 4,203 square feet

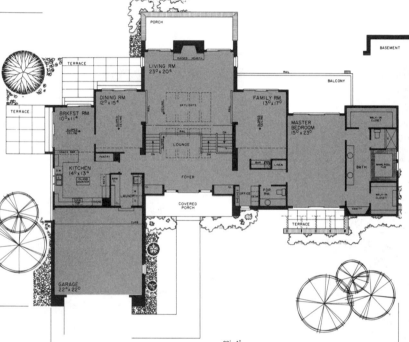

● This contemporary hillside is ideal for those with a flair for something different. A large kitchen with adjacent breakfast room offers easy access to the terraces as does the dining room. Other main floor areas include: a master bedroom suite with private terrace and access to the rear balcony, a family room, powder room and a sunken living room. Special features include a skylight in the living room, wet bar in family room and sloped ceilings. The lower level has two more bedrooms, activity room and lounge with built-in bar. Note the special bath facilities on both levels.

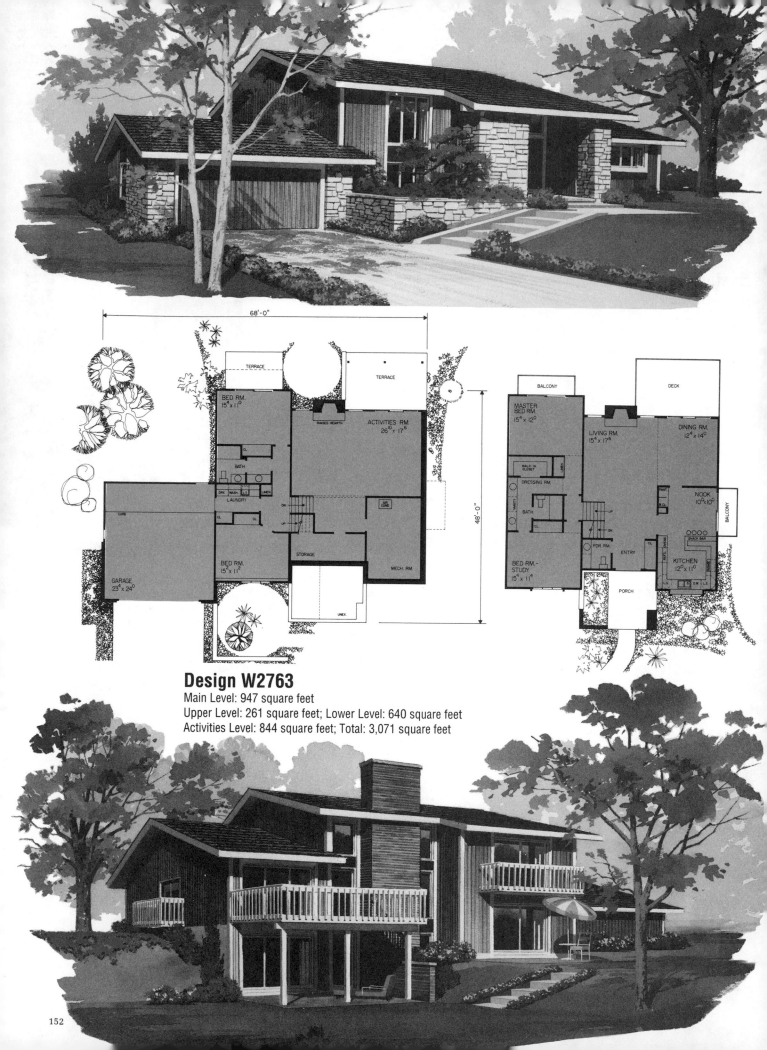

Design W2763

Main Level: 947 square feet
Upper Level: 261 square feet; Lower Level: 640 square feet
Activities Level: 844 square feet; Total: 3,071 square feet

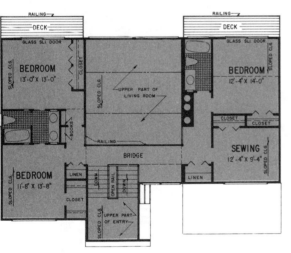

LIFESTYLE
HOME PLANS

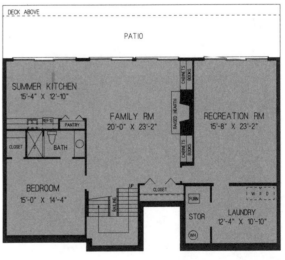

Design W4141

Main Level: 1,809 square feet
Upper Level: 1,293 square feet
Lower Level: 1,828 square feet
Total: 4,930 square feet

● A spacious two-story living room is the centerpiece of this plan with its large fireplace and access to the rear deck. Next door is the kitchen and breakfast room and adjacent formal dining room. Also on this level, an enormous master bedroom with fireplace. Upstairs are three bedrooms and a sewing room linked by a balcony overlooking the living room.

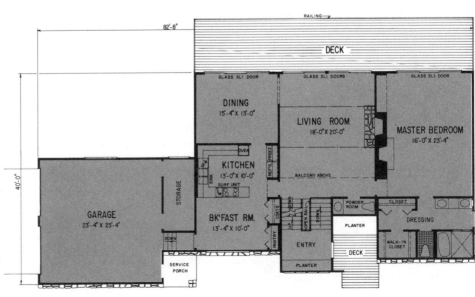

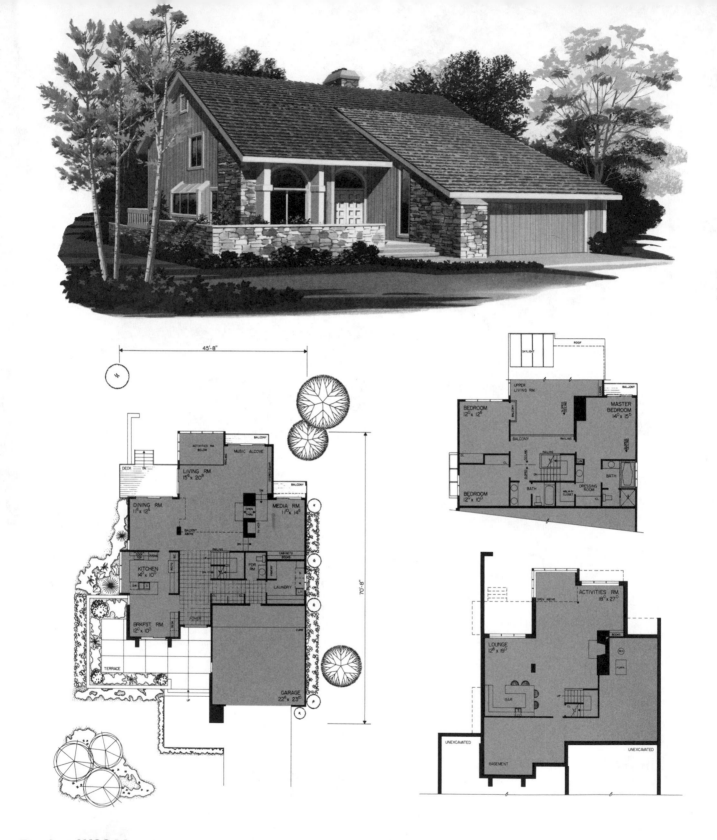

Design W2944 Main Level: 1,545 square feet; Upper Level: 977 square feet; Lower Level: 933 square feet; Total: 3,455 square feet

● This eye-catching contemporary features three stacked levels of livability. And what livability it will truly be! The main level has a fine U-shaped kitchen which is flanked by the informal breakfast room and formal dining room. The living room will be dramatic, indeed. Its sloping ceiling extends through the upper level. It overlooks the lower level activities room and has wonderfully expansive window areas for full enjoyment of surrounding vistas. A two-way fireplace can be viewed from dining, living and media rooms. A sizable deck and two cozy balconies provide for flexible outdoor living. Don't miss the music alcove with its wall for stereo equipment. Upstairs, the balcony overlooks the living room. It serves as the connecting link for the three bedrooms. The lower level offers more cheerful livability with the huge activities room plus lounge area. Note bar, fireplace.

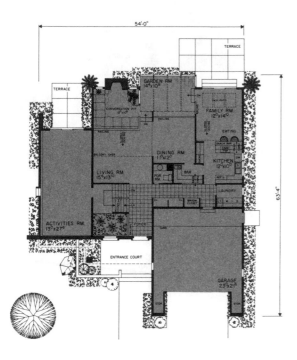

Design W2901

Main Level: 1,449 square feet
Upper Level: 665 square feet
Master Bedroom Level: 448 square feet
Activity Room Level: 419 square feet
Total: 2,981 square feet

L

● An appealing split, this plan has more than a little personality. The main level features a conversation pit in the living room (with a fireplace to boot), 150-square-foot garden room, family room with a trio of skylights and sliding glass doors leading to a rear terrace, and a sizable U-shaped kitchen (note the bevy of built-ins). The master bedroom suite enjoys one whole level—150 square feet of living space—as well as a private balcony. Two other pluses: a huge activity room on the lower level and extra storage throughout.

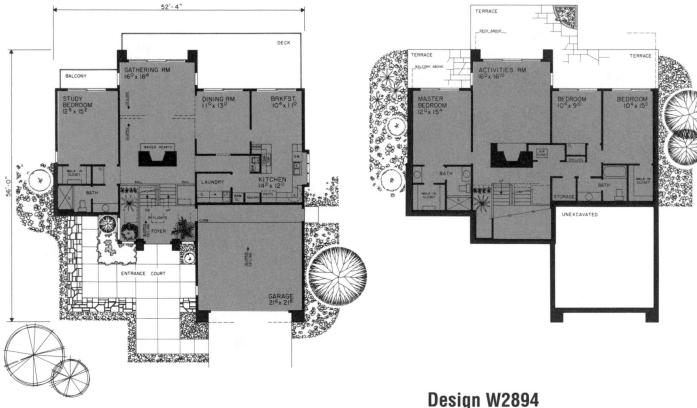

Design W2894
Upper Level: 1,490 square feet
Lower Level: 1,357 square feet
Total: 2,847 square feet

● Contemporary, bi-level living will be enjoyed by all members of the family. Upon entering the foyer, complimented by skylights, stairs will lead you to the upper and lower levels. Up a few steps, you will find yourself in the large gathering room. The fire-place, sloped ceiling and the size of this room will make this a favorite spot. To the left is a study/bedroom with a full bath and walk-in closet. Notice the efficient kitchen and break-fast room with nearby wet bar. The lower level houses two bedrooms and a bath to one side; and a master bed-room suite to the other. Centered is a large activity room with raised-hearth fireplace. It will be enjoyed by all. Note - all of the rear rooms on both levels have easy access to the outdoors for excellent indoor-outdoor livability.

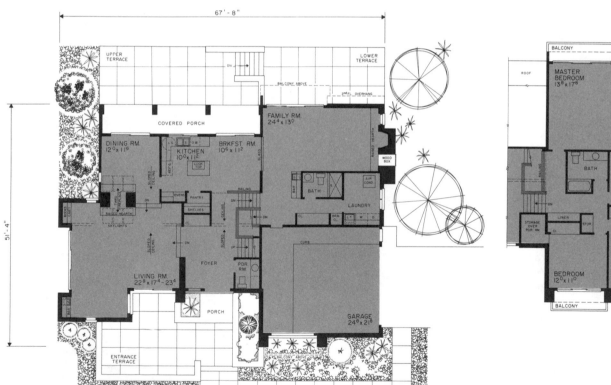

Design W2893

Main Level: 1,297 square feet
Upper Level: 1,256 square feet
Lower Level: 654 square feet
Total: 3,207 square feet

D

● Here is a contemporary split-level with a lot of appeal. To the right of the foyer and up a few steps you will find three bedrooms and a bath. Also, a master bedroom suite with an over-sized tub, shower, walk-in closet and sliding glass doors to a balcony. (One of the front bedrooms also has a balcony.) A sunken living room is on the main level. It has a wet bar and shares with the dining room a thru-fireplace, sloped ceiling and a skylight. A spacious kitchen and breakfast room are nearby. They offer easy access to the covered porch - ideal for summer meals. The lower level has a large family room with sliding glass doors to the lower terrace, another wet bar and a fireplace. The laundry, full bath, large closet and garage access are just steps away.

157

Design W2734 Main Level: 1,626 square feet; Upper Level: 1,033 square feet
Lower Level: 1,273 square feet; Total: 3,932 square feet

● If you have a desire for something delightfully different that offers unique, yet practical and enjoyable living patterns, then this house deserves careful study by all the members of your family. Having three bedrooms and a study on the upper level and a guest (or hobby) room on the lower level offers sleeping flexibility for the growing family. Notice how the living area looks down on the delightful planting area of the lower level. Also it shares a through-fireplace with the study. Other features of the study include a seven-foot-high book shelf, private balcony and separate stairs to the master bedroom. The outstanding U-shaped kitchen is flanked by the family and dining room. In addition to the living room, there is a huge, 32-foot activity room on the lower level. An abundance of storage space will be found in the three-car garage and the basement.

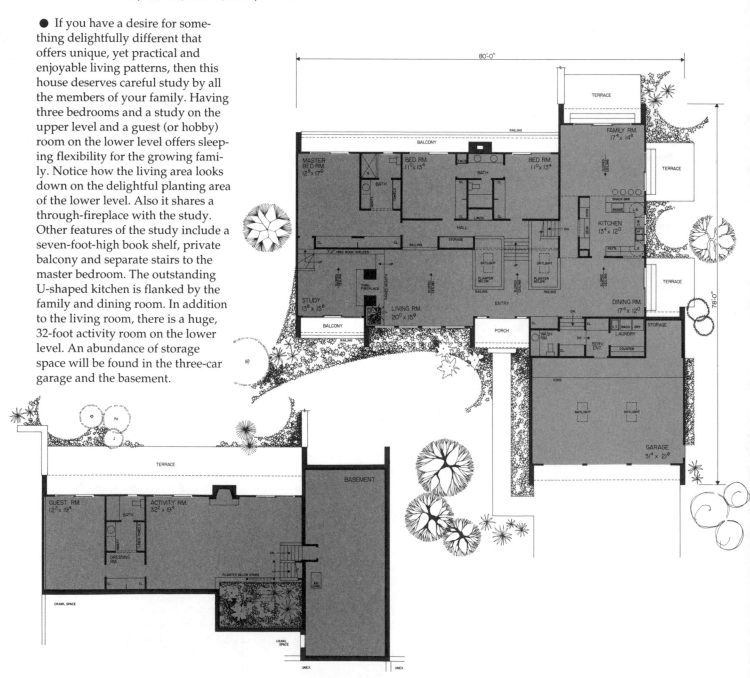

Design W2846

Main Level: 2,341 square feet; Lower Level: 1,380 square feet
Total: 3,721 square feet

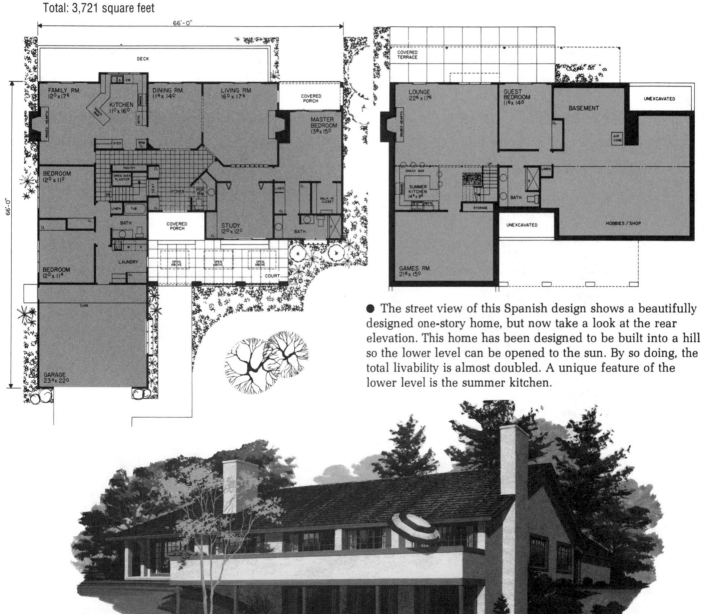

● The street view of this Spanish design shows a beautifully designed one-story home, but now take a look at the rear elevation. This home has been designed to be built into a hill so the lower level can be opened to the sun. By so doing, the total livability is almost doubled. A unique feature of the lower level is the summer kitchen.

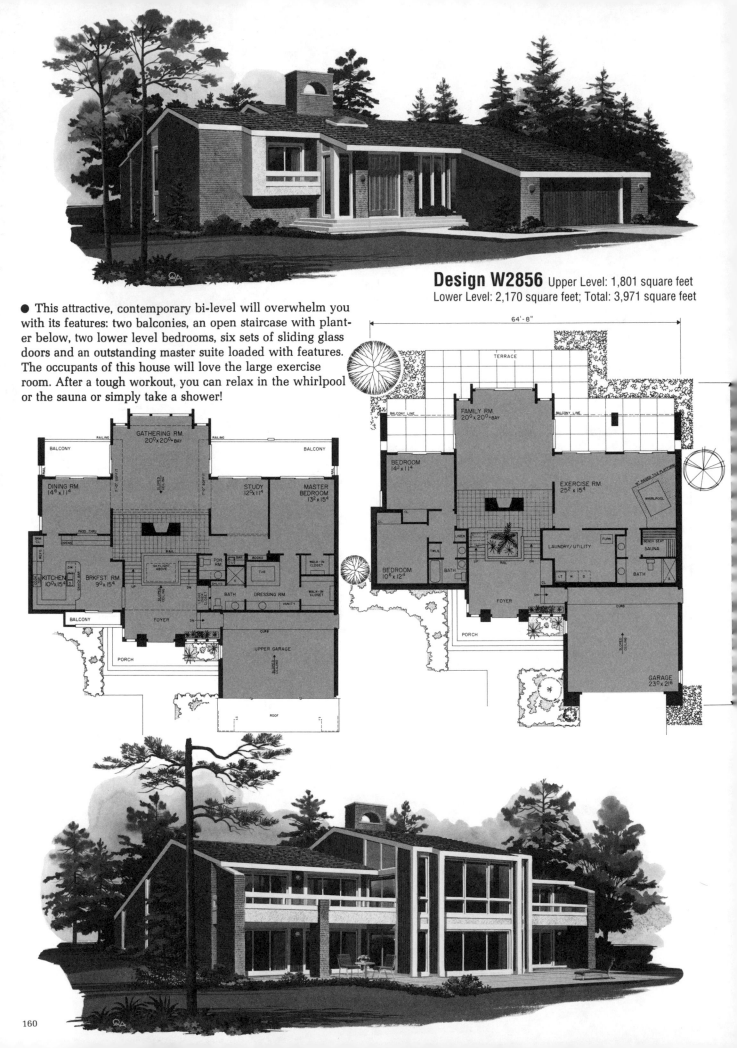

Design W2856 Upper Level: 1,801 square feet
Lower Level: 2,170 square feet; Total: 3,971 square feet

● This attractive, contemporary bi-level will overwhelm you with its features: two balconies, an open staircase with planter below, two lower level bedrooms, six sets of sliding glass doors and an outstanding master suite loaded with features. The occupants of this house will love the large exercise room. After a tough workout, you can relax in the whirlpool or the sauna or simply take a shower!

Design W2896

Upper Level: 1,856 square feet; Lower Level: 1,454 square feet
Total: 3,310 square feet

● This design is very inviting with its contemporary appeal. A large kitchen with an adjacent snack bar makes light meals a breeze. The adjoining breakfast room offers a scenic view through sliding glass doors. Notice the sloped ceiling in the dining and gathering rooms. A fireplace in the gathering room adds a cozy air. An interesting feature is the master bedroom's easy access to the study. Also, take note of the sliding doors in the master bedroom which lead to a private balcony. On the lower level, a large activities room will be a frequently used spot by family members. The fireplace and wet bar add a nice touch for entertaining friends. Also, notice the sliding glass doors which lead to the terrace. Take note of the two or optional three bedrooms - the choice is yours.

Design W2868

Upper Level: 1,203 square feet
Lower Level: 1,317 square feet; Total: 2,520 square feet

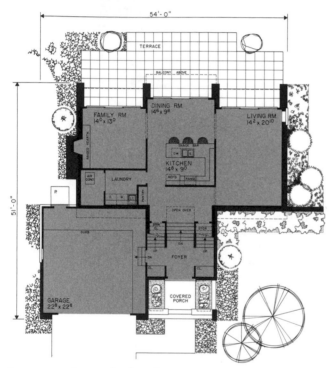

● Two couples sharing the expense of a house has got to be ideal and, of course, economical. The occupants of this house could do just that. The lower level, housing the kitchen, dining room, family and living rooms and the laundry facilities, is the common area to be shared by both couples. Centrally located, the kitchen and dining room act as a space divider to the living and family rooms so both couples can enjoy privacy.

Separate stairways lead to the upper level from the skylit foyer. Each private area has two bedrooms, a dressing room and a full bath. Individual entrances can be locked for additional privacy. Sliding glass doors are in each of the rear rooms on both levels so the outdoors can be enjoyed to its fullest.

Design W2735

Upper Level: 1,545 square feet
Lower Level: 1,633 square feet
Total: 3,178 square feet

● Whether entering this house through the double front doors, or from the garage, access is gained to the lower level by descending seven stairs. Here, there is a bonus of livability. If desired, this level could be used to accommodate a live-in relative while still providing the family with a fine informal activities room and a separate laundry/hobby room and extra powder room. Up seven risers form the entry is the main living level. It has a large gathering room; a sizable nook which could be called upon to function as a separate dining room; an efficient kitchen with pass-through to a formal dining area and a two-bedroom, two-bath and study-sleeping zone. Don't miss the balconies and deck.

Design W2588 Main Level: 1,354 square feet; Upper Level: 1,112 square feet; Lower Level: 562 square feet; Total: 3,028 square feet

● A through-fireplace with an accompanying planter for the formal dining room and living room. That's old—fashioned good cheer in a contemporary home. The dining room has an adjacent screened-in porch for outdoor dining in the summertime. There are companions for these two formal areas, an informal breakfast nook and a family room. Each having sliding glass doors to separate rear terraces. Built-in desk, pantry, ample work space and is-land range are features of the L-shaped kitchen. The large laundry on the lower level houses the heating and cooling equipment. Three family bedrooms, bath and master bedroom suite are on the upper level.

Design W1704

Upper Level: 1,498 square feet
Lower Level: 870 square feet
Total: 2,368 square feet

● The bi-level concept of living has become popular. This is understandable, for it represents a fine way in which to gain a maximum amount of extra livable area beneath the basic floor plan.

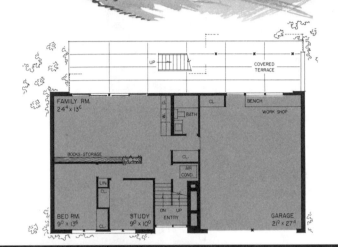

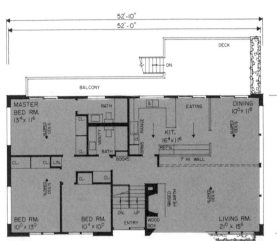

Design W2393

Entry Level: 392 square feet; Upper Level: 841 square feet
Lower Level: 848 square feet; Total: 2,081 square feet

● For those with a flair for something refreshingly contemporary both inside and out, this modest-sized multi-level has a unique exterior and an equally interesting interior. The low-pitched, wide-overhanging roof protects the inviting double front doors and the large picture window. The raised planter and the side balcony add an extra measure of appeal. Inside, the formal living room looks down into the dining room. Like the front entry, the living room has direct access to the lower level. The kitchen is efficient and spacious enough to accommodate an informal breakfast eating area. The laundry room is nearby. The all-purpose family room has a beamed ceiling, fireplace and sliding glass doors to a rear terrace. The angular, open stair-well to the upper level is dramatic. Notice how each bedroom has direct access to an outdoor balcony.

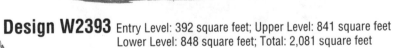

Design W2628

Main Level: 649 square feet
Upper Level: 672 square feet
Lower Level: 624 square feet
Total: 1,945 square feet

D

● For a growing family on a budget, this plan has a good-looking face and plenty of affordable space—plus a few extras. Open to the dining room, the living room has a fireplace with bookshelves built in. The L-shaped kitchen has just enough room for a nook, which, like the dining room, leads out to a rear terrace. On the lower level are a large family room with beamed ceiling and wet bar, fourth bedroom (or quiet study), and extra storage. The upper level has three bedrooms, including a cozy master suite.

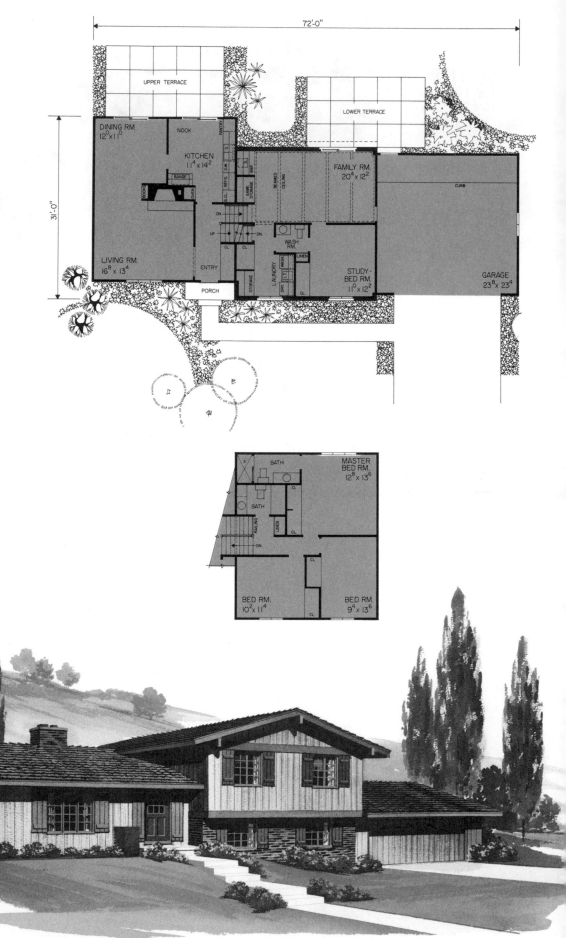

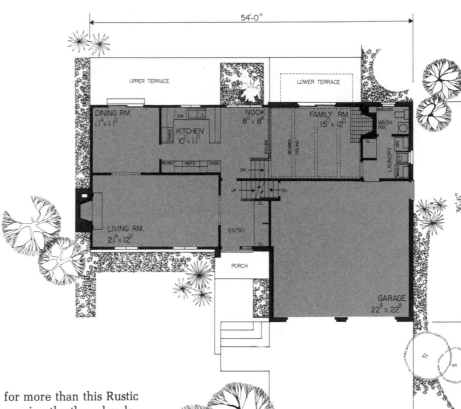

● Tri-level living could hardly ask for more than this Rustic design has to offer. Not only can one enjoy the three levels but also there is a fourth basement level for bulk storage and perhaps, a shop area. The interior livability is outstanding. The main level has an L-shaped formal living/dining area with a fireplace in the living room and sliding glass doors in the dining room to the upper terrace, a U-shaped kitchen and an informal eating area. Down a few steps to the lower level is the family room with another fireplace and sliding doors to the lower terrace, a washroom and laundry. The upper level houses all of the sleeping facilities including three bedrooms, bath and master suite.

Design W2608

Main Level: 728 square feet
Upper Level: 874 square feet
Lower Level: 310 square feet
Total: 1,912 square feet

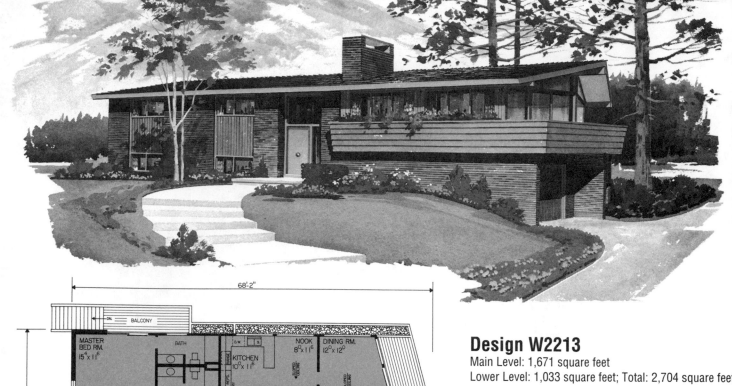

Design W2213

Main Level: 1,671 square feet
Lower Level: 1,033 square feet; Total: 2,704 square feet

● Whether you locate this contemporary bi-level home on a sloping or flat site, it will certainly command its share of attention and provide the family with wonderful living patterns. The front entry is a separate level with stairs leading directly to the lower and the upper levels.

The most captivating feature of this home may very well be the spacious living and dining areas. An exposed beam is the apex of sloped ceilings. The projecting, glass-gabled end allows for a full measure of natural light. Two pairs of sliding glass doors open onto the balcony. The living balcony wraps around both front and rear to provide appealing planting areas. The kitchen is an efficient one in which to work, while the breakfast nook is but a step away. The sleeping zone has three bedrooms plus two full baths. Don't overlook the fireplace with its wood box.

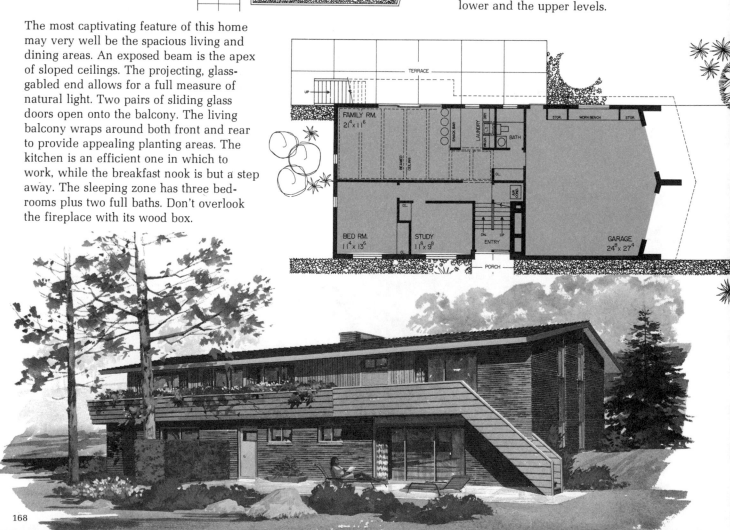

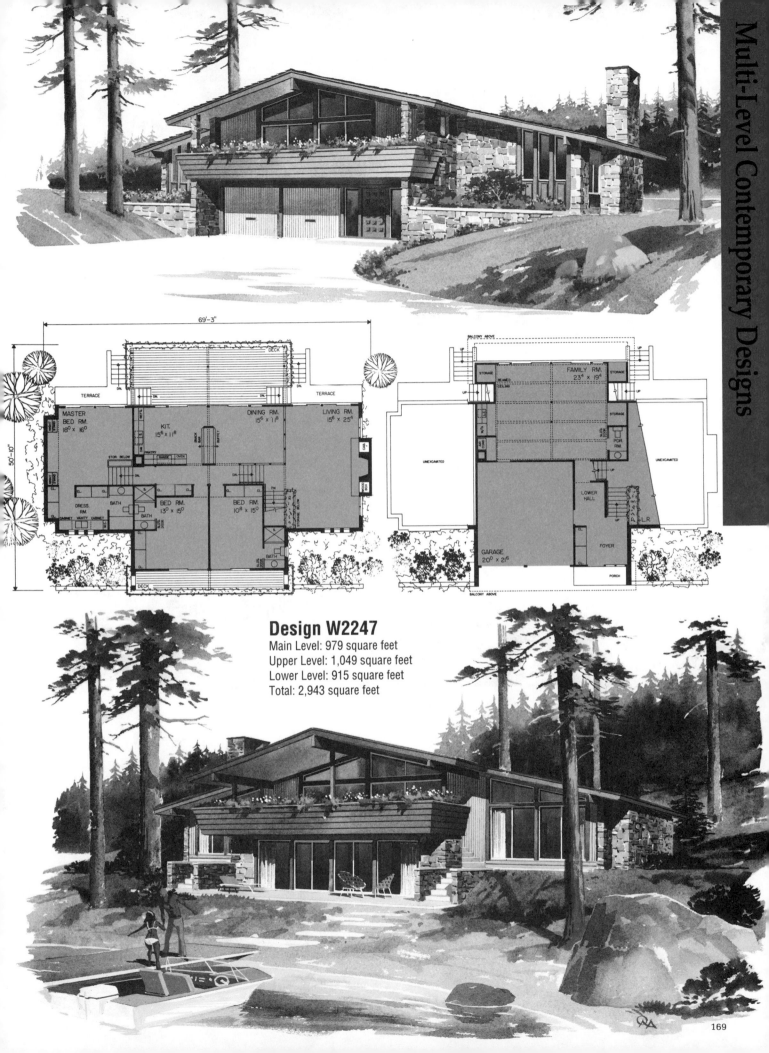

Design W2247

Main Level: 979 square feet
Upper Level: 1,049 square feet
Lower Level: 915 square feet
Total: 2,943 square feet

Design W2716

Main Level: 1,013 square feet
Upper Level: 885 square feet
Lower Level: 1,074 square feet
Total: 2,972 square feet

L

● Stuck with a hilly site?
If so, this plan may fit right
in. The upper-level master
suite is one highlight. It's
got a huge sitting and
dressing room, as well as a
private balcony. The main
level is a welcome combi-
nation of open floor planning and traditional room
layout. The combo gather-
ing room (which is open to
the upper level) and dining
area total just under 400
square feet; note the
through-fireplace (to a
comfy study off the entry)
and access to the balcony in
back. On the lower level are
a large family room, where
there's another fireplace;
guest bedroom and full
bath; and rear terrace.

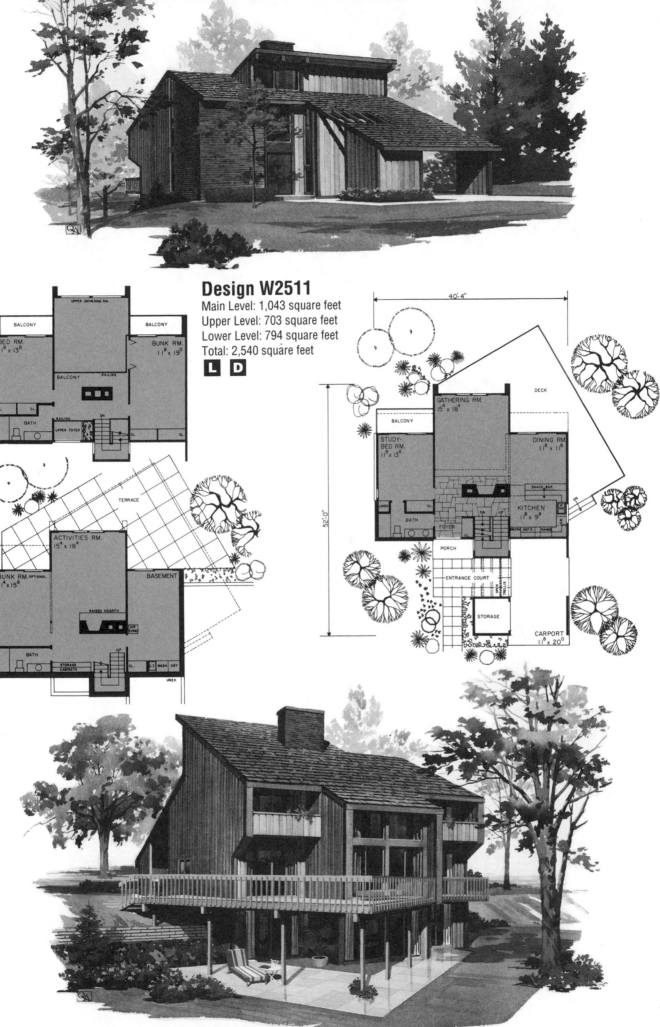

Design W2511

Main Level: 1,043 square feet
Upper Level: 703 square feet
Lower Level: 794 square feet
Total: 2,540 square feet

L **D**

UPPER GATHERING RM.

BALCONY

BED RM.
11⁸ x 13⁸

BALCONY

BUNK RM.
11⁸ x 19⁰

BALCONY   RAILING

CL.   CL.

BATH   RAILING

UPPER FOYER   DN.   CL.   CL.

TERRACE

ACTIVITIES RM.
15⁴ x 18⁴

BUNK RM. OPTIONAL
11⁴ x 15⁸

BASEMENT

RAISED HEARTH

AIR COND.

BATH

STORAGE CABINETS   UP   H.T.   WASH   DRY

CL.   UNEX.

40'-4"

52'-0"

GATHERING RM.
15⁴ x 18⁴

DECK

BALCONY

STUDY-BED RM.
11⁸ x 13⁸

DINING RM.
11⁸ x 11⁸

SNACK BAR

LINEN   CL.

KITCHEN
11⁸ x 9⁸

BATH   DN.   UP

FOYER   PANTRY   REF.   RANGE

PORCH

ENTRANCE COURT   OPEN TRELLIS

STORAGE

CARPORT
11⁸ x 20⁰

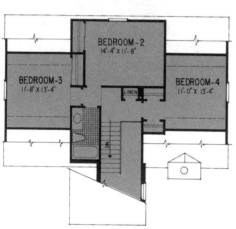

BEDROOM-2
14'-4" X 11'-8"

BEDROOM-3
11'-8" X 13'-4"

BEDROOM-4
11'-0" X 13'-4"

LINEN

DN

Design W4254

Main Level: 1,160 square feet
Upper Level: 715 square feet
Lower Level: 614 square feet
Total: 2,489 square feet

LIFESTYLE
HOME PLANS

● Unique siding and masonry work make this hillside home a showplace. Inside there's plenty of living space in the lower-level family room and main-level great room. The kitchen with breakfast area is conveniently adjacent to the great room. The split sleeping area thoughtfully places the master bedroom on the main level and the remaining three bedrooms on the upper level for utmost peace and quiet.

40'-8"

DECK

WINDOW GREENHOUSE

SLD. GL. DOOR   SLD. GL. DOOR

MASTER
BEDROOM
13'-8" X 14'-0"

BREAKFAST

RANGE

KITCHEN

SINK

DINING

D

W

REFG.

GREAT ROOM
15'-0" X 25'-4"

WALK-IN
CLOSET   LINEN

LINEN

DRESSING

DN

LIVING

36'-5"

PORCH   ENTRY

COATS

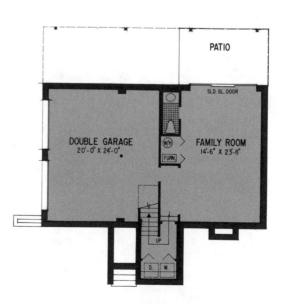

PATIO

SLD. GL. DOOR

DOUBLE GARAGE
20'-0" X 24'-0"

W/H

FURN.

FAMILY ROOM
14'-6" X 23'-8"

UP

D.   W.

Design W4129

Entry Level: 802 square feet
Upper Level: 576 square feet
Lower Level: 577 square feet
Total: 1,955 square feet

● This design with its stacked levels of livability is ideal for a sloping site. The entry level contains the kitchen and the multi-purpose great room with its flanking decks. A large triangular projection contains a sunken conversation pit with fireplace — a cozy spot for chatting or curling up with a book. The two-bedroom lower level includes a deck; both parents and children will appreciate this extra space for playing or relaxing. The master suite is found on the upper level. Notice the large closet and oversized tub.

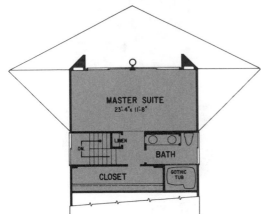

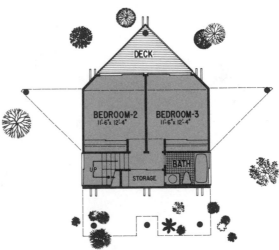

LIFESTYLE
HOME PLANS

Design W4115

Entry Level: 1,494 square feet
Upper Level: 597 square feet
Total: 2,091 square feet

● Interior spaces are dramatically proportioned because of the long and varied roof lines of this contemporary. The two-story living area has a sloped ceiling as does the master bedroom and two upper-level bedrooms. Two fireplaces, a huge rear wooden deck, a small upstairs sitting room, and a liberal number of windows make this a most comfortable vacation residence.

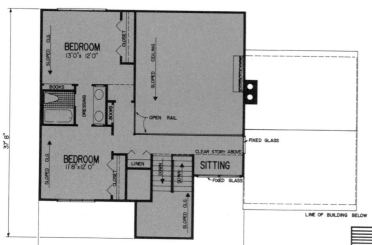

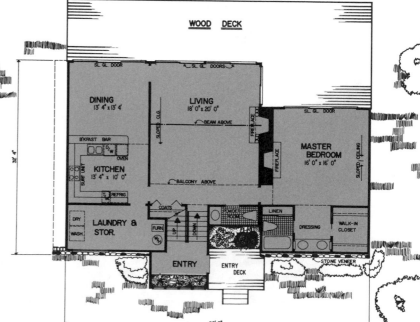

Design W4102

Main Level: 1,237 square feet
Upper Level: 982 square feet
Total: 2,219 square feet

● Varying rooflines create an attractive exterior for this home. Inside, the well-planned interior includes a two-story living room, formal dining room and kitchen with breakfast area. Also found on this level, the master bedroom opens onto the rear terrace. Three more bedrooms are upstairs as well as a balcony family room overlooking the living room.

LIFESTYLE HOME PLANS

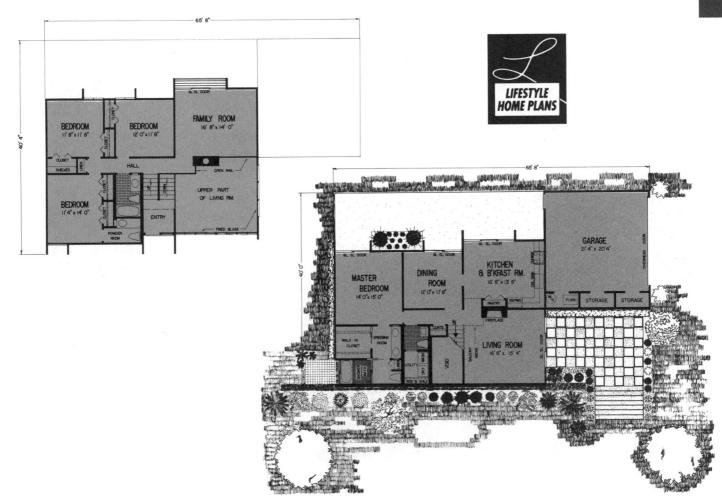

Design W2835

Upper Level: 1,626 square feet
Lower Level: 2,038 square feet
Total: 3,664 square feet

● Loaded with goodies, this striking contemporary is a sunstruck wonder. Fed by multiple skylights, the lower-level sunroom (nearly 600 square feet) is a perfect passive solar feature; plus, it's got a large whirlpool. Also down below are a spacious family room with semi-circular bar, two bedrooms, two baths, room for a wine cellar extra built-ins, and a back-up active solar system. Upstairs, there's lots more going on: huge living room and dining area, L-shaped kitchen, and master bedroom suite, which has twin vanities, exercise room, step-up tub, and plenty of closet space.

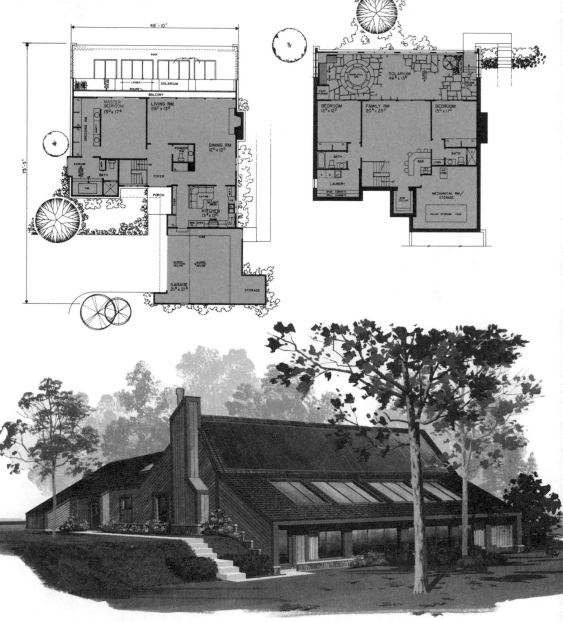

Design W2834

First Floor: 1,775 square feet
Second Floor: 1,041 square feet
Lower Level: 1,128 square feet
Total: 3,944 square feet

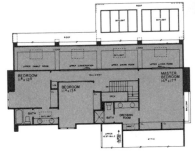

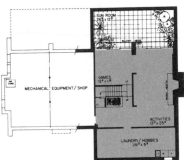

● This passive solar design offers 3,900 square feet of livability situated on three levels. The primary passive element will be the lower level sun room which admits sunlight for direct-gain heating. The solar warmth collected in the sun room will radiate into the rest of the house. During the warm summer months, shades are put over the skylight. Solar heating panels may be installed on the south-facing portion of the roof. An attic fan exhausts any hot air out of the house in the summer and circulates air in the winter.

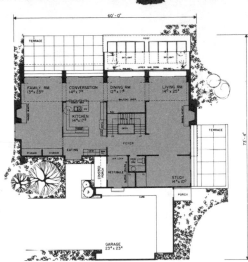

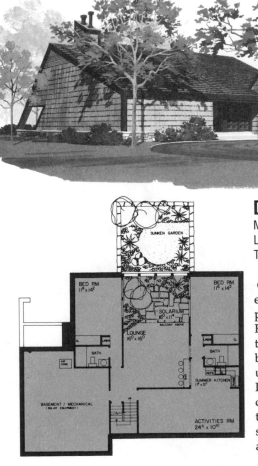

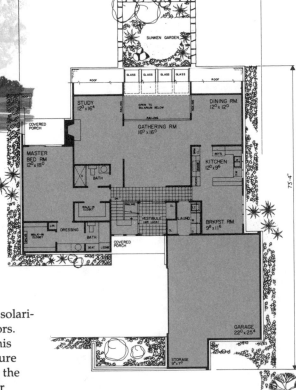

Design W2830

Main Level: 1,795 square feet
Lower Level: 1,546 square feet
Total: 3,341 square feet

● This home has been created with the advantages of passive solar heating in mind. For optimum energy savings, this delightful design combines a passive solar device, the solarium, with optional active collectors. Included with the purchase of this design are four plot plans to assure that the solar collectors will face the south. Schematic details for solar application are also included.

Design W2848 Main Level: 2,028 square feet
Lower Level: 1,122 square feet; Total: 3,150 square feet

● This contemporary design is characterized by the contrast in diagonal and vertical wood siding. The private front court adjacent to the covered porch is a nice area for evening relaxation and creates an impressive entry. Once inside the house, the livability begins to unfold. Three bedrooms are arranged to one side of the entry with two baths sharing back-to-back plumbing. The master bedroom has a balcony. A view of the front court will be enjoyed from the kitchen and breakfast room. Along with the breakfast room, both the formal dining room and the screened porch will have easy access to the kitchen. A formal living room will be enjoyed on many occasions. It is detailed by a sloped ceiling and the warmth of a fireplace. A fourth bedroom is on the lower level. This level is opened to the outdoors by three sets of sliding glass doors. A second fireplace, this one with a raised hearth, is in the family room. A full bath and two work rooms also are located on the lower level.

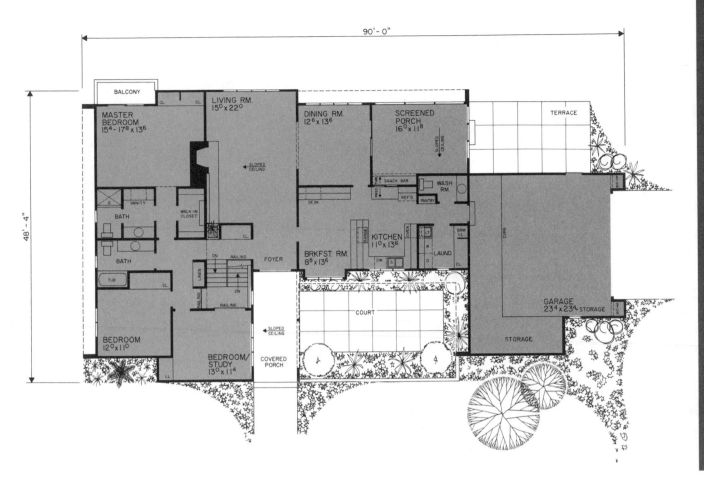

Contemporary Hillside Living

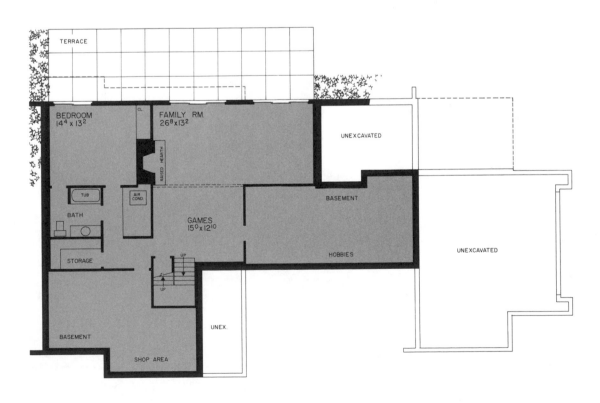

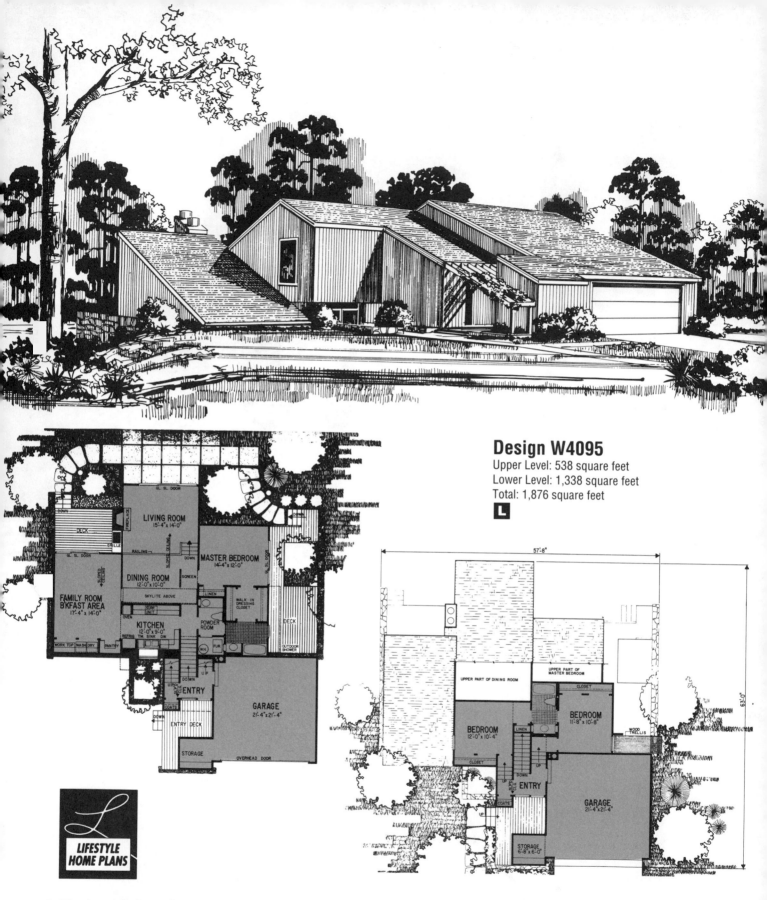

Design W4095

Upper Level: 538 square feet
Lower Level: 1,338 square feet
Total: 1,876 square feet

L

● Here's a split-foyer design with lots of visual appeal. Steeply pitched rooflines and sloped ceilings create a dramatic appearance both inside and out. From the entry, stairs lead down to a galley kitchen with lots of counter space for food preparation. Next door is a large family room and breakfast area with adjacent deck and barbecue. Beyond the kitchen is a formal dining room which overlooks the sunken living room with fireplace. The master suite is also on this level and features a large private deck. The upper level contains two bedrooms with separate staircases.

Design W4168

Entry and Upper Levels: 1,487 square feet

D

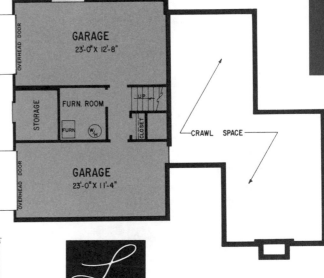

GARAGE
23'-0" X 12'-8"

OVERHEAD DOOR

STORAGE

FURN. ROOM

FURN

W/H

UP

CLOSET

CRAWL SPACE

GARAGE
23'-0" X 11'-4"

OVERHEAD DOOR

48'-0"

DECK

GL SLI DR

WALK-IN CLOSET

T/M SINK D/W

RANGE

MASTER BEDROOM
23'-6" X 13'-0"

REF'G

PANT

COUNTRY KITCHEN
13'-4" X 15'-0"

GLASS SLI DOOR

DECK

38'-4"

WASH DRY

DOWN

GLASS SLI DOOR

LIN

UP

ENTRY

40'-0"

COATS

BEDROOM
11'-8" X 11'-6"

BEDROOM
11'-8" X 11'-6"

BRIDGE

GREAT ROOM
15'-4" X 20'-0"

STONE

CLOSET

CLOSET

STEP

FIREPLACE

STONE

L

LIFESTYLE HOME PLANS

● Having two garages and storage space below the living levels of this plan gives it a more low-slung appearance than most multi-levels. The country kitchen and great room share a large outdoor deck and are separate from bedrooms on the upper level. Notice that the master suite has a small private deck and huge walk-in closet. Washer/dryer space is found near the bedrooms.

Design W4122

Main Level: 1,711 square feet
Lower Level: 1,322 square feet
Total: 3,033 square feet

D

● This distinctive design features diagonal and horizontal siding, projecting wings and a clerestory above the entry. For gathering and entertaining there's a spacious great room off the foyer. Notice the large fireplace. Next door is an enormous country kitchen with efficient work area and space for both dining and sitting areas. Three large bedrooms occupy their own wing. Note lower-level potential.

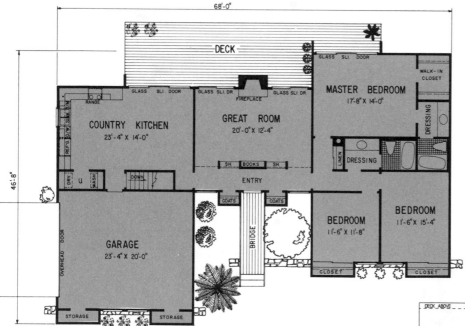

LIFESTYLE HOME PLANS

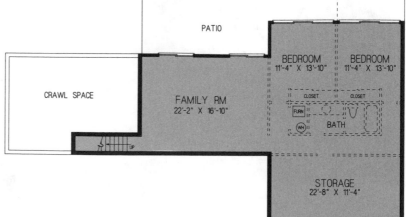

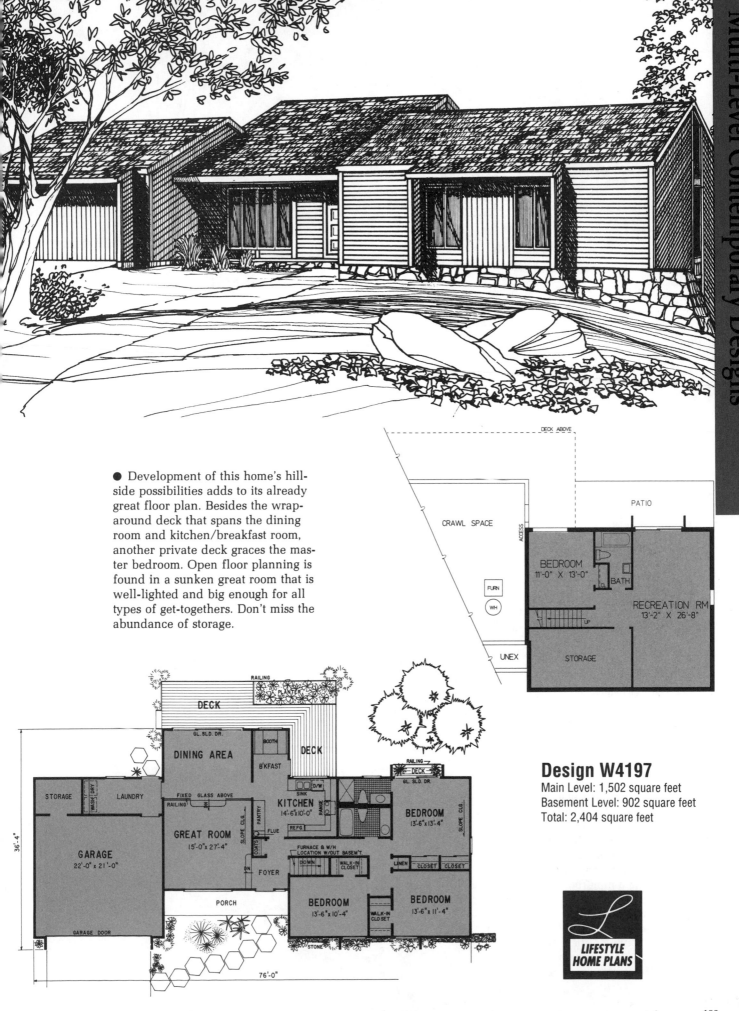

● Development of this home's hillside possibilities adds to its already great floor plan. Besides the wraparound deck that spans the dining room and kitchen/breakfast room, another private deck graces the master bedroom. Open floor planning is found in a sunken great room that is well-lighted and big enough for all types of get-togethers. Don't miss the abundance of storage.

Design W4197

Main Level: 1,502 square feet
Basement Level: 902 square feet
Total: 2,404 square feet

LIFESTYLE
HOME PLANS

LIFESTYLE HOME PLANS

Design W4240

Entry Level: 1,781 square feet
Lower Level: 931 square feet
Total: 2,712 square feet

D

● This design has the appearance of a cozy cottage yet boasts tremendous living space inside. Off the foyer is a spacious living room with a fireplace flanked by built-in shelves and cabinets, a sloped ceiling, and bay window. Also on this level, the well-equipped kitchen includes a pantry, barbecue, lots of counter space, and a pass-through to the dining room which has its own fireplace. The sleeping area is contained on the upper level with three nice-sized bedrooms and two baths. A fourth bedroom is found on the lower level along with a mammoth playroom and tavern. Also notice the laundry room.

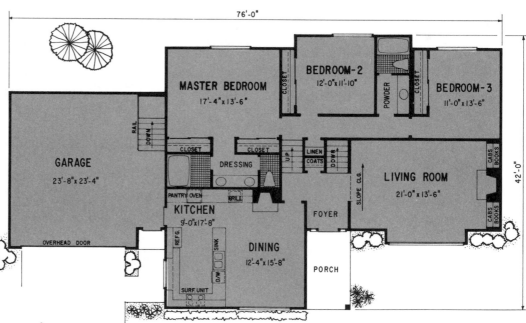

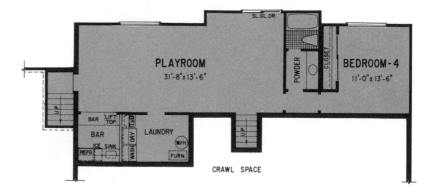

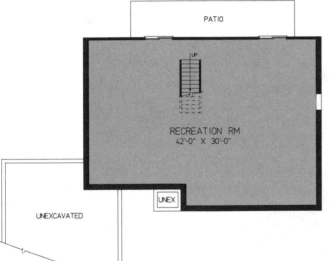

PATIO

UP

RECREATION RM.
42'-0" X 30'-0"

UNEX

UNEXCAVATED

Design W4175

Main Level: 1,374 square feet
Lower Level: 1,336 square feet
Total: 2,710 square feet

LIFESTYLE
HOME PLANS

● If a dramatic entry
appeals to you, then
this hillside residence
will catch your eye.
The design boasts a
simple peaked roof
and board-and-batten
siding enhanced by a
soaring covered porch
and trellis. The interior
plan contains a living
room with fireplace, L-
shaped kitchen with
dining area and out-
side patio, three bed-
rooms, two full baths
and a basement recre-
ation area.

RAILING

DECK

FIREPLACE   GL. SLI. DR.   DRESSING   GL. SLI. DR.

LIVING ROOM
17'-8" X 15'-8"

WASH

DOWN

DRY

MASTER BEDRM.
12'-4" X 15'-8"

PATIO

DINING & KIT.
12'-4" X 11'-4"

REFG.

ENTRY

HALL

CLOSET
CLOSET
LIN

STORAGE

PANTRY

RANGE   D/W

CLOSET   COATS

BEDROOM
10'-4" X 10'-10"

BEDROOM
12'-6" X 10'-10"

DESK

50'-0"

PORCH

GARAGE
21'-4" X 21'-4"

COVERED
WALK

OVERHEAD   DOOR

59'-0"

FURN

UTL.

DRY. WASH

ALTERNATE PLAN
FOR CRAWL SPACE

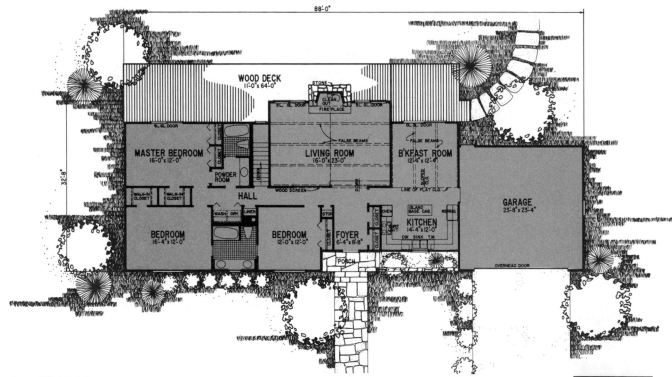

Design W4300

Main Level: 1,824 square feet
Lower Level: 811 square feet
Total: 2,635 square feet

● This cozy ranch house makes a great starter home. Directly off the foyer is the spacious living room with beamed ceiling and enormous stone fireplace. Nearby is the kitchen with island work center and breakfast room. The three-bedroom sleeping area features a master with access to the rear deck. A walk-out basement provides room for future expansion.

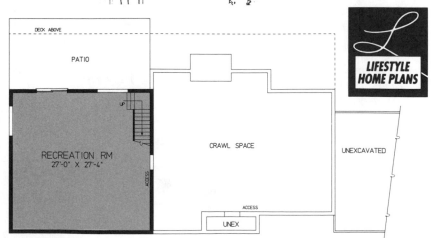

LIFESTYLE
HOME PLANS

Design W4101

Main Level: 2,154 square feet
Lower Level: 2,154 square feet
Total: 4,308 square feet

● Board-and-batten and stone lend a rustic appearance to this home's exterior. Inside the living areas include a sunken living room, formal dining room and family room with sloped ceiling and corner fireplace. The kitchen features a U-shaped work area, breakfast room, and access to the rear deck. The sleeping wing contains four bedrooms (two with window seats) and two baths.

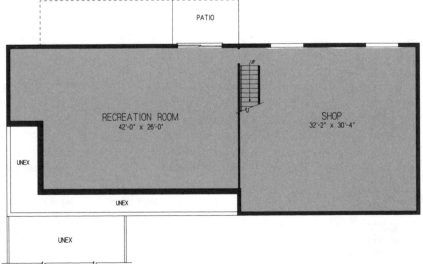

LIFESTYLE
HOME PLANS

● This attractive exterior comes with a floor plan in three different sizes to accommodate different size budgets. Each plan features a sunken great room with sloped ceiling and fireplace, dining room, kitchen with island cooktop and breakfast area, and a three-bedroom sleeping area with two baths. An optional walk-out basement adds extra living and storage space.

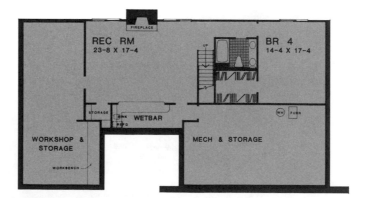

Lower Level: 1,130 square feet

LIFESTYLE
HOME PLANS

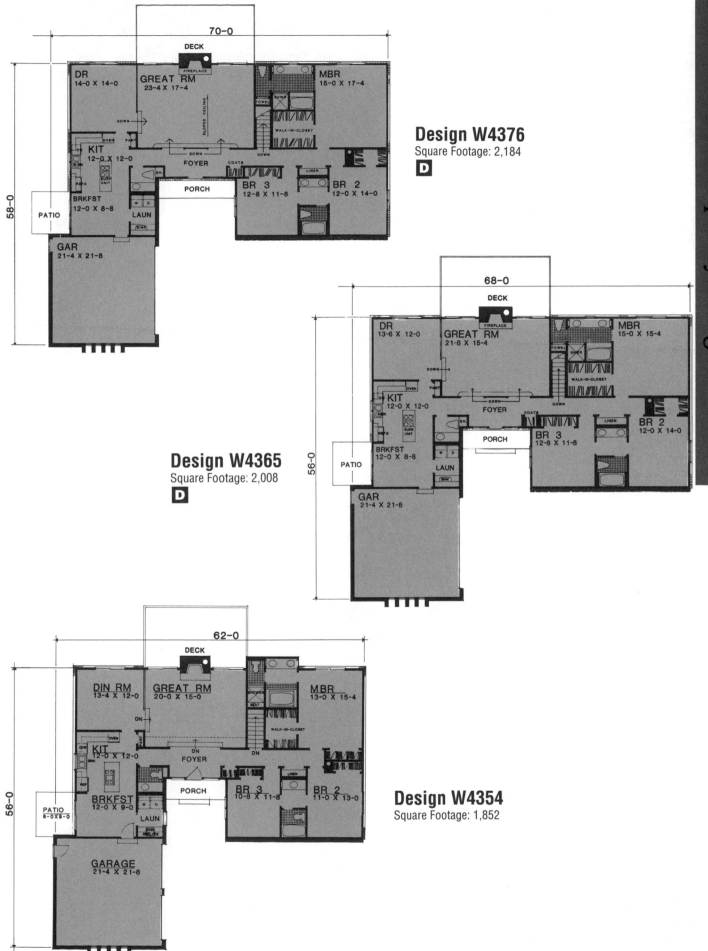

Design W4376
Square Footage: 2,184
D

Design W4365
Square Footage: 2,008
D

Design W4354
Square Footage: 1,852

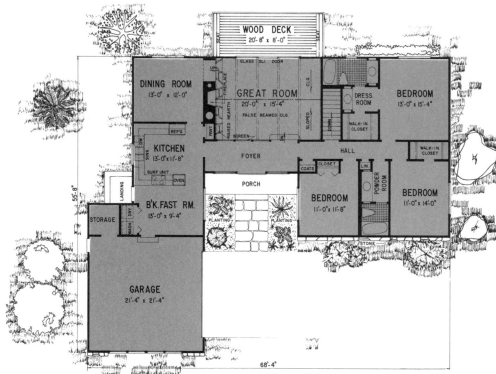

LIFESTYLE HOME PLANS

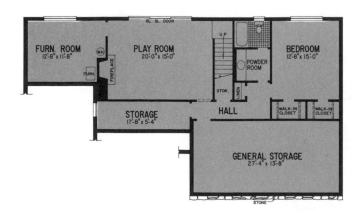

Design W4090

Main Level: 1,858 square feet
Lower Level: 1,538 square feet
Total: 3,396 square feet

● A wonderful combination of wood and stone accents the exterior of this clean-lined home while a gracious floor plan meets the needs of a busy family. Besides a great room with attached deck on the main level, there is a children's play room and plenty of storage area on the lower level. Three bedrooms on the main level are complemented by a fourth below. Note the convenient placement of baths and the many extras such as a raised-hearth fireplace and large walk-in closets.

Design W4052

Upper Level: 1,843 square feet
Lower Level: 1,495 square feet
Total: 3,338 square feet

DECK ABOVE

PATIO

STORAGE

RECREATION RM
20'-0" X 14'-10"

WH

FURN

BATH

LINEN

BEDROOM
12'-2" X 14'-10"

STORAGE

WALK-IN CLOSET

WALK-IN CLOSET

SHOP
26'-6" X 13'-8"

RAILING

WOOD DECK

BENCH

BENCH

DINING ROOM
13'-0 x 12'-0"

GLASS SLIDING DOOR

LIVING ROOM
20'-0" x 15'-4"
SLOPED BEAMED CEILING

UP
ATTIC

DRESS. ROOM

BEDROOM
13'-0" x 15'-4"

FIREPLACE
RAISED HEARTH

BOTTLE GLASS SCREEN

PANT.

SURF UNIT

OVEN

REF'G

DW

SINK

CABT'S

BAR

DOWN
BSMT.

WALK-IN CLOSET

WALK-IN CLOSET

KITCHEN & BR'FAST AREA
13'-0" x 21'-0"

LANDING

STORAGE

FOYER
17'-8" x 5'-8"

PLANTING

FLAGSTONE WALK

PLANTING

COATS

CLOSET

LIN

POWDER ROOM

BEDROOM
11'-0" x 11'-8"

BEDROOM
11'-0" x 14'-0"

FENCE

FENCE

POST LANTERN

STONE

W

D

GARAGE
21'-4" x 21'-4"

OVERHEAD DOOR

55'-8"

68'-4"

● This design has the appearance of a one-story with the livability of a multi-level. Directly off the foyer is a sunken living room and large kitchen with adjacent dining room. Also on this level is the three-bedroom sleeping area. A walkout basement provides additional living space.

LIFESTYLE HOME PLANS

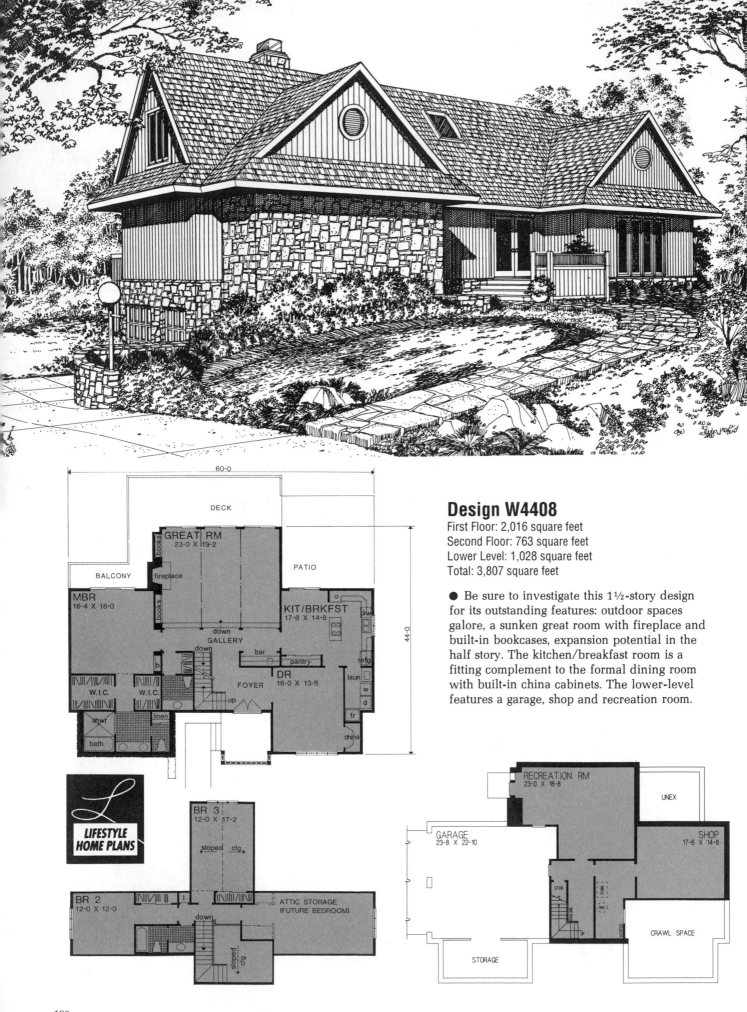

Design W4408

First Floor: 2,016 square feet
Second Floor: 763 square feet
Lower Level: 1,028 square feet
Total: 3,807 square feet

● Be sure to investigate this 1½-story design for its outstanding features: outdoor spaces galore, a sunken great room with fireplace and built-in bookcases, expansion potential in the half story. The kitchen/breakfast room is a fitting complement to the formal dining room with built-in china cabinets. The lower-level features a garage, shop and recreation room.

Floor plan labels:

60-0

DECK

GREAT RM
23-0 X 19-2

BALCONY

PATIO

fireplace

MBR
16-4 X 16-0

KIT/BRKFST
17-8 X 14-8

44-0

books

down
GALLERY

down
bar
pantry

refg

W.I.C.   W.I.C.

DR
16-0 X 13-8

laun

FOYER   up   w

shwr   linen

d

fr

bath

china

LIFESTYLE HOME PLANS

BR 3
12-0 X 17-2

sloped clg

RECREATION RM
23-0 X 18-8

UNEX

BR 2
12-0 X 12-0

ATTIC STORAGE
(FUTURE BEDROOM)

GARAGE
23-8 X 22-10

SHOP
17-6 X 14-8

down

sloped clg

STOR

CRAWL SPACE

STORAGE

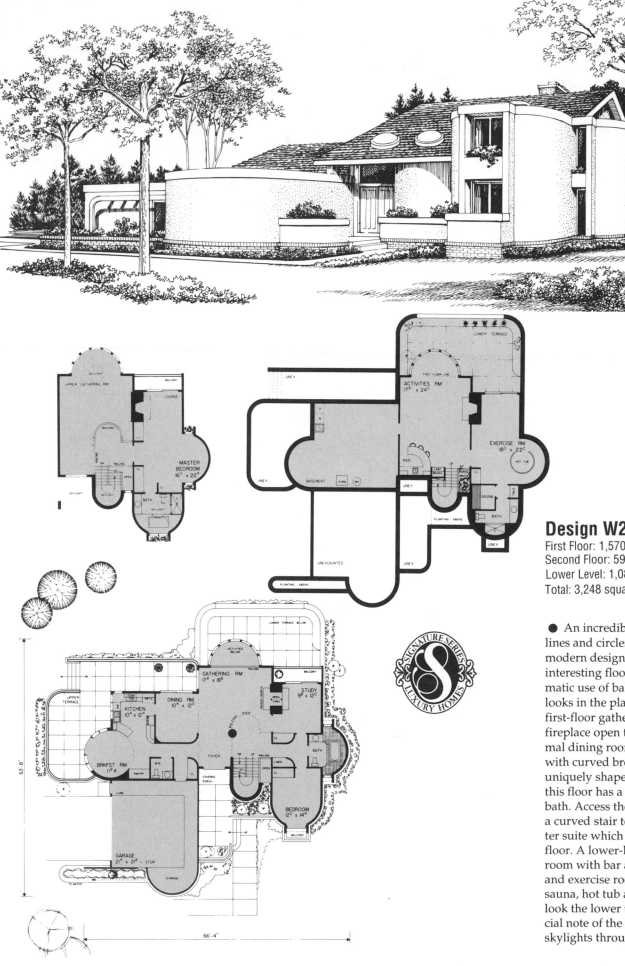

Design W2926

First Floor: 1,570 square feet;
Second Floor: 598 square feet
Lower Level: 1,080 square feet;
Total: 3,248 square feet

● An incredible use of curving lines and circles in this ultra modern design makes for an interesting floor plan. The dramatic use of balconies and overlooks in the plan highlights a first-floor gathering room with fireplace open to the study, formal dining room and kitchen with curved breakfast room. A uniquely shaped bedroom on this floor has a balcony and full bath. Access the second floor by a curved stair to to find the master suite which dominates this floor. A lower-level activities room with bar and fireplace, and exercise room with attached sauna, hot tub and bath overlook the lower terrace. Take special note of the generous use of skylights throughout.

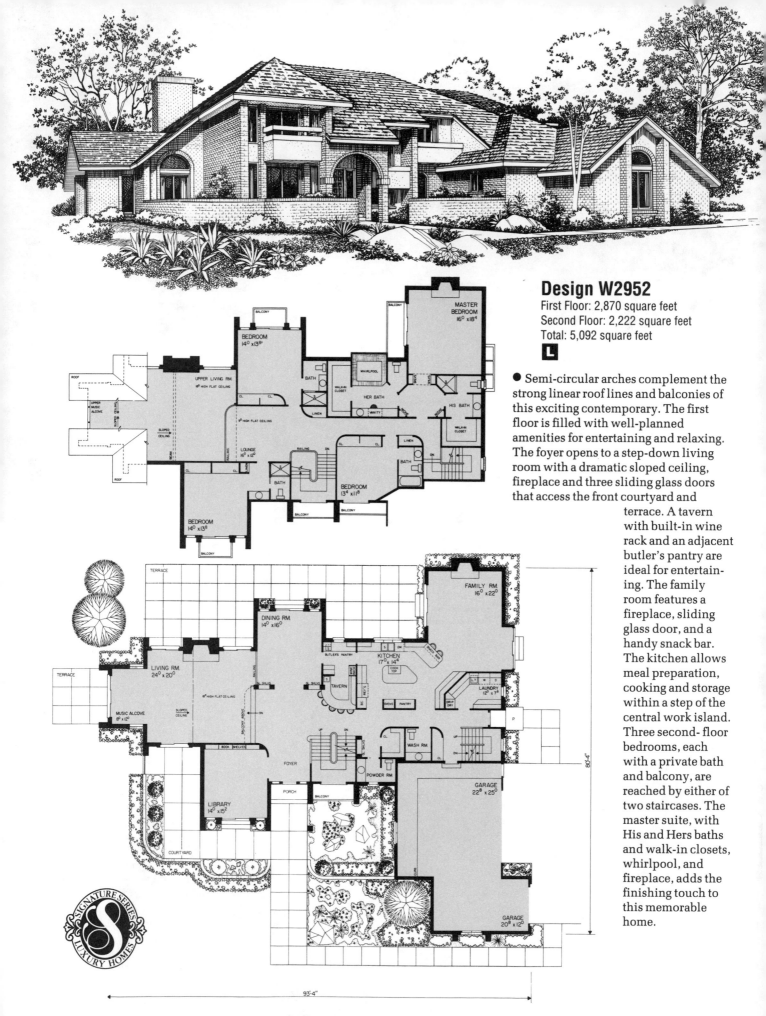

Design W2952

First Floor: 2,870 square feet
Second Floor: 2,222 square feet
Total: 5,092 square feet

L

● Semi-circular arches complement the strong linear roof lines and balconies of this exciting contemporary. The first floor is filled with well-planned amenities for entertaining and relaxing. The foyer opens to a step-down living room with a dramatic sloped ceiling, fireplace and three sliding glass doors that access the front courtyard and terrace. A tavern with built-in wine rack and an adjacent butler's pantry are ideal for entertaining. The family room features a fireplace, sliding glass door, and a handy snack bar. The kitchen allows meal preparation, cooking and storage within a step of the central work island. Three second-floor bedrooms, each with a private bath and balcony, are reached by either of two staircases. The master suite, with His and Hers baths and walk-in closets, whirlpool, and fireplace, adds the finishing touch to this memorable home.

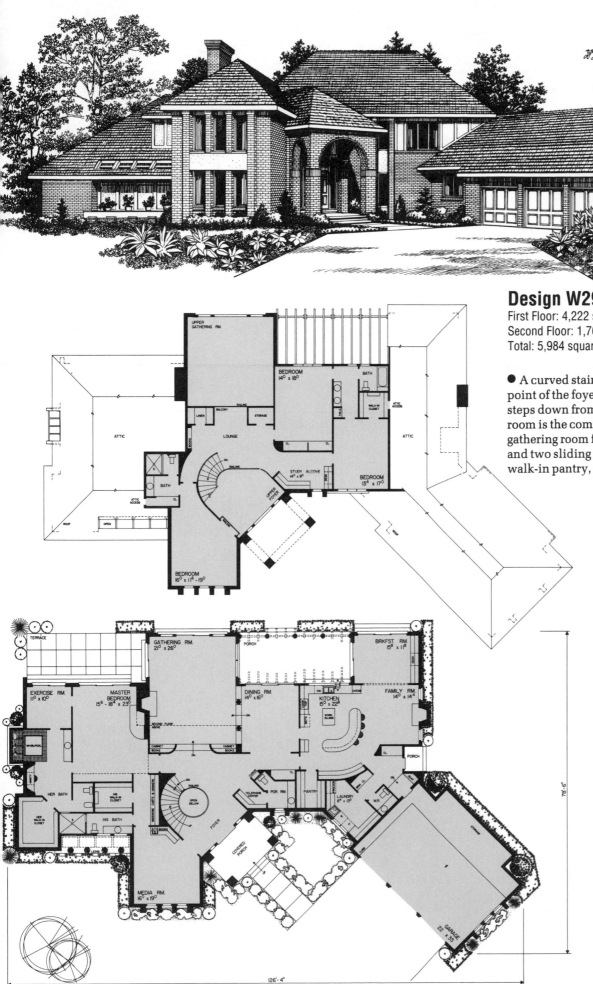

Design W2956

First Floor: 4,222 square feet
Second Floor: 1,762 square feet
Total: 5,984 square feet

● A curved staircase is the focal point of the foyer of this home. Two steps down from the foyer or dining room is the comfortable, two-story gathering room featuring a fireplace and two sliding glass doors. A large walk-in pantry, work island, snack bar, and view of the family room fireplace make the kitchen functional and comfortable. The master suite is secluded in its own wing. The bedroom, with a curved-hearth fireplace, and exercise room opens to the terrace through sliding glass doors. A media room with wet bar, accessible from the master bedroom and foyer, is the perfect place to relax. The second-floor stairs open to a lounge which overlooks the gathering room. Three additional bedrooms and a quiet study alcove on the second floor round out this gracious home.

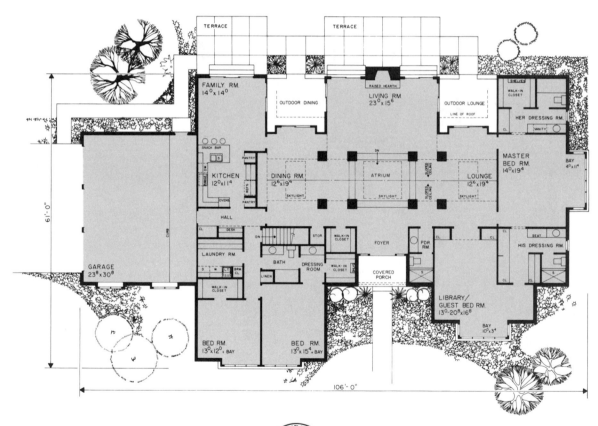

Design W2791

Square Footage: 3,809

● The use of vertical paned windows and the hipped roof highlight the exterior of this unique design. Upon entrance one will view a charming sunken atrium with skylight above plus a skylight in the dining room and one in the lounge. Formal living will be graciously accommodated in the living room. It features a raised-hearth fireplace, two sets of sliding glass doors to the rear terrace plus two more sliding doors, one to an outdoor dining terrace and the other to an outdoor lounge. Informal living will be enjoyed in the family room with snack bar and in the large library. All will praise the fine planning of the master suite. It features a bay window, His and Hers dressing room with private baths and an abundance of closet space.

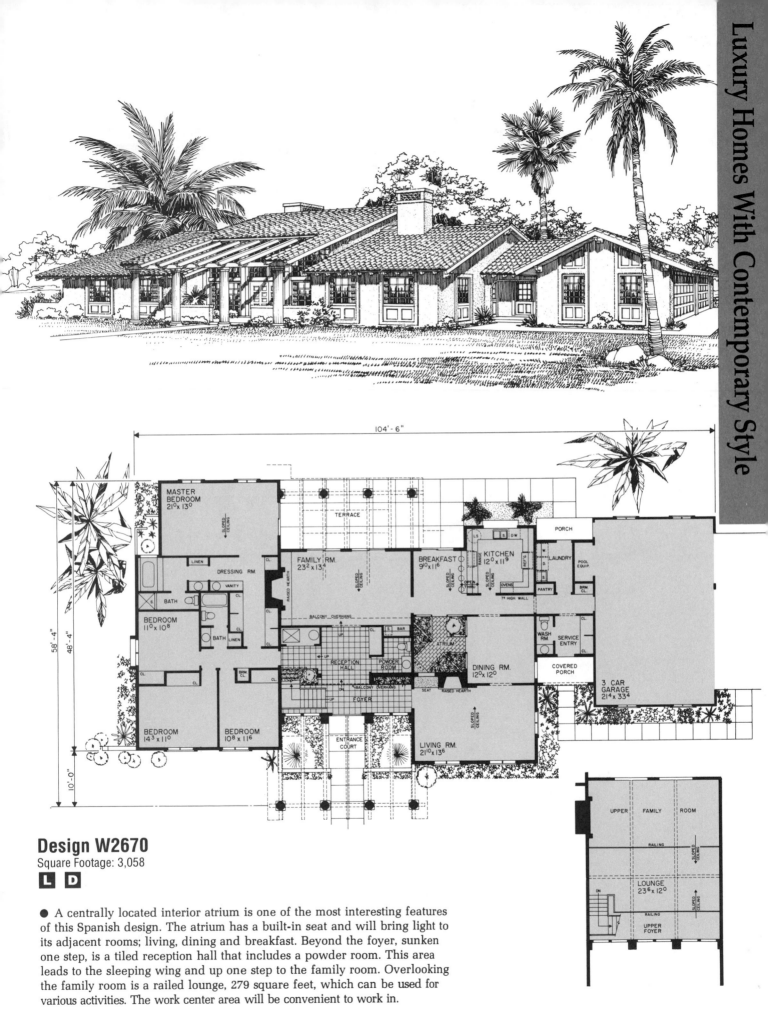

104'- 6"

58'- 4"

48'- 4"

10'- 0"

MASTER BEDROOM
21⁰ x 13⁰

SLOPED CEILING

TERRACE

LINEN

DRESSING RM.

VANITY

BATH

CL.

BEDROOM
11⁰ x 10⁸

BATH LINEN

CL.

FAMILY RM.
23² x 13⁴

SLOPED CEILING

RAISED HEARTH

BREAKFAST
9⁰ x 11⁶

SLOPED CEILING

OPEN THRU

KITCHEN
12⁰ x 11⁹

RANGE

OVENS

REF'G

7' HIGH WALL

PORCH

W

D

LAUNDRY

POOL EQUIP.

PANTRY

BRM CL.

BALCONY OVERHANG

S. BAR

CL.

ATRIUM

WASH RM

SERVICE ENTRY

CL.

RECEPTION HALL

POWDER ROOM

UP

UP

DINING RM.
12⁰ x 12⁰

RAISED HEARTH

COVERED PORCH

3 CAR GARAGE
21⁴ x 33⁴

BRM CL.

CL.

CL.

BEDROOM
14³ x 11⁰

BEDROOM
10⁸ x 11⁶

FOYER

UP

BALCONY OVERHANG

SEAT

ENTRANCE COURT

LIVING RM.
21¹⁰ x 13⁶

SLOPED CEILING

UPPER FAMILY ROOM

RAILING

SLOPED CEILING

LOUNGE
23⁶ x 12⁰

DN

RAILING

SLOPED CEILING

UPPER FOYER

Design W2670

Square Footage: 3,058

L **D**

● A centrally located interior atrium is one of the most interesting features
of this Spanish design. The atrium has a built-in seat and will bring light to
its adjacent rooms; living, dining and breakfast. Beyond the foyer, sunken
one step, is a tiled reception hall that includes a powder room. This area
leads to the sleeping wing and up one step to the family room. Overlooking
the family room is a railed lounge, 279 square feet, which can be used for
various activities. The work center area will be convenient to work in.

Design W3361

Main Level: 3,548 square feet
Lower Level: 1,036 square feet
Total: 4,584 square feet

● Here's a dandy hillside home that can easily accommodate the largest of families and is perfect for both formal and informal entertaining. Straight back from the entry foyer is a grand gathering room/dining room combination. It is complemented by the breakfast room and a front-facing media room. The sleeping wing contains three bedrooms and two full baths. On the lower level is an activities room with summer kitchen and a fourth bedroom that makes the perfect guest room.

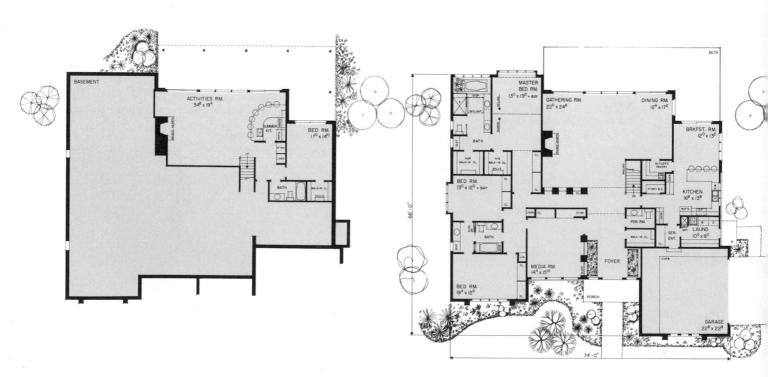

Design W2934

Main Level: 2,472 square feet; Lower Level: 2,145 square feet
Total: 4,617 square feet

D

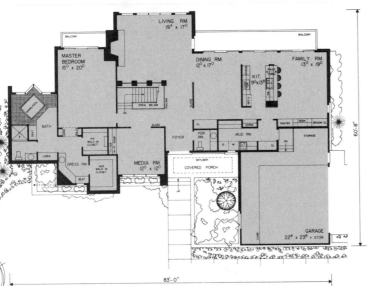

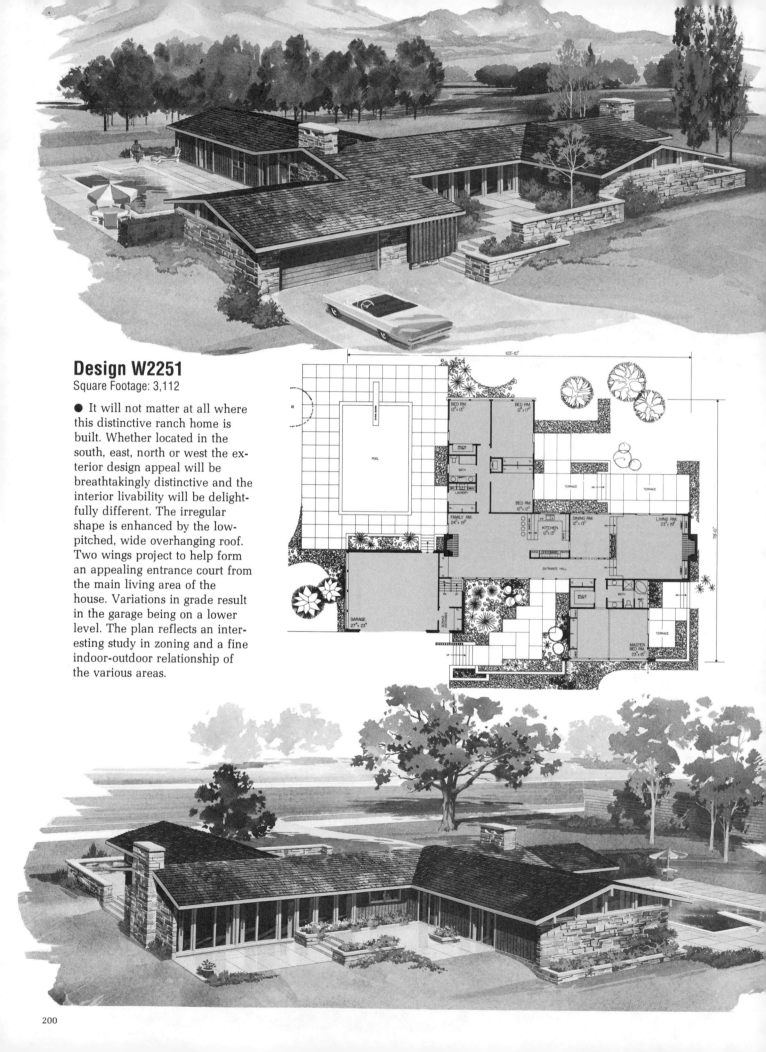

Design W2251
Square Footage: 3,112

● It will not matter at all where this distinctive ranch home is built. Whether located in the south, east, north or west the exterior design appeal will be breathtakingly distinctive and the interior livability will be delightfully different. The irregular shape is enhanced by the low-pitched, wide overhanging roof. Two wings project to help form an appealing entrance court from the main living area of the house. Variations in grade result in the garage being on a lower level. The plan reflects an interesting study in zoning and a fine indoor-outdoor relationship of the various areas.

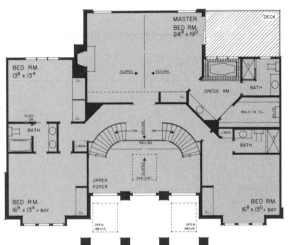

Design W3364

First Floor: 2,883 square feet
Second Floor: 1,919 square feet
Total: 4,802 square feet

L **D**

● The impressive stonework facade of this contemporary home is as dramatic as it is practical — and it contains a grand floor plan. Notice the varying levels — a family room, living room, media room, and atrium are down a few steps from the elegant entry foyer. The large L-shaped kitchen is highlighted by an island work center and a pass-through snack bar. A double curved staircase leads to a second floor where four bedrooms and three full baths are found.

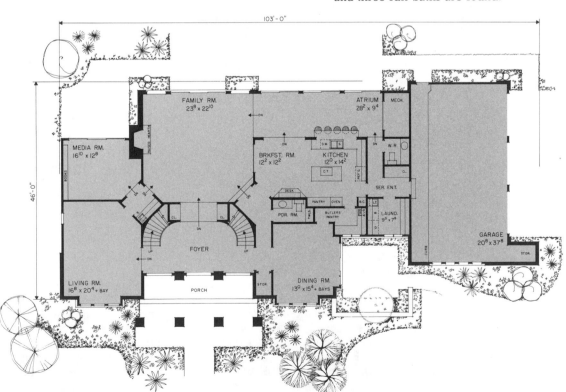

Design W2938
First Floor: 4,518 square feet
Second Floor: 882 square feet
Total: 5,400 square feet

● A semi-circular fanlight and sidelights grace the entrance of this striking contemporary. The lofty foyer, with balcony above, leads to an elegant, two-story living room with fireplace. The family room, housing a second fireplace, leads to a glorious sunroom; both have dramatic sloped ceilings.

The kitchen and breakfast room are conveniently located for access to the informal family room or to the formal dining room via the butler's pantry. The large adjoining clutter room with work island offers limitless possibilities for the seamstress, hobbyist, or indoor gardener. An executive-sized, first-

floor master suite offers privacy and relaxation; the bath with whirlpool tub and dressing area with twin walk-in closets open to a study that could double as an exercise room. Two second-floor bedrooms with private baths and walk-in closets round out the livability in this gracious home.

Design W2879 Living Area Including Atrium: 3,173 square feet
Upper Lounge/Balcony: 267 square feet
Total: 3,440 square feet

● This plush modern design seems to have it all, including an upper lounge, upper family room, and upper foyer. There's also an atrium with skylight centrally located downstairs. A modern kitchen with snack bar service to a breakfast room also enjoys its own greenhouse window. A deluxe master bedroom includes its own whirlpool and bay window. Three other bedrooms also are isolated at one end of the house downstairs to allow privacy and quiet. A spacious family room in the rear enjoys its own raised-hearth fireplace and view of a rear covered terrace. A front living room with its own fireplace looks out upon a side garden court and the central atrium. There's also a formal dining room situated between the kitchen and living room, plus a three-car garage, covered porches, and sizable laundry with washroom just off the garage.

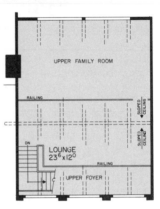

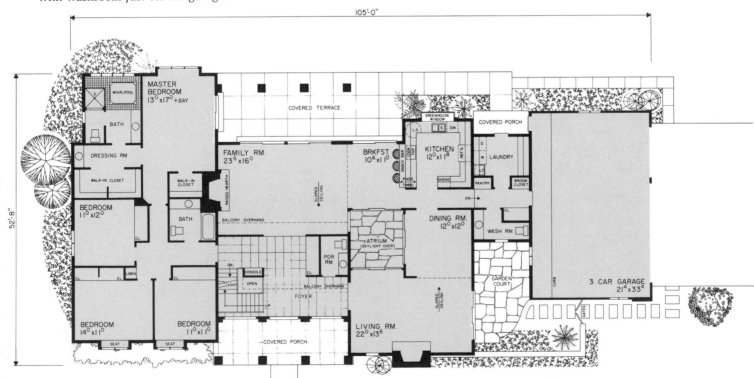

● You can't help but feel spoiled by this design. Behind the handsome facade lies a spacious, amenity-filled plan. Downstairs from the entry is the large living room with sloped ceiling and fireplace. Nearby is the U-shaped kitchen with a pass-through to the din-

ing room — a convenient step-saver. Also on this level, the master suite boasts a fireplace and a sliding glass door onto the deck. The living and dining rooms also feature deck access. Upstairs are two bedrooms and shared bath. A balcony sitting area overlooks

the living room. The enormous lower-level playroom includes a fireplace, a large bar, and sliding glass doors to the patio. Also notice the storage room with built-in workbench.

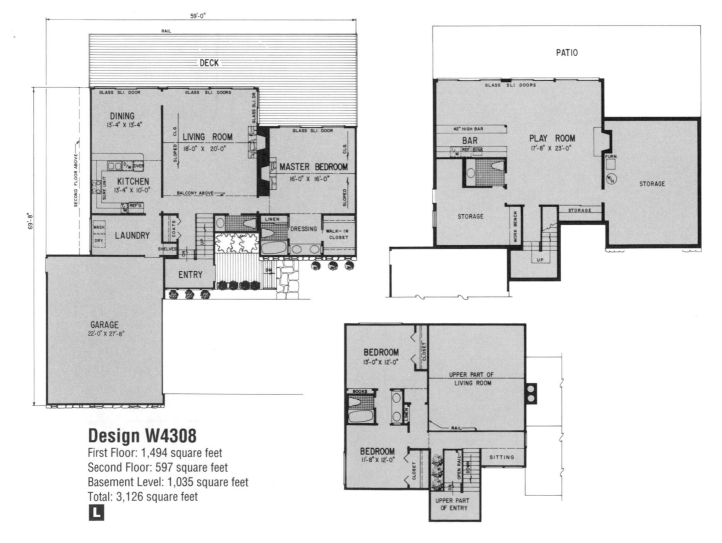

Design W4308

First Floor: 1,494 square feet
Second Floor: 597 square feet
Basement Level: 1,035 square feet
Total: 3,126 square feet

● This home is a showplace both inside and out. A handsome contemporary exterior houses a spacious interior. The first floor features a dramatic living room, formal dining room, kitchen with breakfast area, library with built-in shelves and the master bedroom. Four more bedrooms and two baths are on the second floor. The basement recreation room has a sliding glass door leading outside.

Design W4548
First Floor: 3,064 square feet
Second Floor: 1,450 square feet
Basement: 1,115 square feet
Total: 5,629 square feet

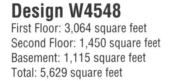

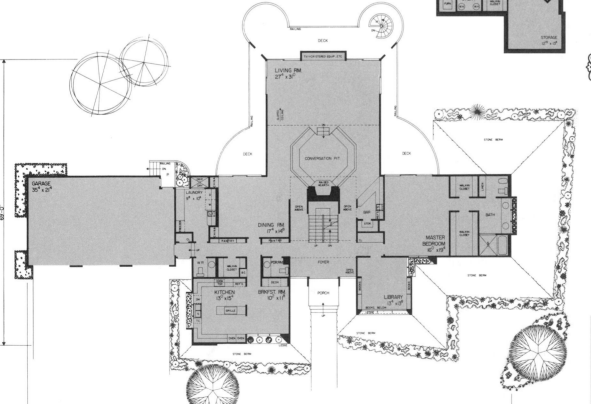

LIFESTYLE
HOME PLANS

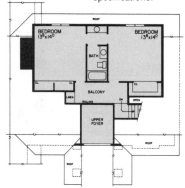

CUSTOMIZABLE

Custom Alterations? See page 301 for customizing this plan to your specifications.

Design W2920
First Floor: 3,067 square feet
Second Floor: 648 square feet; Total: 3,715 square feet

L D

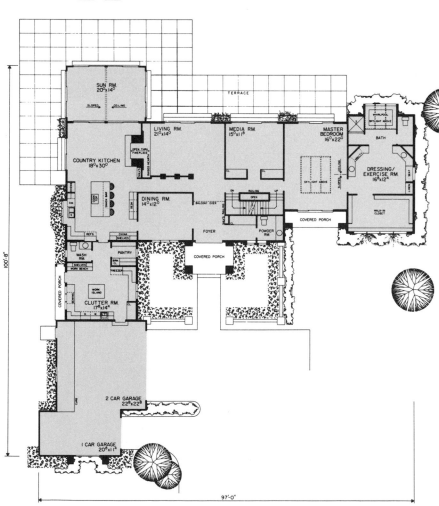

● This contemporary design also has a great deal to offer. Study the living areas. A fireplace opens up to both the living room and country kitchen. Privacy is the key word when describing the sleeping areas. the first floor master bedroom is away from the traffic of the house and features a dressing/exercise room, whirlpool tub and shower and a spacious walk-in closet. Two more bedrooms and a full bath are on the second floor. The three car garage is arranged so that the owners have use of a double-garage with an attached single on reserve for guests. The cheerful sun room adds 296 sq. ft. to the total.

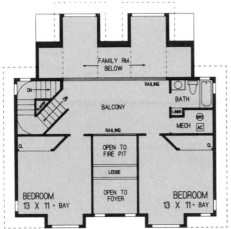

Design W3404

First Floor: 3,358 square feet
Second Floor: 868 square feet
Total: 4,226 square feet

L **D**

● Farmhouse design does a double take in this unusual and elegant rendition. Notice that most of the living takes place on the first floor: formal living room and dining room, gigantic family room with enormous firepit and porch access, guest bedroom or den and master bedroom suite. Upstairs there are two smaller bedrooms and a dramatic balcony overlook to the family room below.

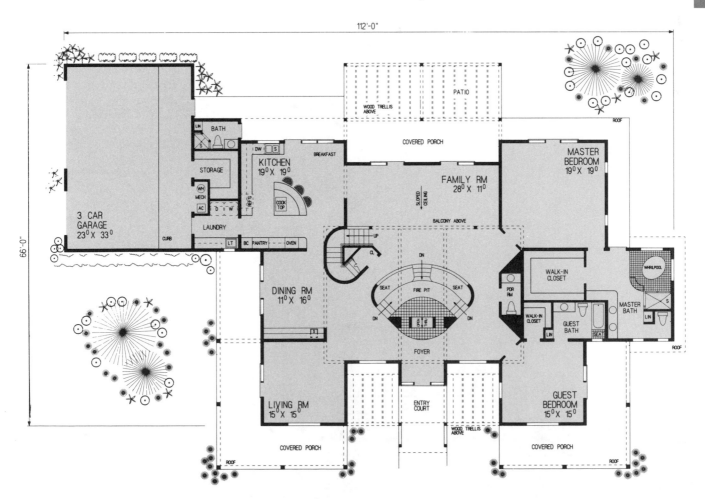

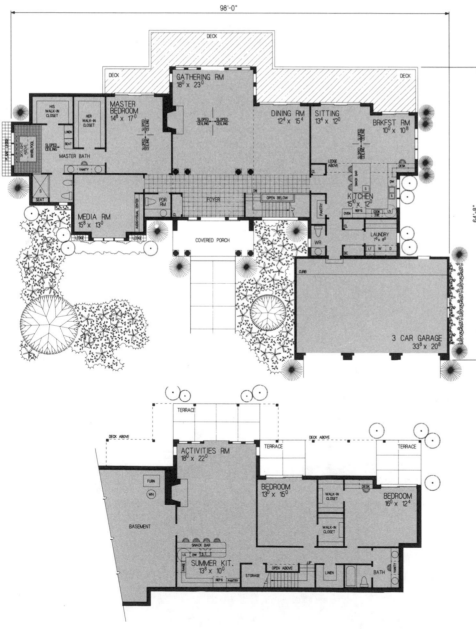

Design W3311

Main Level: 2,662 square feet
Lower Level: 1,548 square feet
Total: 4,210 square feet

L **D**

● Here's a hillside haven
for family living with plenty
of room to entertain in style.
Enter the main level from a
dramatic columned portico
that leads to a large entry
hall. The gathering room is
straight back and adjoins a
formal dining area. A true
gourmet kitchen with plenty
of room for casual eating
and conversation is nearby.
The abundantly appointed
master suite on this level is
complemented by a luxuri-
ous bath. Note the media
room to the front of the
house. On the lower level
are two more bedrooms, a
full bath, a large activity
area with fireplace and a
convenient summer kitchen.

Design W3409

First Floor: 1,481 square feet
Second Floor: 1,287 square feet
Total: 2,768 square feet

L

● Glass block walls and a foyer with barrel vaulted ceiling create an interesting exterior. Covered porches to the front and rear provide for excellent indoor/outdoor living relationships. Inside, a large planter and through-fireplace enhance the living room and family room. The dining room has a stepped ceiling. A desk, eating area and snack bar are special features in the kitchen. The master suite features a large walk-in closet, bath with double bowl vanity and separate tub and shower, and a private deck. Three additional bedrooms share a full bath.

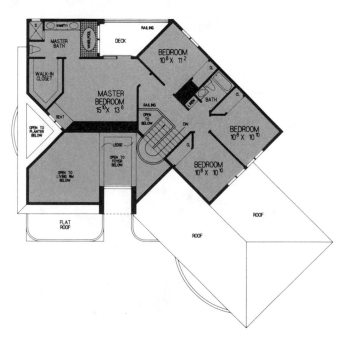

Design W3562

First Floor: 1,182 square feet
Second Floor: 927 square feet
Total: 2,109 square feet

L **D**

● Interesting detailing marks the exterior of this home as a beauty. Its interior makes it a livable option for any family. Entry occurs through double doors to the left side of the plan. A powder room with curved wall is handy to the entry. Living areas of the home are open and well-planned. The formal living room shares a through fireplace with the large family room. The dining room is adjoining and has a pass-through counter to the L-shaped kitchen. Special details on this floor include a wealth of sliding glass doors to the rear terrace and built-ins throughout. Upstairs are three bedrooms with two full baths.

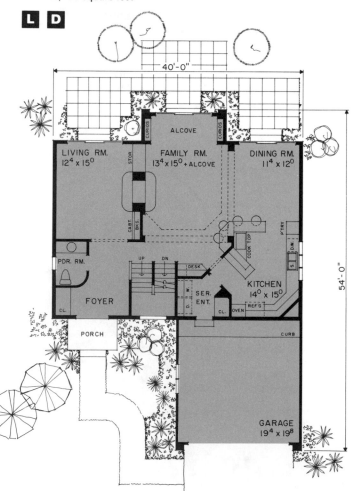

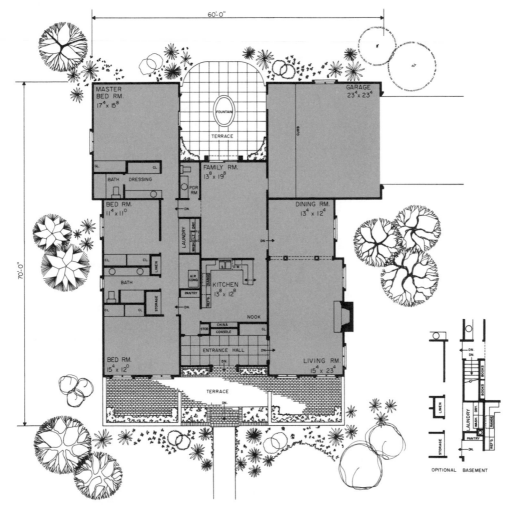

Design W2347
Square Footage: 2,322

● The regal character of this distinctive home is most inviting. The symmetry of the front exterior is enhanced by the raised terrace. The recessed front entrance shelters panelled double doors which open to the formal hall. Traffic may pass to the right directly into the sunken living room. To the left is the sunken three bedroom, two-bath sleeping area. The center of the plan features the efficient kitchen with nook space and the family room. The rear terrace, enclosed on three sides to assure privacy, is accessible form the master bedroom as well as the family room. Separating the formal living and dining rooms are finely proportioned wood columns. Blueprints include details for an optional partial basement.

Design W3450

First Floor: 1,801 square feet
Second Floor: 1,086 square feet
Total: 2,887 square feet

L **D**

● A striking facade includes a covered front porch with four columns. To the left of the foyer is a large gathering room with a fireplace and bay window. The adjoining dining room leads to a covered side porch. The kitchen includes a snack bar, pantry, desk, and eating area. The first-floor master suite provides a spacious bath with walk-in closet, whirlpool and shower. Also on the first floor: a study and a garage workshop. Two bedrooms and a lavish guest suite share the second floor.

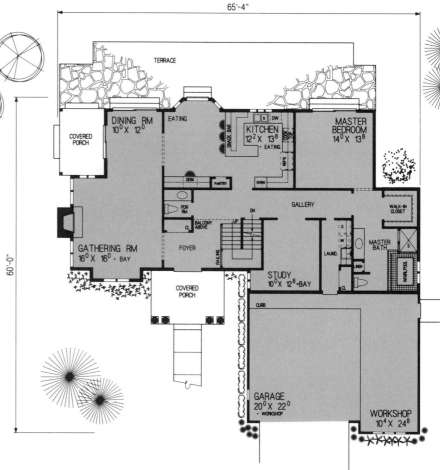

CUSTOMIZABLE

Custom Alterations? See page 301 for customizing this plan to your specifications.

Design W3439

First Floor: 1,425 square feet
Second Floor: 989 square feet
Total: 2,414 square feet

L

● Featuring a facade of wood and window glass, this home presents a striking first impression. It's floor plan is equally as splendid. Formal living and dining areas flank the entry foyer—both are sunken two steps down. Also sunken from the foyer is the family room with attached breakfast nook. A fireplace in this area sits adjacent to a built-in audio-visual center. A nearby study with adjacent full bath doubles as a guest room. Upstairs are three bedrooms including a master suite with whirlpool spa and walk-in closet. Plant shelves adorn the entire floor plan.

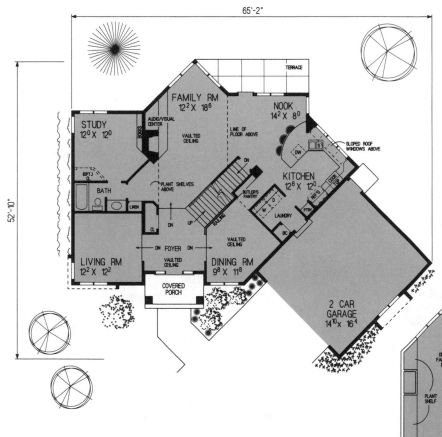

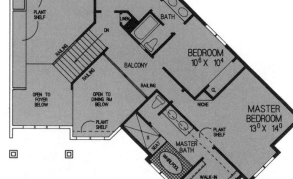

CUSTOMIZABLE

Custom Alterations? See page 301 for customizing this plan to your specifications.

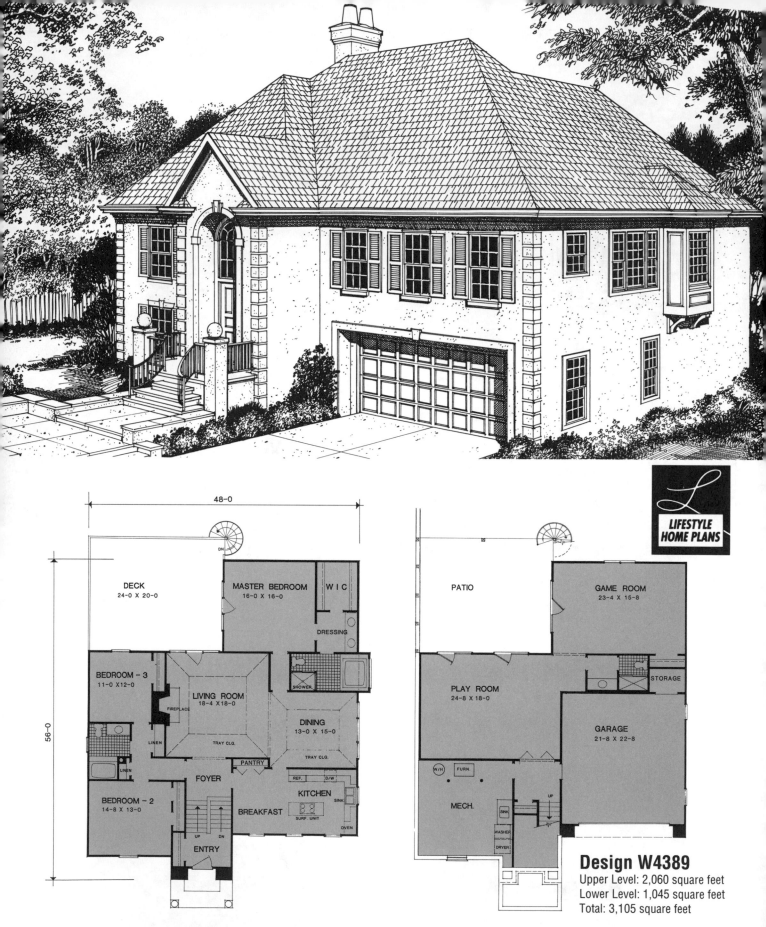

DECK
24-0 X 20-0

MASTER BEDROOM
16-0 X 16-0

W I C

DRESSING

SHOWER

BEDROOM - 3
11-0 X12-0

LIVING ROOM
18-4 X18-0

FIREPLACE

LINEN

TRAY CLG.

DINING
13-0 X 15-0

LINEN

PANTRY

TRAY CLG.

FOYER

BREAKFAST

KITCHEN

UP   DN

SURF. UNIT

REF.   D/W

SINK

OVEN

BEDROOM - 2
14-8 X 13-0

ENTRY

48-0

56-0

DN

PATIO

GAME ROOM
23-4 X 15-8

PLAY ROOM
24-8 X 18-0

STORAGE

GARAGE
21-8 X 22-8

W/H   FURN.

MECH.

SINK

UP

WASHER

DRYER

Design W4389
Upper Level: 2,060 square feet
Lower Level: 1,045 square feet
Total: 3,105 square feet

L
LIFESTYLE
HOME PLANS

● Old world charm greets visitors to this lovely home. Notice the stucco-and-quoin facade, hipped roof, and wrought-iron railings. The living room with tray ceiling and fireplace is the centerpiece of the plan. The adjoining dining room also boasts a tray ceiling and is convenient to the large kitchen with island cooktop. Separated from the other bedrooms, the master suite is to the rear and features a walk-in closet, oversized bath with bay window, and access to the rear deck. The lower level contains a game room and play room, both adjacent to a covered patio.

Design W4391

First Floor: 1,315 square feet
Second Floor: 1,312 square feet
Lower Level: 1,273 square feet
Total: 3,900 square feet

● Hillside living takes on elegant proportions in this thoughtful plan. Formal and informal living areas to the left of the central foyer complement the dining and cooking areas on the right. A large deck to the back adds outdoor enjoyment. The master bedroom, with full bath, upstairs misses nothing in the way of luxury and is joined by two family bedrooms and baths. Bonus space to the front makes a perfect office or computer room. Note recreation room with fireplace.

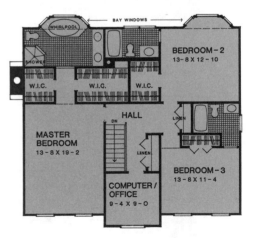

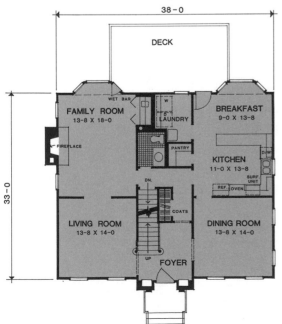

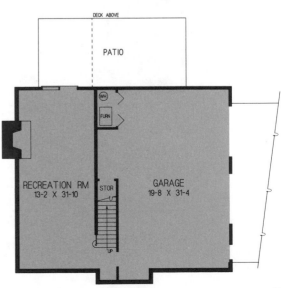

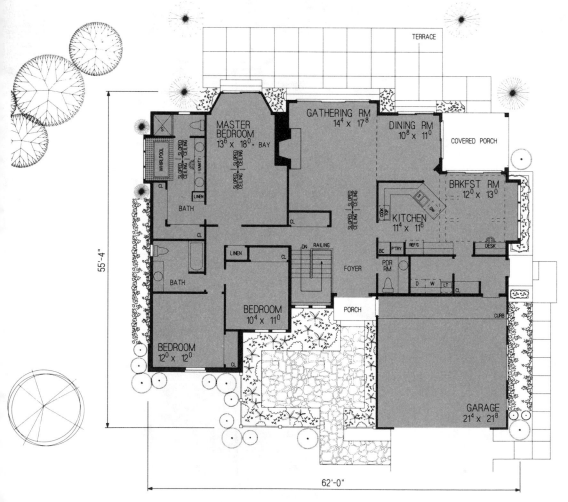

Design W3336
Square Footage: 2,022

● Compact and comfortable! This three-bedrooom home is a good consideration for a small family or empty-nester retirees. Of special note are the covered eating porch and sloped ceilings in the gathering room and master bedroom. A well-placed powder room is found at the front entry.

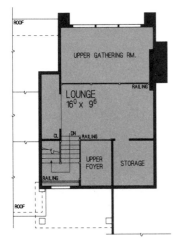

Design W3330

First Floor: 1,394 square feet
Second Floor: 320 square feet
Total: 1,714 square feet

● Outdoor living and open floor planning are highlights of this moderately sized plan. Amenities include a private hot tub on a wooden deck that is accessible via sliding glass doors in both bedrooms, and a two-story gathering room. An optional second-floor plan allows for a full 503 square feet of space with a balcony.

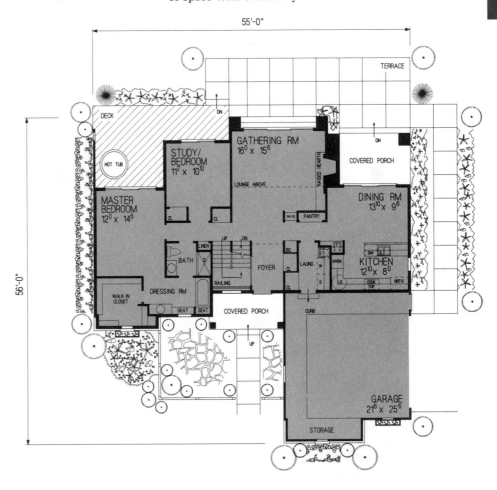

OPTIONAL FLOOR PLAN

Design W2927

First Floor: 1,425 square feet
Second Floor: 704 square feet
Total: 2,129 square feet

D

CUSTOMIZABLE

Custom Alterations? See page 301 for customizing this plan to your specifications.

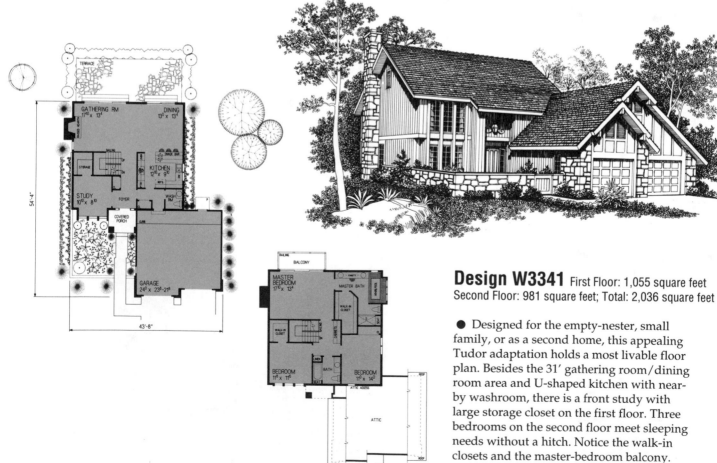

Design W3341

First Floor: 1,055 square feet
Second Floor: 981 square feet; Total: 2,036 square feet

● Designed for the empty-nester, small family, or as a second home, this appealing Tudor adaptation holds a most livable floor plan. Besides the 31' gathering room/dining room area and U-shaped kitchen with near-by washroom, there is a front study with large storage closet on the first floor. Three bedrooms on the second floor meet sleeping needs without a hitch. Notice the walk-in closets and the master-bedroom balcony.

CUSTOMIZABLE

Custom Alterations? See page 301 for customizing this plan to your specifications.

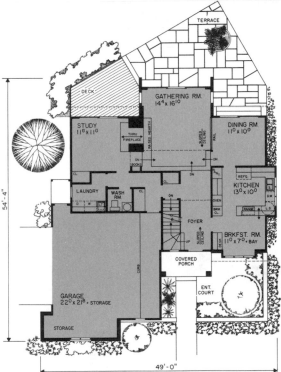

Design W2826 First Floor: 1,112 square feet
Second Floor: 881 square feet; Total: 1,993 square feet

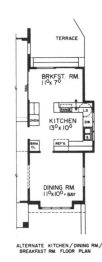

ALTERNATE KITCHEN / DINING RM./
BREAKFAST RM. FLOOR PLAN

● This is an outstanding example of the type of informal, traditional-style architecture that has captured the modern imagination. The interior plan houses all of the features that people want most - a spacious gathering room, formal and informal dining areas, efficient, U-shaped kitchen, master bedroom, two children's bedrooms, second floor lounge, entrance court and rear terrace and deck. Study all areas of this plan carefully.

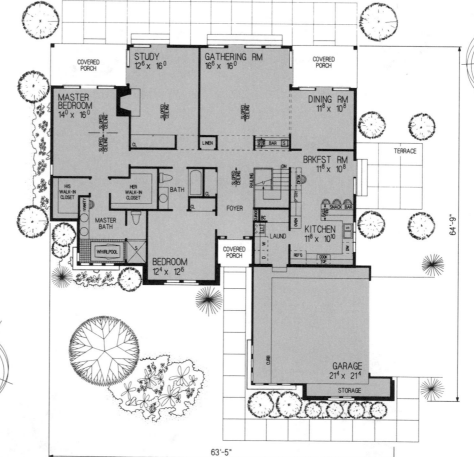

CUSTOMIZABLE

Custom Alterations? See page 301 for customizing this plan to your specifications.

Design W3346

Square Footage: 2,032

● This home boasts a delightful Tudor exterior with a terrific interior floor plan. Though compact, there's plenty of living space: large study with fireplace, gathering room, dining room, and breakfast room. The master bedroom has an attached bath with whirlpool tub. Note the double walk-in closets.

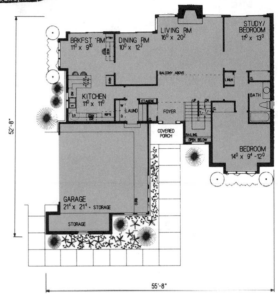

Design W3342

First Floor: 1,467 square feet
Second Floor: 715 square feet
Total: 2,182 square feet

● Just the right amount of living space is contained in this charming traditional house and it's arranged in a great floor plan. The split-bedroom configuration, with two bedrooms (or optional study) on the first floor and the master suite on the second floor with its own studio, assures complete privacy. The living room has a second-floor balcony overlook and a warming fireplace. The full-width terrace in back is counterbalanced nicely by the entry garden court.

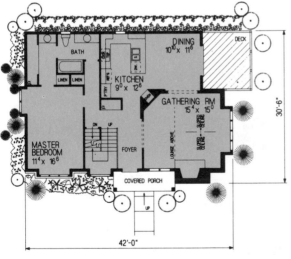

Design W3331

First Floor: 1,115 square feet
Second Floor: 690 square feet
Total: 1,805 square feet

● Who could guess that this compact design contains three bedrooms and two full baths? The kitchen is close to indoor eating space in the dining room and outdoor eating space in an attached deck. A fireplace in the two-story gathering room welcomes company.

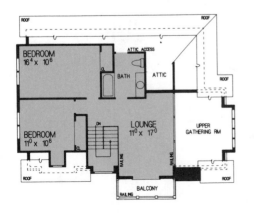

Design W3428 First Floor: 2,623 square feet
Second Floor: 551 square feet; Total: 3,174 square feet

● High sloping ceilings and plenty of windows lend a light, airy feel to this Southwestern design. Flanking the two-story foyer are the sleeping areas, the regal master suite to the left and three more bedrooms (or two plus study) to the right. Overlooking the back yard are the dining room and living room with raised-hearth fireplace. The U-shaped kitchen has a pass-through to the family room which also has a fireplace. Doors here and in the dining room open onto the covered porch. Notice the pot shelves scattered throughout the plan.

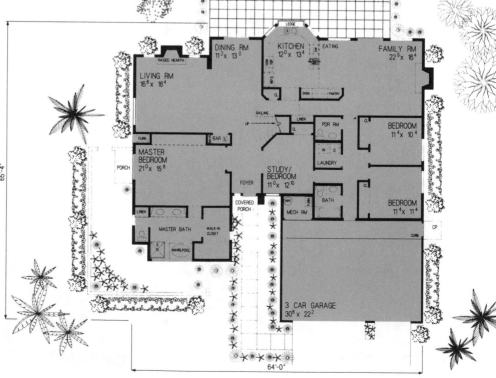

CUSTOMIZABLE
Custom Alterations? See page 301 for customizing this plan to your specifications.

222

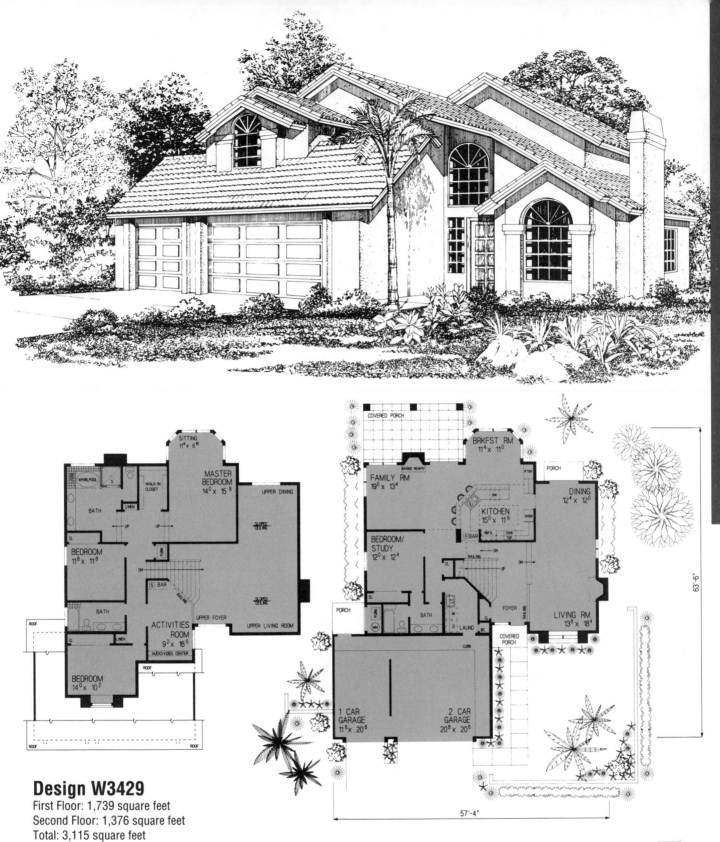

Design W3429

First Floor: 1,739 square feet
Second Floor: 1,376 square feet
Total: 3,115 square feet

● From the dramatic open entry to the covered back porch, this home delivers a full measure of livability in Spanish design. Formal living areas (living room and dining room) have a counter-point in the family room and glassed-in breakfast room. The kitchen is a hub for both areas. Notice that the first-floor study has an adjacent bath, making it a fine guest room when needed. On the second floor, the activities room serves two family bedrooms and a grand master suite.

CUSTOMIZABLE
Custom Alterations? See page 301 for customizing this plan to your specifications.

Design W2950
Square Footage: 2,559

● A natural desert dweller, this stucco, tile-roofed beauty is equally comfortable in any clime. Inside, there's a well-planned design. Common living areas — gathering room, formal dining room, and breakfast room — are offset by a quiet study that could be used as a bedroom or guest room. A master suite features two walk-in closets, a double vanity, and whirlpool spa. The two-car garage has a service entrance; close by is an adequate laundry area and a pantry. Notice the warming hearth in the gathering room and the snack bar area for casual dining.

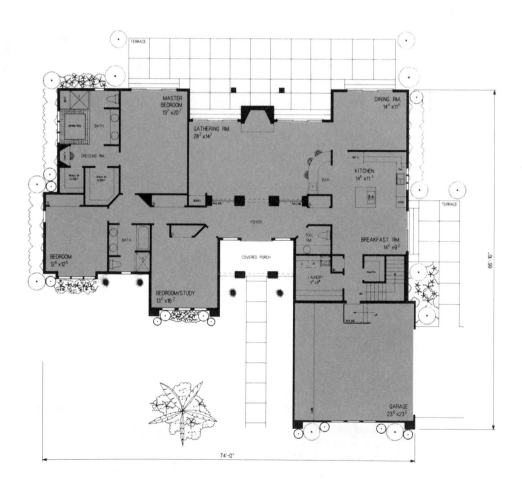

Design W3425

First Floor: 1,776 square feet
Second Floor: 1,035 square feet
Total: 2,811 square feet

● Here's a two-story
Spanish design with an
appealing, angled exterior.
Inside is an interesting
floor plan containing rooms
with a variety of shapes.
Formal areas are to the
right of the entry tower: a
living room with fireplace
and large dining room. The
kitchen has loads of
counter space and is com-
plemented by a bumped-
out breakfast room. Note
the second fireplace in the
family room and the first-
floor bedroom. Three sec-
ond-floor bedrooms radiate
around the upper foyer.

CUSTOMIZABLE

Custom Alterations? See page 301
for customizing this plan to your
specifications.

Design W3560

Square Footage: 2,189

L

● Simplicity is the key to the stylish good
looks of this home's facade. A walled garden
entry and large window areas appeal to
outdoor enthusiasts. Inside, the kitchen forms
the hub of the plan. It opens directly off the
foyer and contains an island counter and
a work counter with eating space on the living
area side. A sloped ceiling, fireplace, and sliding glass doors to a rear terrace are highlights
in living area. The master bedroom also sports
sliding glass doors to the terrace. Its dressing
area is enhanced with double walk-in closets
and lavatories. A whirlpool tub and seated
shower are additional amenities. Two family
bedrooms are found on the opposite side of the
house. They share a full bath with twin
lavatories.

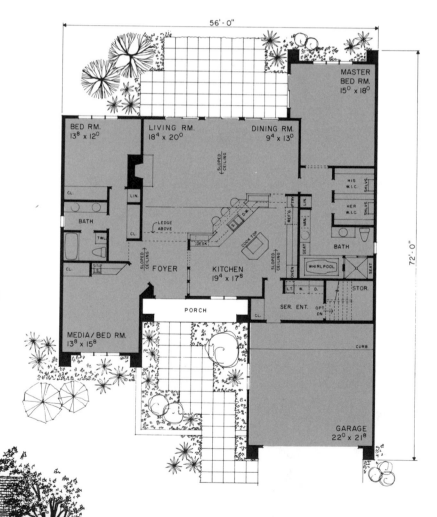

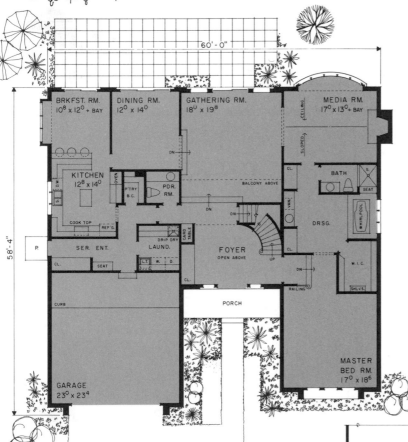

Design W3557

First Floor: 2,897 square feet
Second Floor: 835 square feet
Total: 3,732 square feet

L D

● The owners of this home will be giving themselves a real treat. A large master bedroom is accompanied by a pampering master bath and dressing area with walk-in closet. The master suite also provides access to the media room with bay window and fireplace. A sunken gathering room suits formal or informal occasions. The kitchen contains a snack bar and is convenient to the breakfast and dining rooms. Two large bedrooms upstairs are accompanied by two full baths.

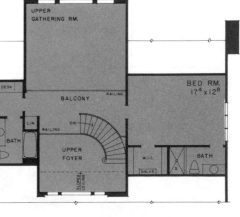

Design W3416

Square Footage: 1,375

● Here's a Southwestern design that will be economical to build and a pleasure to occupy. The front door opens into a spacious living room with corner fireplace and dining room with coffered ceiling. The nearby kitchen serves both easily. A few steps away is the cozy media room with built-in space for audio/visual equipment. Down the hall are two bedrooms and two baths; the master features a whirlpool. A guest room is found around the entry court and includes a fireplace and sloped ceiling.

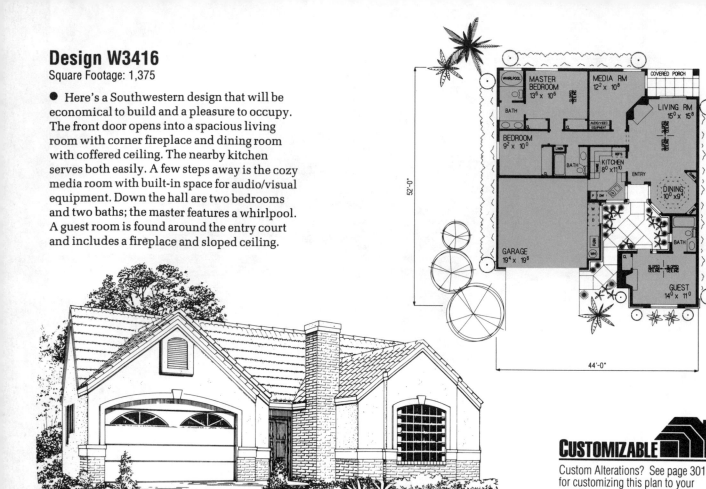

CUSTOMIZABLE

Custom Alterations? See page 301 for customizing this plan to your specifications.

Design W3419

Square Footage: 1,965

● This attractive, multi-gabled exterior houses a compact, livable interior. The entry foyer effectively routes traffic to all areas: left to the family room and kitchen, straight back to the dining room and living room, and right to the four-bedroom sleeping area. The spacious family room provides an informal gathering space while the living and dining rooms are perfect for formal occasions. The highlight of the sleeping area is the master bedroom with its whirlpool, walk-in closet and view of the back yard.

CUSTOMIZABLE

Custom Alterations? See page 301 for customizing this plan to your specifications.

Design W4386

Square Footage: 1,811

● Empty nesters and small families will appreciate the compact design of this home. An island kitchen with breakfast nook and adjacent screened porch serves the dining room/living room. A fireplace warms the occasion. Three bedrooms, one a master suite with a full bath, allow plenty of space for a newborn's nursery or visiting grandchildren.

L
LIFESTYLE HOME PLANS

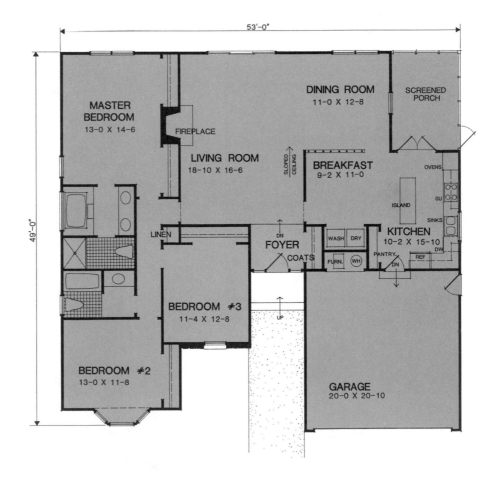

53'-0"

49'-0"

MASTER BEDROOM
13-0 X 14-6

FIREPLACE

LIVING ROOM
18-10 X 16-6

DINING ROOM
11-0 X 12-8

SCREENED PORCH

SLOPED CEILING

BREAKFAST
9-2 X 11-0

OVENS

SU

ISLAND

SINKS

LINEN

FOYER

KITCHEN
10-2 X 15-10

DN

WASH DRY

COATS

FURN. WH

PANTRY

DN

REF

DW

BEDROOM #3
11-4 X 12-8

UP

BEDROOM #2
13-0 X 11-8

GARAGE
20-0 X 20-10

Design W4390

First Floor: 1,507 square feet
Second Floor: 1,086 square feet
Total: 2,593 square feet

● This plan successfully joins elements of contemporary and traditional design for a thoroughly pleasing result. The unusual set of roof lines creates interesting patterns on the inside on all the first-floor rooms. The second floor has a balcony overlook to the living room below and also contains a bonus room with dormer that would make a great playroom.

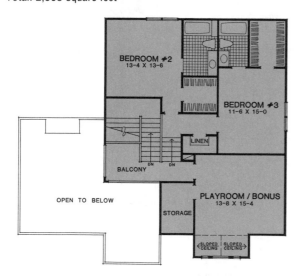

LIFESTYLE
HOME PLANS

Design W2876 First Floor: 1,462 square feet
Second Floor: 1,132 square feet; Total: 2,594 square feet

● This Early American design has received a modern facelift that includes large view windows and a floor plan for Contemporary living patterns. The charm of traditional covered porch and vertical lines have been maintained, along with practical dormer windows that pierce the gable roof line. A front dining room and a living room on either side of the central foyer both enjoy bay windows. There's also a rear family room downstairs, as well as a modern kitchen that incorporates a breakfast room and island cook top in its open planning expanse. Upstairs are three large bedrooms including a master bedroom suite and five cozy dormers with window-ledge seats. Also note the covered side porch that allows handy entry to the laundry, kitchen, or garage.

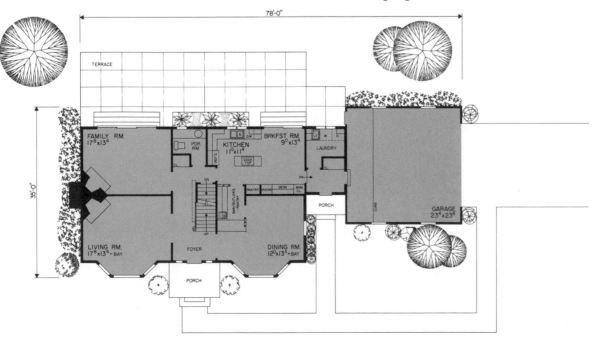

Design W4406

First Floor: 1,497 square feet
Second Floor: 848 square feet
Total: 2,345 square feet

● Tame a narrow lot with this unique side-entry design. The front kitchen and dining room feature high ceilings while the sloped-ceiling living room has a fireplace and built-in bookshelves. The master suite on the first floor is separated from two bedrooms on the second floor, each with its own full bath.

Design W2488 First Floor: 1,113 square feet
Second Floor: 543 square feet; Total: 1,656 square feet

D

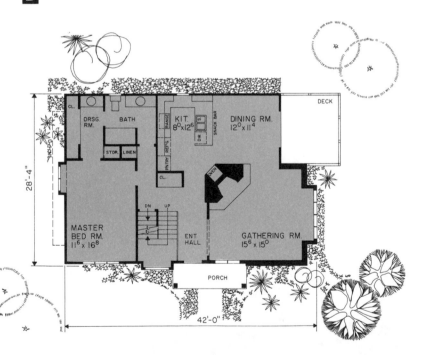

CUSTOMIZABLE

Custom Alterations? See page 301 for customizing this plan to your specifications.

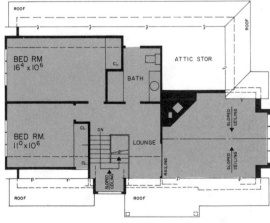

● A cozy cottage for the young at heart! Whether called upon to serve the young active family as a leisure-time retreat at the lake, or the retired couple as a quiet haven in later years, this charming design will perform well. As a year round second home, the up-stairs with its two sizable bedrooms, full bath and lounge area looking down into the gathering room below, will ideally accommodate the younger generation. When called upon to function as a retirement home, the second floor will cater to the visiting family members and friends. Also, it will be available for use as a home office, study, sewing room, music area, the pursuit of hobbies, etc. Of course, as an efficient, economical home for the young, growing family, this design will function well.

Design W2928

First Floor: 1,917 square feet
Second Floor: 918 square feet
Total: 2,835 square feet

● Gambrel-roofed, but contemporary as they come—this home appeals to tastes of every description. Split-bedroom planning puts the master bedroom on the first floor along with the gathering room with music alcove, the country kitchen with greenhouse and the formal dining room. Upstairs there are three bedrooms and a full bath plus a convenient lounge area for studying or relaxing.

Design W2883 First Floor: 1,919 square feet
Second Floor: 895 square feet, Total: 2,814 square feet

● A country-style home is part of America's fascination with the rural past. This home's emphasis of the traditional home is in its gambrel roof, dormers and fanlight windows. Having a traditional exterior from the street view, this home has window walls and a greenhouse, which opens the house to the outdoors in a thoroughly contemporary manner. The interior meets the requirements of today's active family. Like the country houses of the past, it has a gathering room for family get-togethers or entertaining. The adjacent two-story greenhouse doubles as the dining room. There is a pass-through snack bar to the country kitchen here. This country kitchen just might be the heart of the house with its two areas — work zone and sitting room. There are four bedrooms on the two floors — the master bedroom suite on the first floor; three more on the second floor. A lounge, overlooking the gathering room and front foyer, is also on the second floor.

235

Design W2594
Square Footage: 2,294

D

● A spectacular foyer offers double entry to the heart of this home — a large gathering room complete with raised-hearth fireplace and sliding glass doors onto the terrace. There is also a formal dining room. A well-located study (or third bedroom) offers space for undisturbed work. The kitchen features a snack bar and breakfast nook with sliding glass doors onto the terrace. In the master bedroom suite there are sliding glass doors to the terrace and a dressing room with entry to the bath. Another bedroom is located to the front of the plan.

Design W2877
Square Footage: 2,612

D

● Here's a dramatic Post-Modern exterior with a popular plan featuring an outstanding master bedroom suite. The bedroom itself is spacious, has a sloped ceiling, a large walk-in closet and sliding glass doors to the terrace. Along with this bedroom, there are three more served by a full bath. The living area of this plan has the formal areas in the front and informal areas in the rear. Both have a fireplace. The roomy work center is efficiently planned.

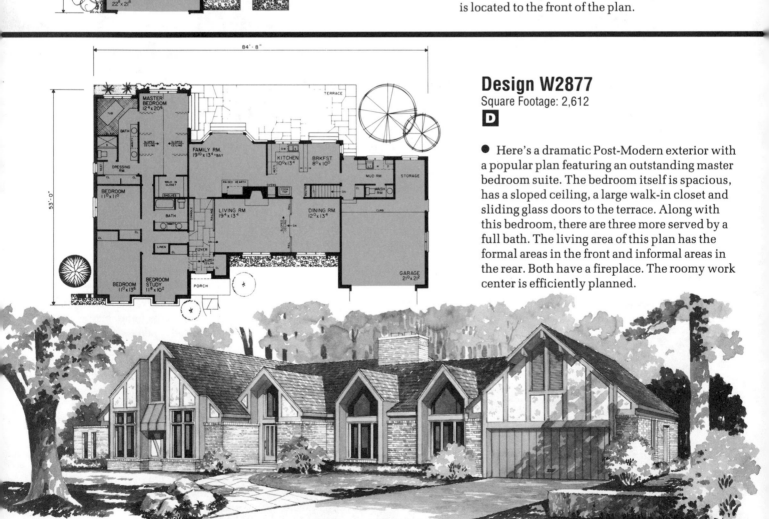

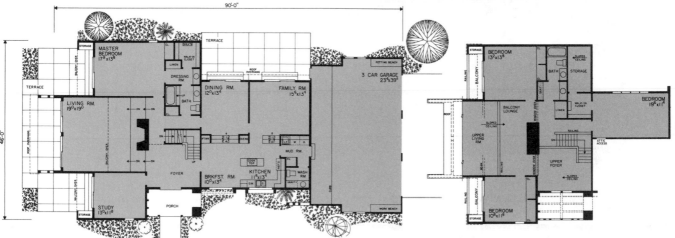

Design W2872 First Floor: 2,148 square feet
Second Floor: 1,126 square feet; Total: 3,274 square feet

● This Post-Modern design is stylistic, indeed, with angles and broken lines that reach for the sky. The downstairs provides excellent terrace views for a master bedroom suite, study, and a large living room with fireplace. A formal dining room and family room near the three-car garage also enjoy terrace views. A modern kitchen area with island cook top includes a breakfast room. Two other bedrooms with bath are located upstairs, along with an upper foyer, balcony lounge, storage areas, and outer balconies.

Design W4382

First Floor: 888 square feet
Second Floor: 888 square feet
Total: 1,776 square feet

L

● Charming and symmetrical design go hand in hand with a country kitchen to one side of the central foyer and a great room to the other. A screened porch and fireplace enhance the great room's usefulness. Three bedrooms and two full baths on the second floor round out this lovely home.

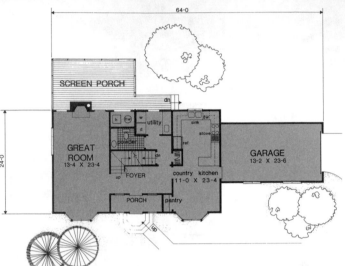

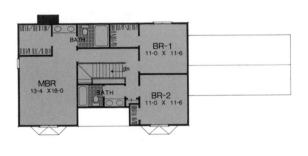

Design W2874
First Floor: 1,661 square feet
Second Floor: 1,808 square feet; Third Floor: 436 square feet; Total: 3,905 square feet

● This Post-Modern design, with its many gables, offers plenty of roomy comfort in a stylish home sure to draw heads. The first floor includes a living room with fireplace and bay window, study with its own bay window, family room with fireplace, formal dining room, modern kitchen with snack bar and breakfast room, and large foyer. The second floor includes a master bedroom suite, three other large bedrooms, and a large studio that could also double as room for hobbies or storage. The third floor includes a guest bedroom with bath and an upper lounge. Note the covered porch, window treatments and overhangs in this lovely design. This is a modernization of classic period architecture, with a modern floor plan and contemporary view windows.

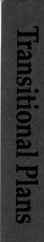

Design W2647 First Floor: 2,104 square feet
Second Floor: 1,230 square feet; Total: 3,334 square feet

L

● Another Neo-Victorian, and what an impressive and unique design it is. Observe the roof lines, the window treatment, the use of contrasting exterior materials and the arched, covered front entrance.

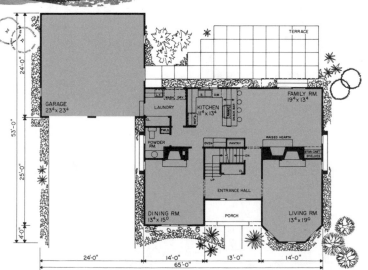

Design W2646 First Floor: 1,274 square feet
Second Floor: 1,322 square feet; Total: 2,596 square feet

L **D**

● What a stylish departure from today's usual architecture. This refreshing exterior may be referred to as Neo-Victorian. Its vertical lines, steep roofs and variety of gables are reminiscent of the Old Victorian houses of yesteryear. Inside, there is an efficiently working floor plan that is delightfully spacious.

Design W2829

First Floor: 2,044 square feet
Second Floor: 1,962 square feet
Total: 4,006 square feet

L **D**

● The architecture of this design is Post-Modern with a taste of Victorian styling. Detailed with gingerbread woodwork and a handsome double-width chimney, this two-story design is breathtaking. Enter this home to the large, tiled receiving hall and begin to explore this very livable floor plan. Formal areas consist of the front living room and the dining room. Each has features to make it memorable. The living room is spacious, has a fireplace and access to the covered porch; the dining room has a delightful bay window and is convenient to the kitchen for ease in meal serving. The library is tucked between these two formal areas. Now let's go to the informal area. The family room will welcome many an explorer. It will be a great place for many family activities. Note the L-shaped snack bar with cabinets below. Onward to the second floor, where the private area will be found. Start with the two bedrooms that have two full bathrooms joining them together. The older children will marvel at this area's efficiency and privacy. A third family bedroom is nearby. Then, there is the master bedroom suite. Its list of features is long, indeed. Begin with the "his" and "her" baths and see how many features you can list. A guest bedroom and bath are on the first floor.

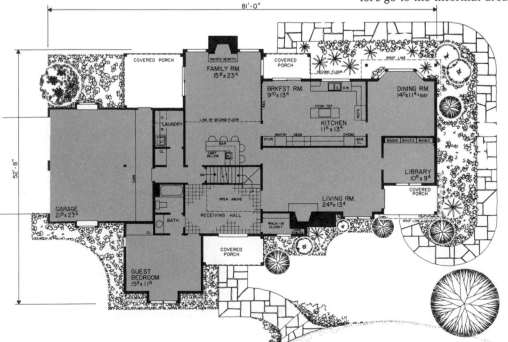

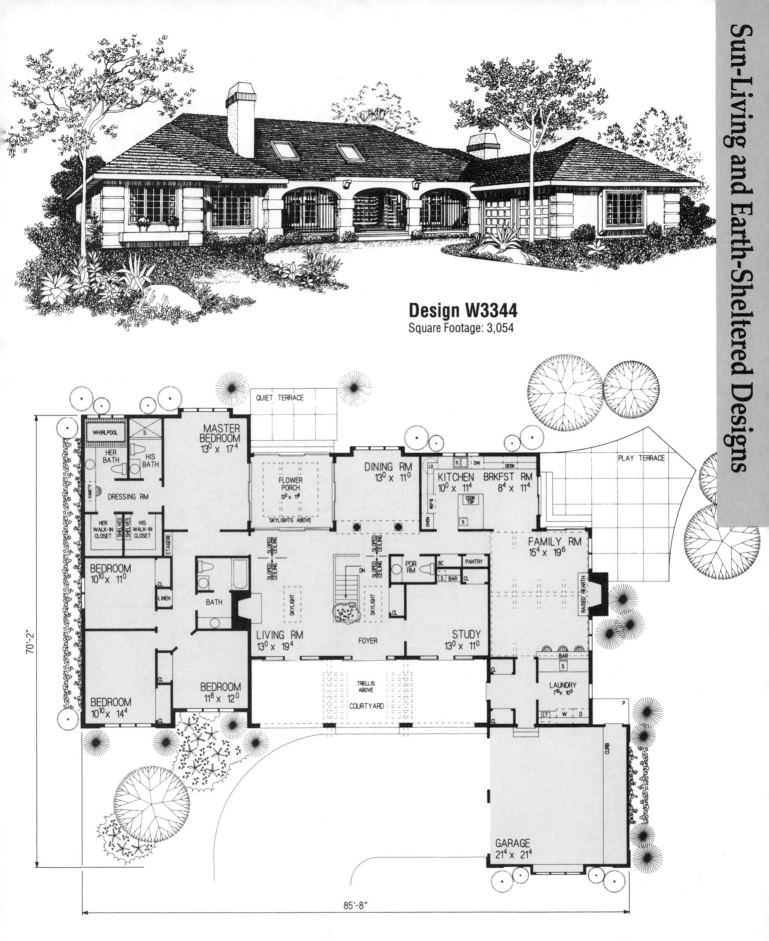

Design W3344
Square Footage: 3,054

● This home features interior planning for today's active family. Living areas include a living room with fireplace, a cozy study and family room with wet bar. Convenient to the kitchen is the formal dining room with attractive bay window overlooking the back yard. The four-bedroom sleeping area contains a sumptuous master suite. Also notice the cheerful flower porch with access from the master suite, living room and dining room.

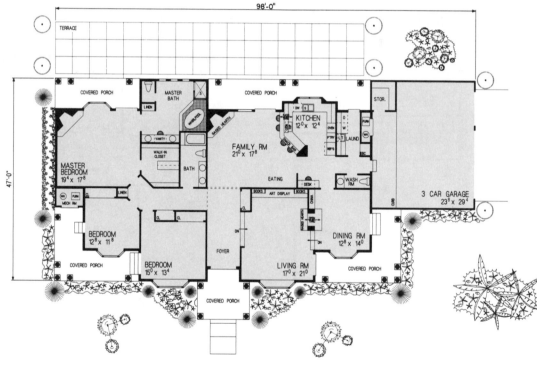

CUSTOMIZABLE

Custom Alterations? See page 301 for customizing this plan to your specifications.

Design W3400

Square Footage: 2,784

● Abundant terrace space favors an outdoor lifestyle in this charming one-story. Each room has access to a porch or terrace; think of the added entertainment possibilities! Interior highlights include corner fireplaces in the master suite and family room, a dining room with bay window, and a regal master bath. Note the dramatic two-story foyer.

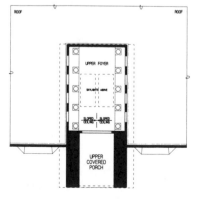

Design W3401
Square Footage: 2,850

● This Southwestern design caters to families who enjoy outdoor living and entertaining. Doors open onto a shaded terrace from the master bedroom and living room, while a sliding glass door in the family room accesses a smaller terrace. Also notice the outdoor bar with pass-through window to the kitchen.

CUSTOMIZABLE
Custom Alterations? See page 301 for customizing this plan to your specifications.

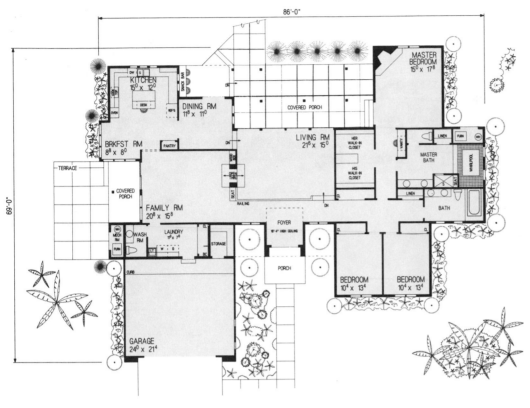

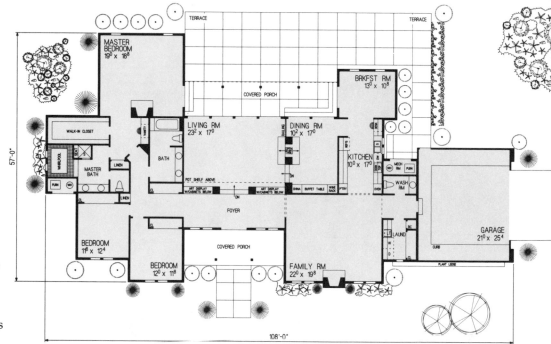

Design W3402
Square Footage: 3,212

● This one-story pairs the customary tile and stucco of Spanish design with a livable floor plan. The sunken living room with its open-hearth fireplace promises to be a cozy gathering place. For more casual occasions, there's a family room with fireplace off the entry foyer. Also noteworthy: a sizable kitchen and a sumptuous master suite.

CUSTOMIZABLE
Custom Alterations? See page 301 for customizing this plan to your specifications.

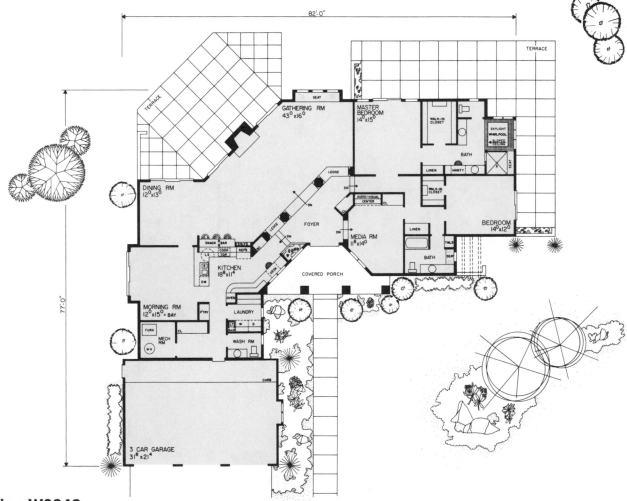

Design W2949

Square Footage: 2,922

D

● Spanish and western influences take center stage in a long, low stucco design. You'll enjoy the Texas-sized gathering room that opens to a formal dining area and has a snack bar through to the kitchen. More casual dining is accommodated in the nook. A luxurious master suite is graced by plenty of closet space and a soothing whirlpool spa. Besides another bed-room and full bath, there is a media room that could easily double as a third bedroom or guest room.

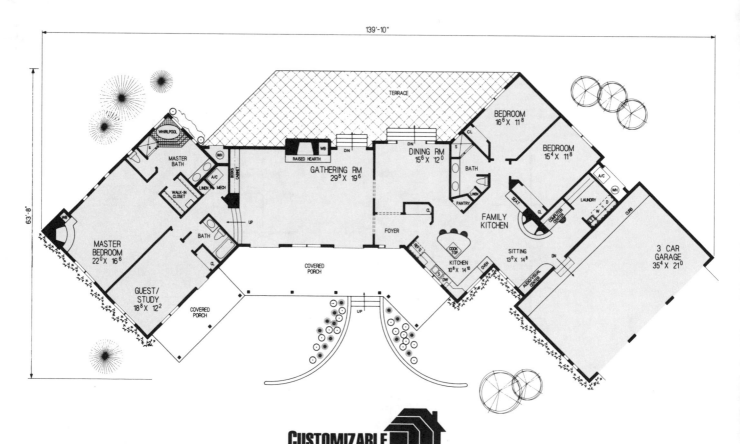

139'-10"

63'-8"

WHIRLPOOL

MASTER BATH

WALK-IN CLOSET

MASTER BEDROOM
22⁰ X 16⁶

BATH

GUEST/ STUDY
18⁸ X 12²

COVERED PORCH

COVERED PORCH

UP

RAISED HEARTH

GATHERING RM
29⁸ X 19⁶

FOYER

TERRACE

DINING RM
15⁶ X 12⁰

BATH

PANTRY

KITCHEN
10⁸ X 14¹⁰

COOK TOP

SITTING
13⁰ X 14⁸

FAMILY KITCHEN

AUDIOVISUAL CENTER

LAUNDRY

BEDROOM
16⁶ X 11⁸

BEDROOM
15⁴ X 11⁸

3 CAR GARAGE
35⁴ X 21⁰

UP

Design W3405

Square Footage: 3,144

L

CUSTOMIZABLE
Custom Alterations? See page 301 for customizing this plan to your specifications.

● In classic Santa Fe style, this home strikes a beautiful combination of historic exterior detailing and open floor planning on the inside. A covered porch running the width of the facade leads to an entry foyer that connects to a huge gathering room with fireplace and formal dining room. The family kitchen allows special space for casual gatherings. The right wing of the home holds two family bedrooms and full bath. The left wing is devoted to the master suite and guest room or study. Built-ins abound throughout the house.

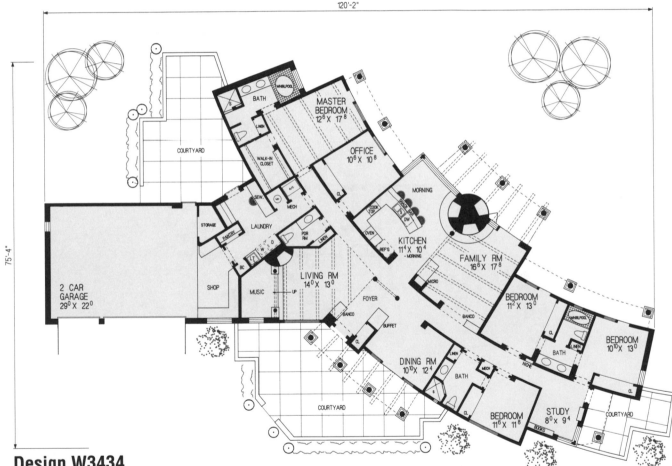

Design W3434
Square Footage: 2,968

L

● An in-line floor plan follows the tradition of the original Santa Fe-style homes. The slight curve to the overall configuration lends an interesting touch. From the front courtyard, the plan opens to a formal living room and dining room complemented by a family room and kitchen with morning room. The master bedroom is found to one side of the plan while family bedrooms share space at the opposite end. There's also a huge office and a study area for private times. With 3½ baths, a workshop garage, full laundry/sewing area, and three courtyards, this plan adds up to great livability.

CUSTOMIZABLE
Custom Alterations? See page 301 for customizing this plan to your specifications.

247

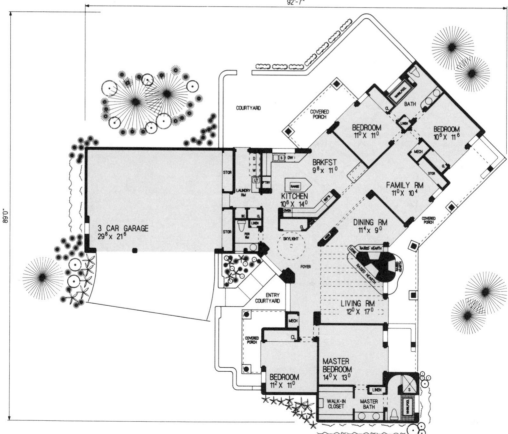

92'-7"

89'0"

COURTYARD

COVERED PORCH

BEDROOM
11⁰ X 11⁰

BATH

BEDROOM
10⁶ X 11⁶

BRKFST
9⁸ X 11⁰

FAMILY RM
11⁰ X 10⁴

KITCHEN
10⁶ X 14⁰

3 CAR GARAGE
29⁸ X 21⁶

LAUNDRY RM

STOR

STOR

DINING RM
11⁴ X 9⁰

COVERED PORCH

SKYLIGHT

FOYER

LIVING RM
12⁰ X 17⁰

ENTRY COURTYARD

MECH

BEDROOM
11² X 11⁰

COVERED PORCH

MASTER BEDROOM
14⁰ X 13⁰

WALK-IN CLOSET

MASTER BATH

LINEN

Design W3433

First Floor: 2,350 square feet

 L

● Santa Fe styling creates interesting angles in this one-story home. A grand entrance leads through a courtyard into the foyer with circular skylight, closet space and niches, and convenient powder room. Turn right to the master suite with deluxe bath and a bedroom close at hand, perfect for a nursery, home office or exercise room. Two more family bedrooms are placed quietly in the far wing of the house. Fireplaces in the living room, dining room and covered porch create various shapes. Make note of the island range in the kitchen, extra storage in the garage, and covered porches on two sides.

CUSTOMIZABLE

Custom Alterations? See page 301 for customizing this plan to your specifications.

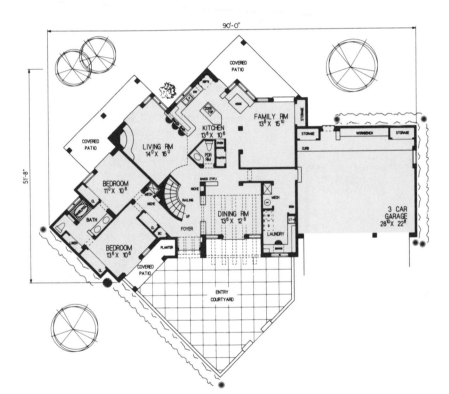

Design W3432

First Floor: 1,966 square feet
Second Floor: 831 square feet
Total: 2,797 square feet

L

● Unique in nature, this two-story
Santa Fe-style home is as practical as
it is lovely. The facade is elegantly
enhanced by a large entry court, over-
looked by windows in the dining
room and a covered patio from one of
two family bedrooms. The entry foyer
leads to living areas at the back of the
plan: a living room with corner fireplace and a family room connected to
the kitchen via a built-in eating nook.
Upstairs, the master suite features a
grand bath and large walk-in closet.
The guest bedroom has a private
bath. Every room in this home has its
own outdoor area.

Custom Alterations? See page 301
for customizing this plan to your
specifications.

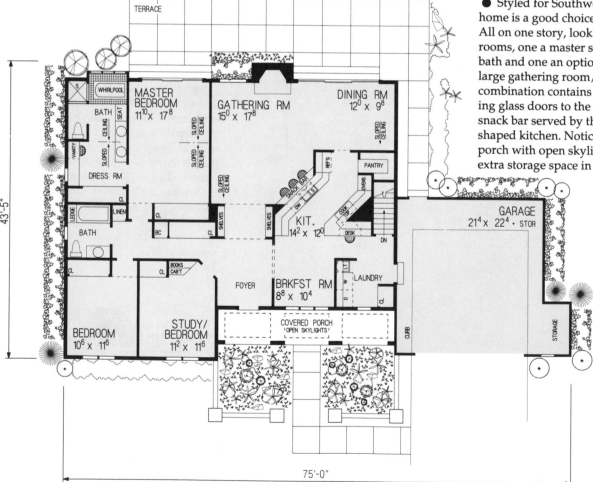

TERRACE

MASTER BEDROOM
11¹⁰ x 17⁸

WHIRLPOOL

BATH SEAT

SLOPED CEILING

VANITY

DRESS RM

S

CL

LINEN

LEDGE

BATH

CL

BC

CL

SHELVES

GATHERING RM
15⁰ x 17⁸

SLOPED CEILING   SLOPED CEILING

SLOPED CEILING

SLOPED CEILING

SHELVES

SNACK BAR

DW

REF'S

PANTRY

OVENS

COOK TOP

DESK

DN

KIT.
14² x 12⁰

DINING RM
12⁰ x 9⁸

SLOPED CEILING

GARAGE
21⁴ x 22⁴ + STOR

CL

BOOKS CAB'T

CL

BEDROOM
10⁶ x 11⁶

STUDY/ BEDROOM
11² x 11⁶

FOYER

BRKFST RM
8⁸ x 10⁴

D   W

LT

LAUNDRY

CL

CURB

STORAGE

COVERED PORCH
OPEN SKYLIGHTS

43'-5"

75'-0"

Design W2948

Square Footage: 1,830

● Styled for Southwest living, this home is a good choice in any region. All on one story, look for three bedrooms, one a master suite with deluxe bath and one an optional study. The large gathering room/dining room combination contains a fireplace, sliding glass doors to the terrace, and a snack bar served by the uniquely shaped kitchen. Notice the covered porch with open skylights and the extra storage space in the garage.

CUSTOMIZABLE
Custom Alterations? See page 301 for customizing this plan to your specifications.

Design W3322 First Floor: 1,860 square feet
Second Floor: 935 square feet; Total: 2,795 square feet

L **D**

● This cleverly designed Southwestern-style home takes its cue from the California Craftsman and Bungalow styles that have seen such an increase in popularity lately. Nonetheless, it is suited to just about any climate. Its convenient floor plan includes living and working areas on the first floor in addition to a master suite. The second floor holds two family bedrooms and a guest bedroom. Note the abundance of window area to the rear of the plan.

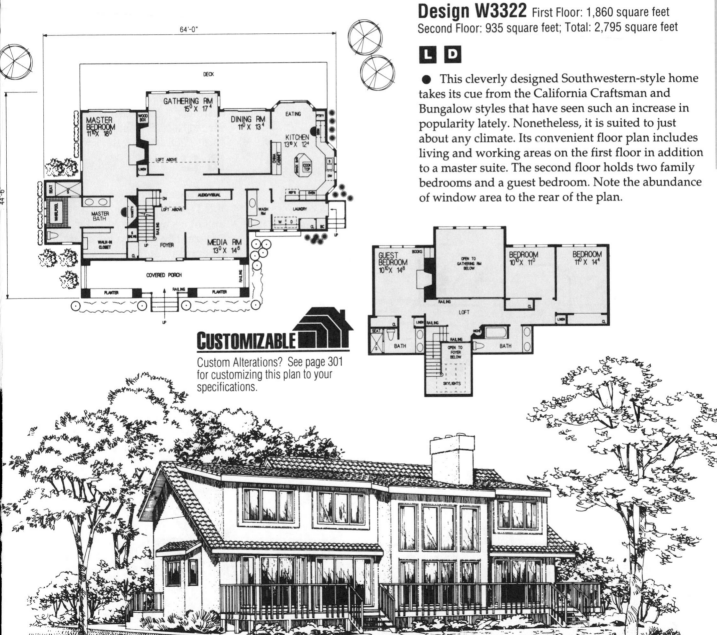

CUSTOMIZABLE

Custom Alterations? See page 301 for customizing this plan to your specifications.

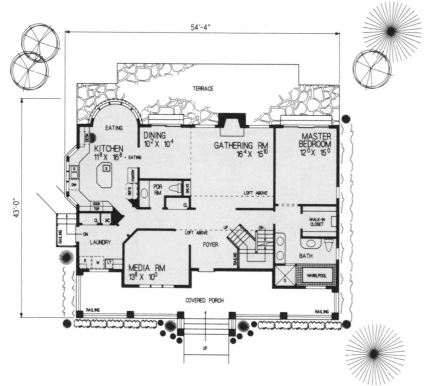

Design W3321
First Floor: 1,636 square feet
Second Floor: 572 square feet
Total: 2,208 square feet

L **D**

● Cozy and completely functional, this 1½-story bungalow has many amenities not often found in homes its size. The covered porch at the front opens at the entry to a foyer with angled staircase. To the left is a media room, to the rear the gathering room with fireplace. Attached to the gathering room is a formal dining room with rear terrace access. The kitchen features a curved casual eating area and island work station. The right side of the first floor is dominated by the master suite. It has access to the rear terrace and a luxurious bath. Upstairs are two family bedrooms connected by a loft area overlooking the gathering room and foyer.

CUSTOMIZABLE

Custom Alterations? See page 301 for customizing this plan to your specifications.

Design W3319

Square Footage: 2,274

L **D**

● This attractive bungalow design separates the master suite from family bedrooms and puts casual living to the back in a family room. The formal living and dining areas are centrally located and have access to a rear terrace, as does the master suite. The kitchen sits between formal and informal living areas. The two family bedrooms are found to the front of the plan. A home office or study opens off the front foyer and the master suite.

CUSTOMIZABLE

Custom Alterations? See page 301 for customizing this plan to your specifications.

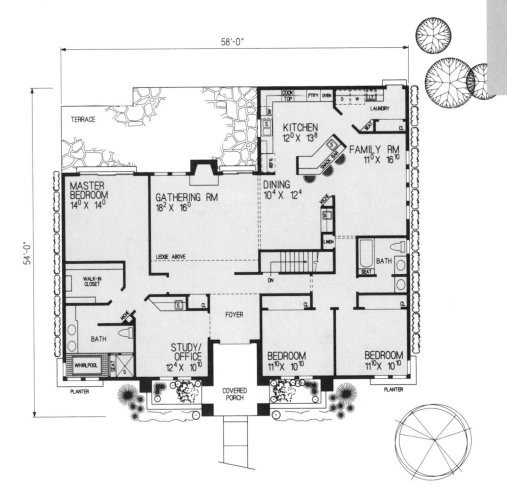

58'-0"

54'-0"

TERRACE

KITCHEN
12⁰ X 13⁸

LAUNDRY

FAMILY RM
11⁰ X 16¹⁰

MASTER
BEDROOM
14⁰ X 14⁰

GATHERING RM
18² X 16⁰

DINING
10⁴ X 12⁴

LEDGE ABOVE

LINEN

BATH

WALK-IN
CLOSET

DN

BATH

WHIRLPOOL

FOYER

STUDY/
OFFICE
12⁴ X 10¹⁰

BEDROOM
11¹⁰ X 10¹⁰

BEDROOM
11¹⁰ X 10¹⁰

PLANTER

COVERED
PORCH

PLANTER

● This design is carefully zoned for utmost livability. The entry foyer routes traffic to all areas of the house. To the rear is the living room/dining room combination with built-in china cabinet. To the left, the kitchen is open to the breakfast room and family room with fireplace. The master bedroom is on the right and features a whirlpool and a private porch. Upstairs-are three more bedrooms and an outdoor balcony.

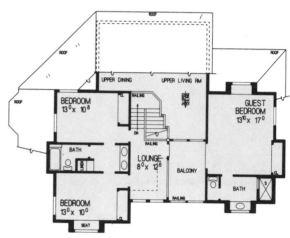

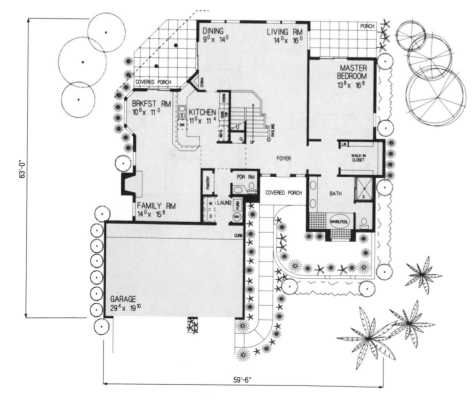

Design W3426
First Floor: 1,859 square feet
Second Floor: 969 square feet
Total: 2,828 square feet

CUSTOMIZABLE

Custom Alterations? See page 301 for customizing this plan to your specifications.

Design W3435

First Floor: 1,946 square feet
Second Floor: 986 square feet
Total: 2,932 square feet

L

● Here's a grand Spanish Mission home designed for family living. Enter at the angled foyer which contains a curved staircase to the second floor. Family bedrooms are here along with a spacious guest suite. The master bedroom is found on the first floor and has a private patio and whirlpool overlooking an enclosed garden area. Besides a living room and dining room connected by a through-fireplace, there is a family room with casual eating space. There is also a library with large closet. You'll appreciate the abundant built-ins and interesting shapes throughout this home.

CUSTOMIZABLE

Custom Alterations? See page 301 for customizing this plan to your specifications.

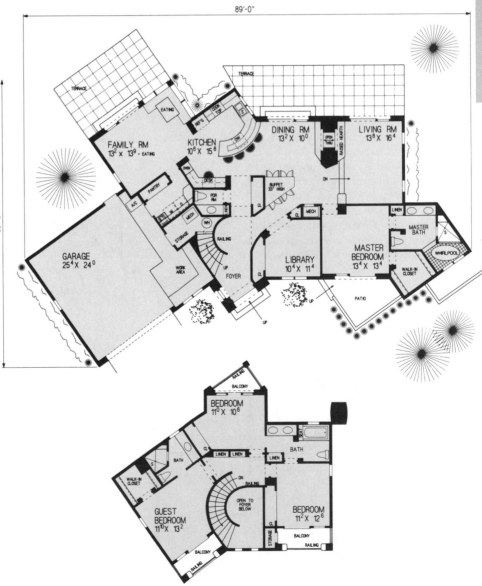

Design W3449

First Floor: 1,336 square feet
Second Floor: 1,186 square feet
Total: 2,522 square feet

L

● A covered porch leads inside to a
wide, tiled foyer. A curving staircase
makes an elegant expression in the open
space including the living and dining
rooms with two-story ceilings. A through-
fireplace warms the nook and family
room with wet bar and glass shelves. The
nook also includes planters on two sides.
Just above, light spills into the whirlpool
in the master bath with dual vanities and
walk-in closet. The master bedroom
includes a sitting area, two more closets,
and access to a private covered deck. Two
family bedrooms share a full bath with
dual vanities.

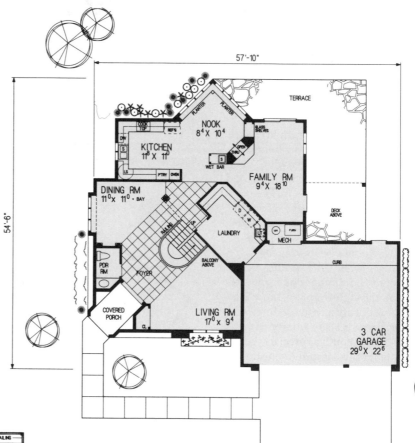

CUSTOMIZABLE

Custom Alterations? See page 301
for customizing this plan to your
specifications.

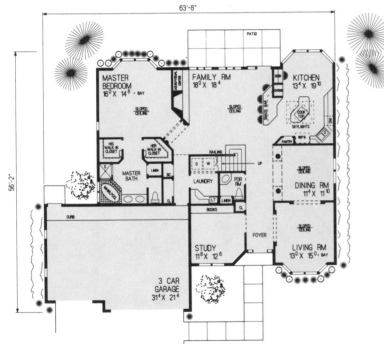

Design W3441

First Floor: 2,022 square feet
Second Floor: 845 square feet
Total: 2,867 square feet

L

● Special details make the difference between a house and a home. A snack bar, audio/visual center and a fireplace make the family room livable. A desk, island cook top, bay, and skylights enhance the kitchen area. The dining room features two columns and a plant ledge. The first-floor master suite includes His and Hers walk-in closets, a spacious bath, and a bay window. On the second floor, one bedroom features a walk-in closet and private bath, while two additional bedrooms share a full bath.

CUSTOMIZABLE

Custom Alterations? See page 301 for customizing this plan to your specifications.

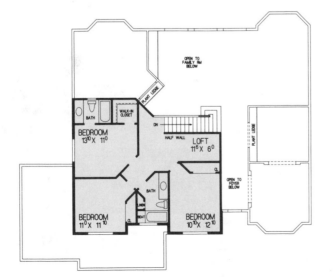

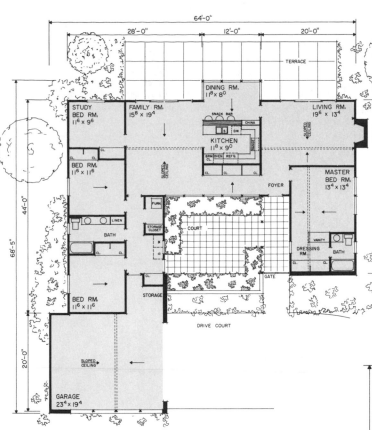

Design W1726
Square Footage: 1,910

● The U-shaped plan has long been honored for its excellent zoning. As the floor plan for this fine Spanish adaptation illustrates, it not only provides separation between parents' area and children's wing, but also it places a buffer area in the center. This makes the kitchen the "control center" for the home - handy to the family room, living room and the dining alcove.

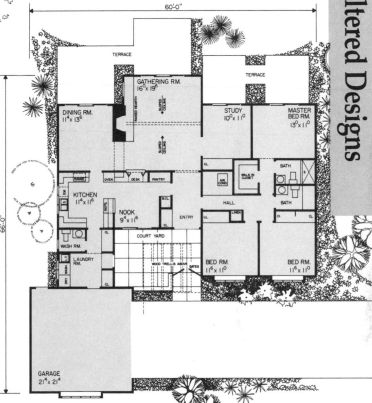

Design W2743
Square Footage: 1,892

● Placing the attached garage at the front cuts down on the size of a site required for this design. It also represents an appealing design factor. The privacy wall and overhead trellis provide a pleasant front courtyard. Inside, the gathering room satisfies the family's more gregarious instincts, while there is always the study nearby to serve as a more peaceful haven. The separate dining room and the nook offer dining flexibility. The two full baths highlight the economical back-to-back plumbing feature.

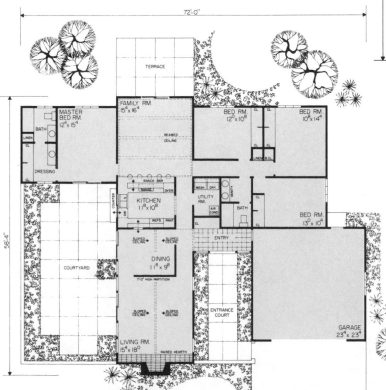

Design W2386
Square Footage: 1,994

L

● This distinctive home may look like the Far West, but don't let that inhibit you from enjoying the great livability it has to offer. Wherever built, you will experience a satisfying sense of pride in ownership. Imagine, an entrance court in addition to a large side courtyard! A central core is made up of the living, dining and family rooms, plus the kitchen. Each functions with an outdoor living area. The younger generation has its sleeping zone separated from the master bedroom. The location of the attached garage provides direct access to the front entry. Don't miss the vanity, utility room with laundry equipment, snack bar or raised hearth fireplace. Note three pass-thrus from the kitchen.

Design W1754

Square Footage: 2,080

D

● Boasting a traditional Western flavor, this rugged U-shaped ranch home has the features to assure grand living. The front flower court, inside the high brick wall, creates a delightfully dramatic atmosphere which carries inside. The floor plan is positively unique and exceptionally livable. Wonderfully zoned, the three bedrooms enjoy their full measure of privacy. The formal living and dining rooms function together in a most pleasing fashion. The laundry, kitchen, informal eating and family room fit together to guarantee efficient living patterns.

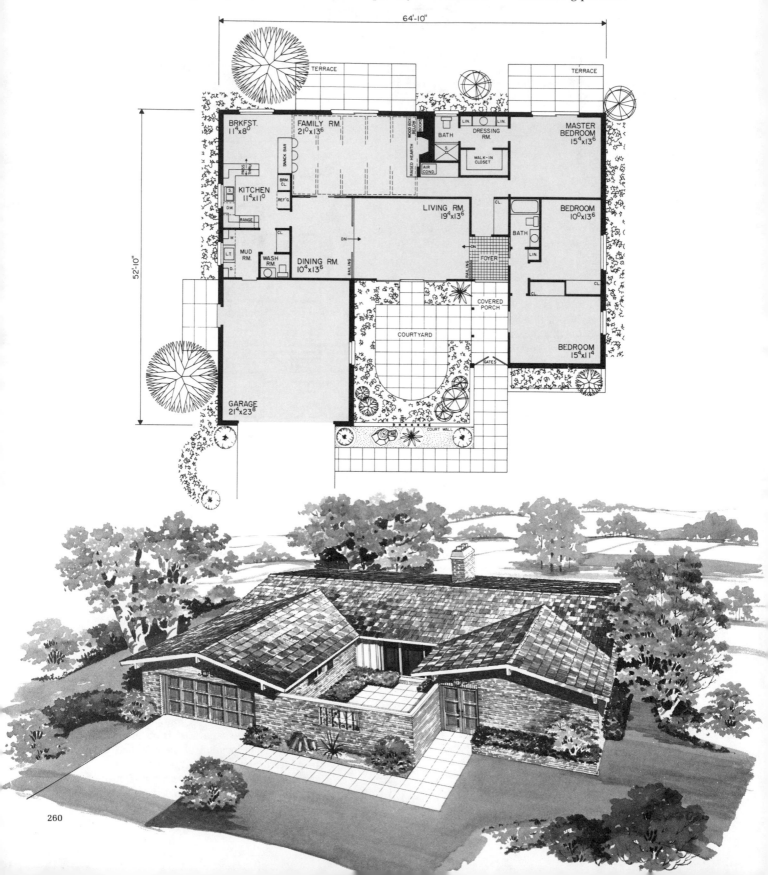

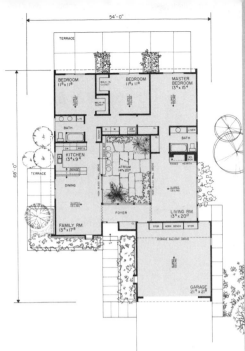

Design W2182
Square Footage: 1,558

● What a great new dimension in living is represented by this unique contemporary design! Each of the major zones comprise a separate unit which, along with the garage, clusters around the atrium. High sloped ceilings and plenty of glass areas assure a feeling of spaciousness. The quiet living room will enjoy its privacy, while activities in the informal family room will be great fun functioning with the kitchen. A snack bar opens the kitchen to the atrium. The view, above right, shows portions of snack bar and the front entry looking through the glass wall. There are two full baths strategically located to service all areas conveniently. Storage facilities are excellent, indeed. Don't miss the storage potential found in the garage. There is a work bench and storage balcony above.

Design W2135
Square Footage: 2,495 (Excluding Atrium)

● The proud occupants of this contemporary home will forever be thrilled at their choice of such a distinguished exterior and such a practical and exciting floor plan. Inside there is a feeling of spaciousness created by the sloping ceilings. The uniqueness of this design is further enhanced by the atrium. Open to the sky, this outdoor area can be enjoyed from all parts of the house. The sleeping zone has four bedrooms, two baths and plenty of closets. The informal living zone has a fine kitchen and breakfast room. The large living/dining area contains a raised-hearth fireplace.

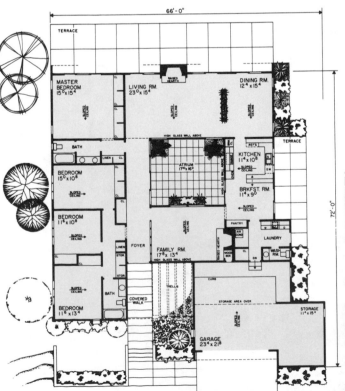

Design W2882

Square Footage: 2,832

● This plan is designed to be oriented on a west-facing site to take best advantage of energy efficiency. It reflects interesting living patterns and excellent indoor/outdoor relationships. Notice the wide, overhanging roofs, skylights, glass gables, vented walkways, wind-buffering privacy fences and terraces. The 2x6 construction adds to the energy oriented features.

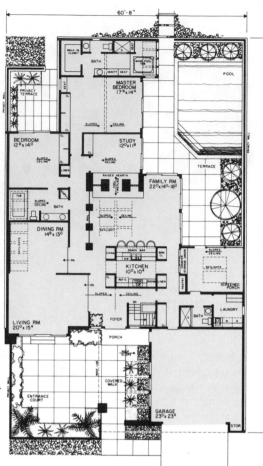

Design W2881

Square Footage: 2,770

● Energy-efficiency was a major consideration in this contemporary design. It was planned for a south-facing lot in temperate zones. Note the variety of outdoor living areas and the centrally located kitchen. Three bedrooms dominate the back of the house, including a master suite with a private terrace. There are two fireplaces: one in the living room and one in the family room.

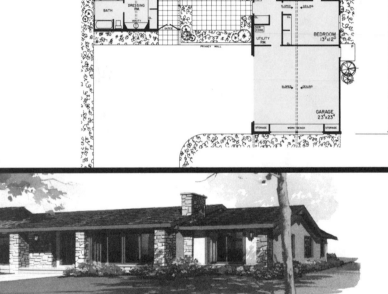

Design W2229

Square Footage: 2,728

● The irregular shape of this rustic ranch home creates an enclosed front entrance court. Twin gates open to a covered walk that looks out upon the delightful private court on the way to the front door. The house also is specially zoned to provide maximum privacy in the living room and master bedroom. At the other end of the house are children's rooms and an informal family room. The kitchen is strategically located. A dining room projects outward onto a terrace with an abundance of glass for full enjoyment of the outdoors during meals. This one-story design also enjoys two fireplaces and sloped ceilings.

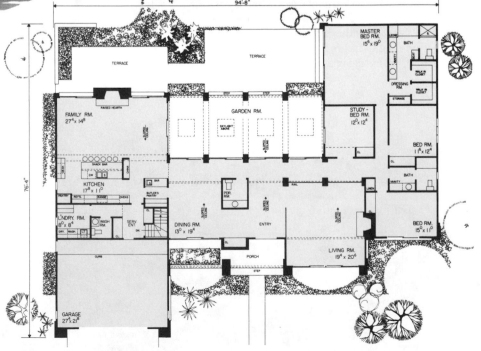

Design W2765

Square Footage: 3,365

D

● This three (optional four) bedroom contemporary is a most appealing design. It offers living patterns that will add new dimensions to your everyday routine. The sloped ceilings in the family room, dining room and living room add much spaciousness to this home. The efficient kitchen has many fine features including the island snack bar and work center, built-in desk, china cabinet and wet bar. Adjacent to the kitchen is a laundry room, washroom and stairs to the basement. Formal and informal living will each have its own area. A raised hearth fireplace and sliding glass doors to the rear terrace in the informal family room. Another fireplace in the front formal living room. You will enjoy all that nature light in the garden room from the skylights in the sloped ceiling.

Design W2871

Living Area: 1,824 square feet
Greenhouse Area: 81 square feet
Total: 1,905 square feet

D

● A greenhouse off the dining room and living room provides a cheerful focal point for this comfortable three-bedroom home. The spacious living room features a cozy fireplace and sloped ceiling. In addition to the dining room, there's a less formal breakfast room just off the modern kitchen. Stairs just off the foyer lead down to a recreation room. The master bedroom suite opens to a terrace. The mud room and washroom off the garage allow rear entry to the house during inclement weather.

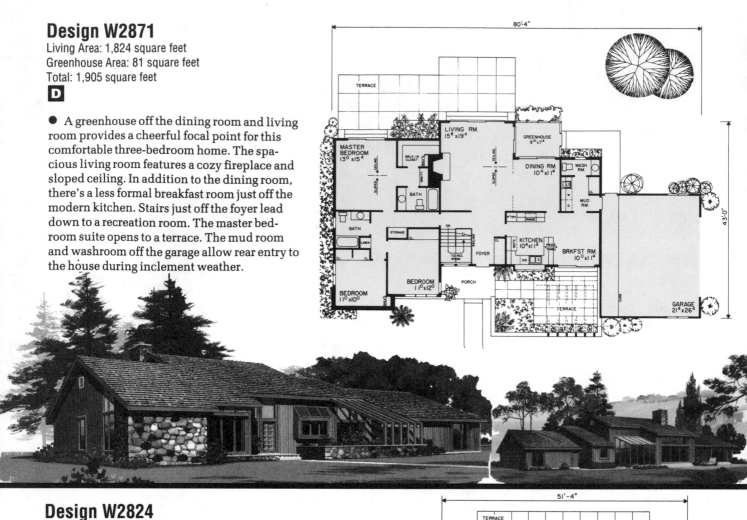

Design W2824

Square Footage: 1,550

● Low maintenance and economy in building are the outstanding exterior features of this sharp one-story design. The entrance opens to a charming courtyard garden and covered walk to the front porch. Sliding glass doors are featured in each of the main rooms for easy access to the outdoors. A sun porch is tucked between the study and gathering rooms. Optional non-basement details are included with the blueprints for this design.

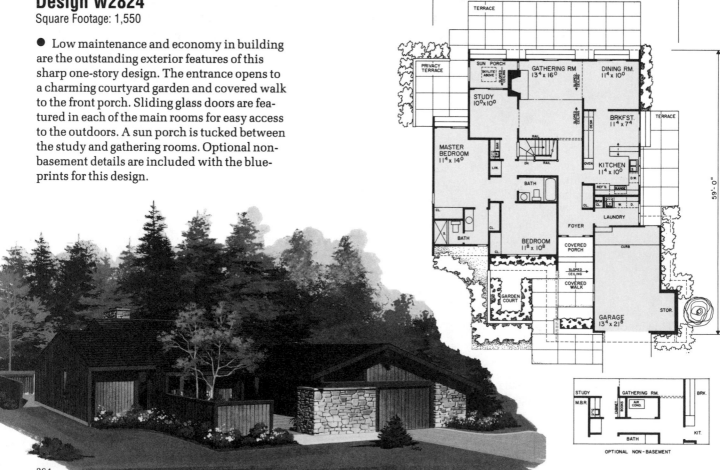

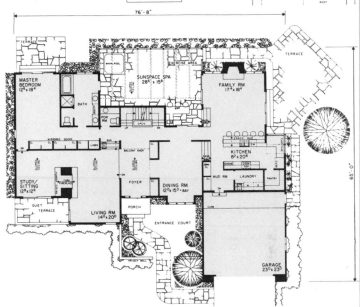

Design W2900

First Floor: 2,332 square feet
Second Floor: 953 square feet
Total: 3,285 square feet

● Contemporary in exterior styling, this house is energy oriented. It calls for 2 x 6 exterior wall construction with placement on a north facing lot. Traffic flows through the interior of this plan by way of the foyer. Excellent living areas are throughout. A spacious, sunken living room is to the left of the foyer. It shares a through-fireplace, faced with fieldstone, with the study. Informal activities can take place in the family room. It, too, has a fireplace and is adjacent to the work center. Two of the bedrooms are on the second floor with a lounge overlooking the gathering room below. The master bedroom is on the first floor.

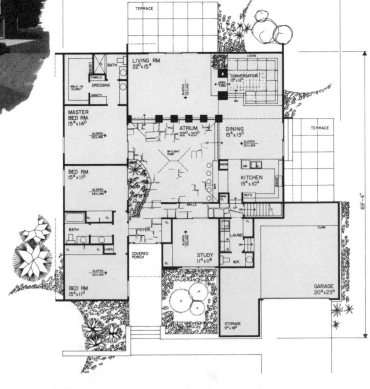

Design W2832

Square Footage: 2,805

D

● The advantage of passive solar heating is a significant highlight of this contemporary design. The huge skylight over the atrium provides shelter during inclement weather, while permitting natural light to enter below. The stone floor of this area absorbs an abundance of heat from the sun during the day and permits the circulation of warm air to other areas at night. Sloping ceilings highlight each of the major rooms: three bedrooms, formal living and dining rooms and the study. Broad expanses of roof can accommodate solar panels, if desired, to complement this design.

Design W2858
Square Footage: 2,231

● This sun oriented design was created to face the south. By doing so, it has minimal northern exposure. It has been designed primarily for the more temperate U.S. latitudes using 2 x 6 wall construction. The morning sun will brighten the living and dining rooms along with the adjacent terrace. Sun enters the garden room by way of the glass roof and walls. In the winter, the solar heat gain from the garden room should provide relief from high energy bills. Solar shades allow you to adjust the amount of light that you want to enter in the warmer months. Interior planning deserves mention, too. The work center is efficient. The kitchen has a snack bar on the garden room side and a serving counter to the dining room. The breakfast room with laundry area is also convenient to the kitchen. Three bedrooms are on the northern wall. The master bedroom has a large tub and a separate shower with a four foot square skylight above. When this design is oriented toward the sun, it should prove to be energy efficient and a joy to live in.

Design W2857
Square Footage: 2,982

L

● You'll applaud the many outstanding features of this home. Notice first the master bedroom. It has His and Hers baths, each with a large walk-in closet, sliding glass doors to a private terrace, and an adjacent study. Two family bedrooms are separate from the master for total privacy. The gathering room is designed for entertaining. It has its own balcony and a fireplace as a focal point. The U-shaped kitchen is efficient and has an attached breakfast room and snack bar pass-through to the dining room.

Design W2343
Square Footage: 3,110

● If yours is a growing active family the chances are good that they will want their new home to relate to the outdoors. This distinctive design puts a premium on private outdoor living. And you don't have to install a swimming pool to get the most enjoyment from this home. Developing this area as a garden court will provide the indoor living areas with a breathtaking awareness of nature's beauty. Notice the fine zoning of the plan and how each area has its sliding glass doors to provide an unrestricted view. Three bedrooms plus study are serviced by three baths. The family and gathering rooms provide two great living areas. The kitchen is most efficient.

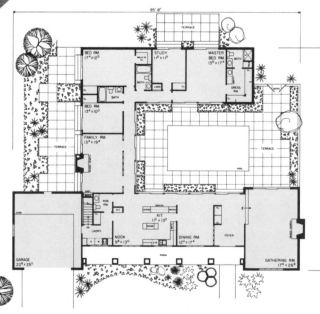

Design W2862
Square Footage: 2,808

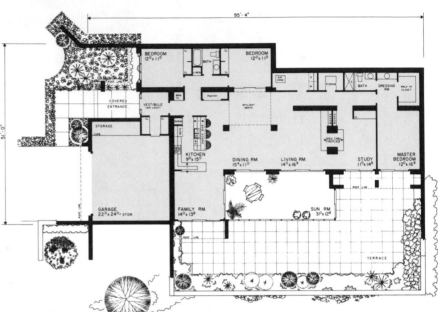

● Earth shelters the interior of this house from both the cold of winter and the heat of the summer. This three-bedroom design has passive solar capabilities. The sun room, south-facing for light, has a stone floor which will absorb heat. When needed, the heat will be circulated to the interior by opening the sliding glass doors or by mechanical means. Entrance to this home will be obtained through the vestibule or the garage. Both have a western exposure. A large, centrally located skylight creates an open feeling and lights up the interior of this plan where the formal and informal living areas are located. The sun room contains 425 square feet not included in the total.

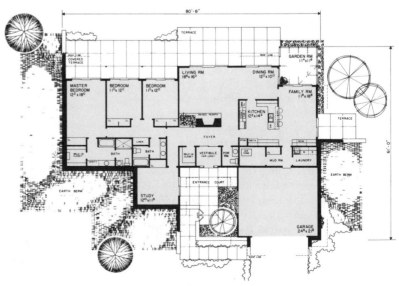

Design W2903
Square Footage: 2,555

● Earth berms on the sides of this house help it achieve energy-efficiency. The maximum amount of light enters this home by way of the many glass areas on the southern exposure. Every room in this plan, except the study, has the benefit of the southern sun. A garden room, tucked between the family and dining rooms, can be used for passive solar capabilities. A front privacy wall and the entrance court will shield the interior from the harsh northern winds. The air-locked vestibule also will be an energy saver. Summer heat gain will be reduced by the wide overhanging roof. The occupants of this home will appreciate the excellent interior planning. The garden room contains 114 square feet not included in the total.

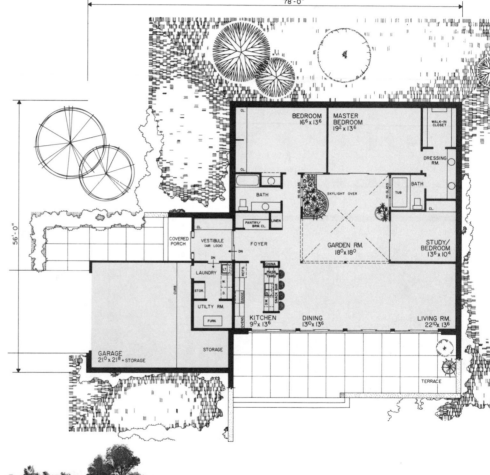

Design W2861
Square Footage: 2,499

● Berming the earth against the walls of a structure prove to be very energy efficient. The earth protects the interior from the cold of the winter and the heat of the summer. Interior lighting will come from the large skylight over the garden room. Every room will benefit from this exposed area. The garden room will function as a multi-purpose area for the entire family. The living/dining room will receive light from two areas, the garden room and the wall of sliding glass doors to the outside. Family living will be served by the efficient floor plan. Three bedrooms and two full baths are clustered together. The kitchen is adjacent to the air-locked vestibule where the laundry and utility rooms are housed. The section is cut through the dining, garden and master bedroom facing the kitchen.

Design W2860
Square Footage: 2,240

● This three-bedroom home is the very embodiment of what's new and efficient in planning and technology. Orienting this earth-sheltered house toward the south assures a warm, bright and cheerful interior. Major contributions to energy-efficiency result from the earth-covered roof, the absence of northern wall exposure and the lack of windows on either end of house. This means a retention of heat in the winter and cool air in the summer. An effective use of skylights provides the important extra measure of natural light to the interior. Sliding glass doors in the living and dining rooms also help bring the light to the indoors.

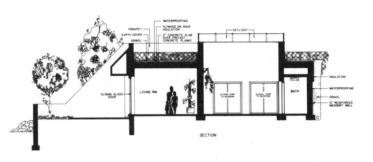

Design W2838
Square Footage: 2,309

● Here is a dramatic earth-sheltered home which will function well with the sun. The spaciousness of the living area in this design is enhanced by the central location of the dramat-

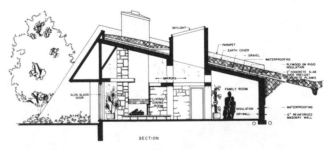

ic skylight. In addition to the passive solar heating gain for the living and bedroom areas, the impressively designed "mansard" roof effect lends itself to the installation of active solar heating panels. The illustration above shows panels only on the garage wing. Consultation with local solar heating experts will determine the effectiveness in your area of additional panels. A special room adjacent to the garage will accommodate mechanical equipment.

● Earth berms are banked against all four exterior walls of this design to effectively reduce heating and cooling demands. The berming is cost-efficient during both hot and cold seasons. In the winter, berming reduces heat loss through the exterior walls and shields the structure from cold winds. It helps keep warm air out during the summer. The two most dramatic interior highlights are the atrium and thru-fireplace. Topped with a large skylight, the atrium floods the interior with natural light. Shades are used to cover the atrium in the summer to prevent solar heat gain. Three bedrooms are featured in this plan and they each open via sliding glass doors to the atrium. This would eliminate any feeling of being closed in. An island with range and oven is featured in the kitchen. Informal dining will be enjoyed at the snack bar. The family/dining room can house those more formal dining occasions. The section at the right is cut through the study, atrium and rear bedroom looking toward master bedroom.

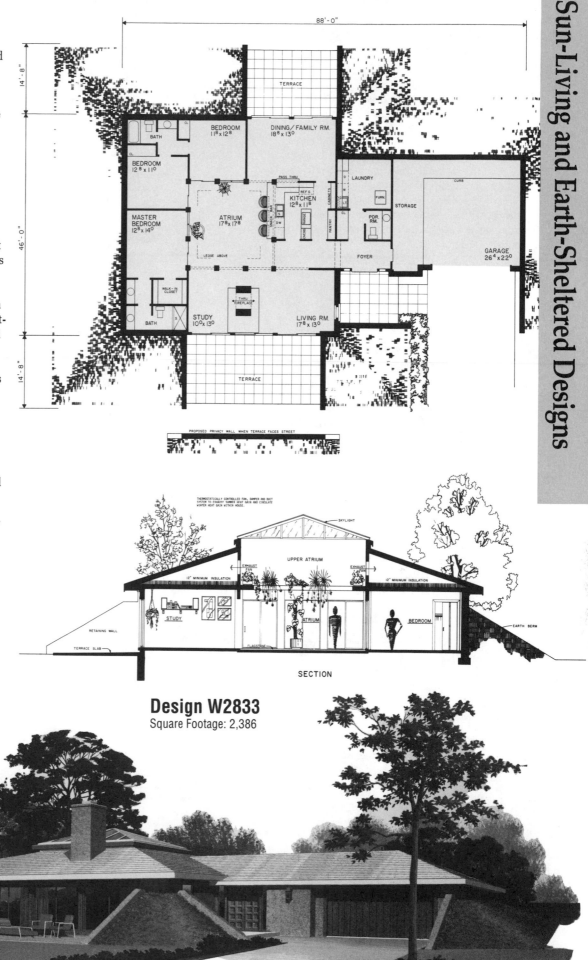

Design W2833
Square Footage: 2,386

Design W2902

Square Footage: 1,632

L

● A sun space highlights this passive solar design. It has access from the kitchen, dining room and garage. Three skylights illuminate the interior — one in the kitchen, one in the laundry and one in the master bath. The living room/dining room has a sloped ceiling, fireplace and two sets of sliding glass doors to the terrace. Three bedrooms and two baths are found in the sleeping wing. The area of the sunspace is 216 square feet not included in the above total.

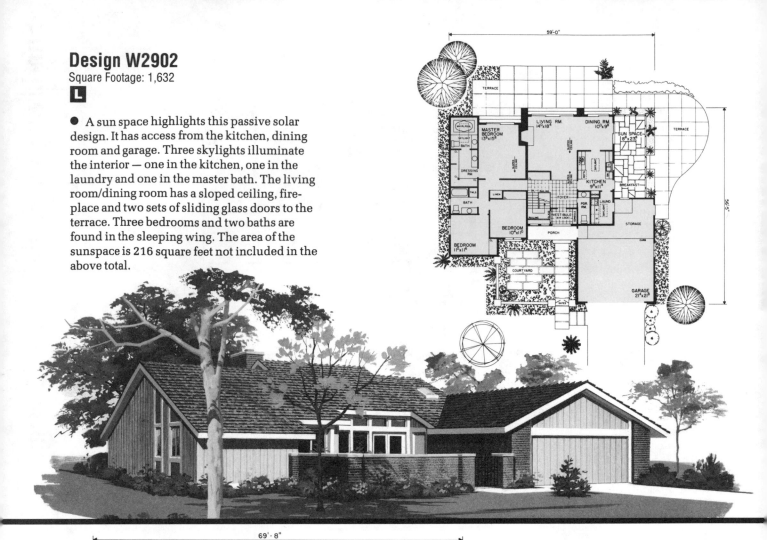

Design W2886

Square Footage: 1,733

● This one-story house is attractive with its contemporary exterior. Note the spacious gathering room with sliding glass doors that allow easy access to the greenhouse. An efficient kitchen has an attached breakfast room with eating terrace. Besides two family bedrooms (one could be a study) there is a roomy master suite with access to a second greenhouse containing a hot tub. The combined area of the greenhouses is 394 square feet, not included in the above total.

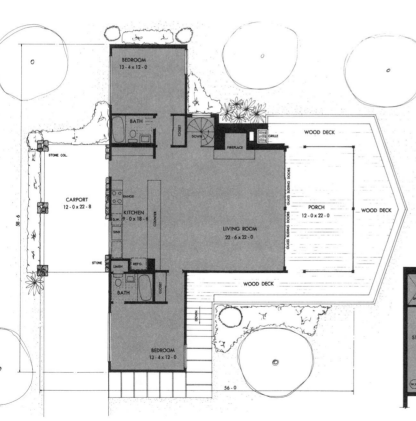

● This plan features the kind of indoor-outdoor relationship found in vacation homes. Sliding glass doors in the living room open onto a screened porch which, in turn, leads to a large deck. Note the built-in grille. The large living room with welcoming fireplace has enough space to accommodate an eating area. The sleeping quarters are split with two private bedrooms and baths on the entry level and a spacious dormitory with fireplace on the lower level. Just steps away is a covered patio.

Design W4012

Main Level: 1,250 square feet
Lower Level: 740 square feet
Total: 1,990 square feet

LIFESTYLE
HOME PLANS

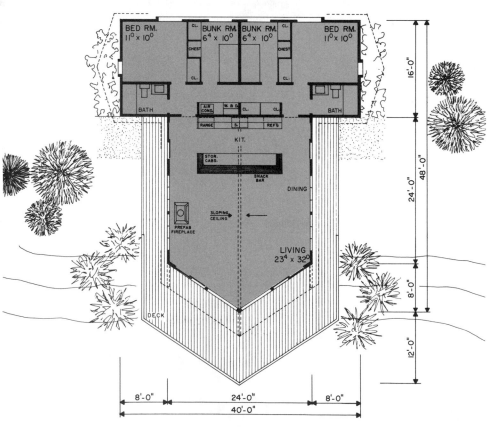

Design W2439
Square Footage: 1,312

● Here is a wonderfully organized plan with an exterior that will command the attention of each and every passerby. Certainly the roof lines and the pointed glass gable-end wall will be noticed immediately. The delightful deck will be quickly noticed, too. Inside a visitor will be thrilled by the spaciousness of the huge living room. The ceilings slope upward to the exposed ridge beam. A free-standing fireplace will make its contribution to a cheerful atmosphere. The sleeping zone has two bedrooms, two bunk rooms, two full baths, two built-in chests and fine closet space.

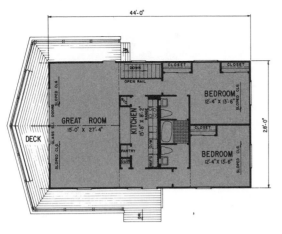

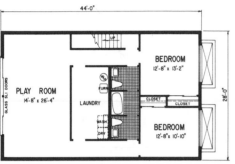

Optional Basement

Design W4027
Square Footage: 1,232

● Good things come in small packages, too! The size and shape of this design will help hold down construction costs without sacrificing livability. The enormous great room is a multi-purpose living space with room for a dining area and several seating areas. Also notice the sloped ceilings. Sliding glass doors provide access to the wraparound deck and sweeping views of the outdoors. The well-equipped kitchen includes a pass-through and pantry. Two bedrooms, each with sloped ceiling and compartmented bath, round out the plan.

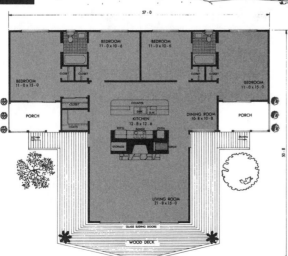

Design W4015
Square Footage: 1,420

● The perfect vacation home combines open, formal living spaces with lots of sleeping space. Study this plan carefully. The spacious living room has a warming fireplace and sliding glass doors onto the deck. Convenient to the dining room, the efficient kitchen is carefully placed so as not to interfere with the living room. Notice the four spacious bedrooms — there is plenty of room for accommodating guests. Two of the bedrooms boast private porches.

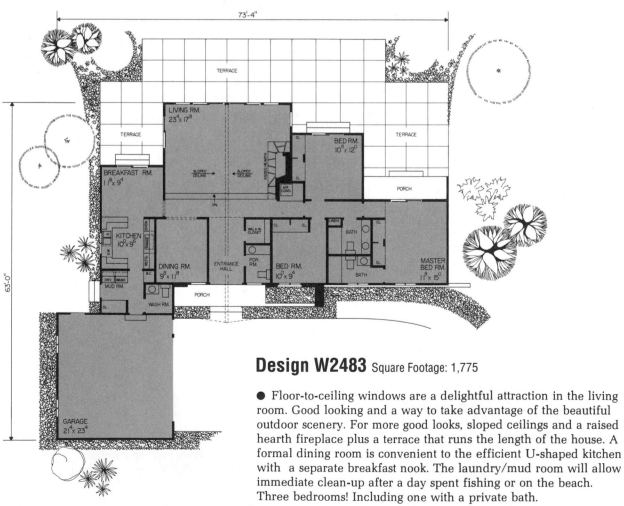

Design W2483 Square Footage: 1,775

● Floor-to-ceiling windows are a delightful attraction in the living room. Good looking and a way to take advantage of the beautiful outdoor scenery. For more good looks, sloped ceilings and a raised hearth fireplace plus a terrace that runs the length of the house. A formal dining room is convenient to the efficient U-shaped kitchen with a separate breakfast nook. The laundry/mud room will allow immediate clean-up after a day spent fishing or on the beach. Three bedrooms! Including one with a private bath.

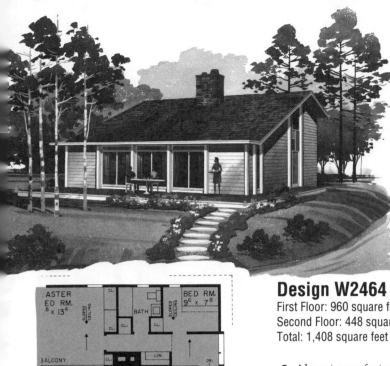

Design W2464

First Floor: 960 square feet
Second Floor: 448 square feet
Total: 1,408 square feet

● Almost a perfect square (32 x 30) feet, this economically built leisure home has a wealth of features. The list might begin with a wood deck just outside the sliding glass doors of the 31-foot living area. The list continues with the U-shaped kitchen, the snack bar, the pantry and closet storage wall, the two full baths (one with stall shower), three bedrooms and raised-hearth fireplace. Perhaps the favorite highlight will be the manner in which the second floor overlooks the first floor. The second-floor balcony adds even a greater dimension of spaciousness and interior appeal. Don't miss side and rear entries. Observe coat closets placed nearby.

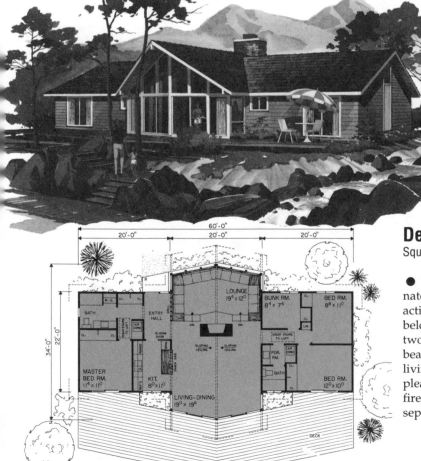

Design W2417

Square Footage: 1,520

● The picturesque exterior of this vacation home is dominated by a projecting gable with a wide, overhanging roof acting as a dramatic sun visor for the large glass area below. Effectively balancing this 20-foot center section are two 20-foot wings. Inside, and below the high, sloping, beamed ceiling, is the huge living area. In addition to the living/dining area, there is a spacious sunken lounge. This pleasant area has a built-in seating arrangement and a cozy fireplace. The parents' and children's sleeping areas are separated and each has a full bath.

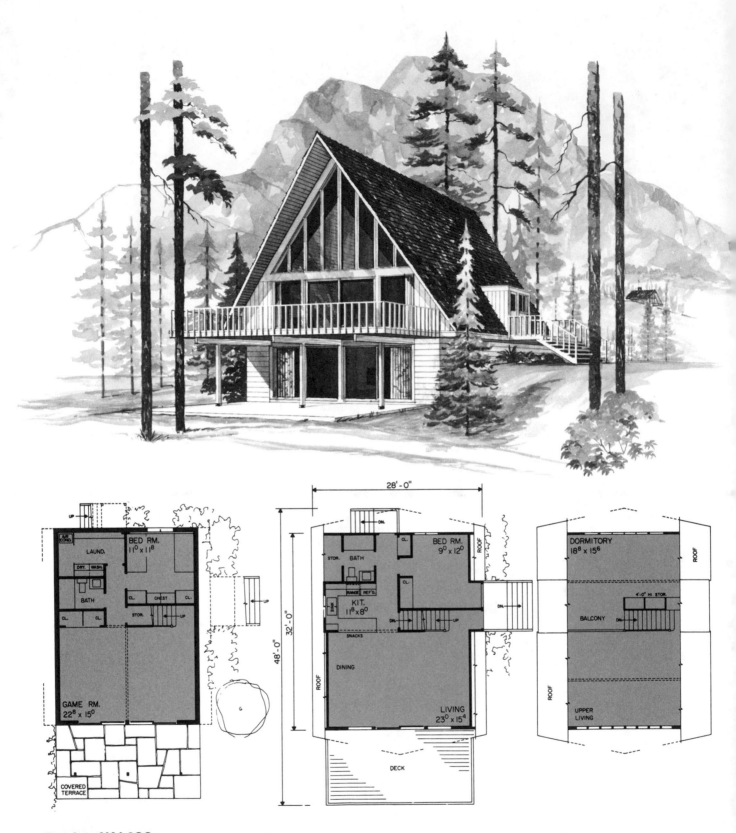

Design W1499 Main Level: 896 square feet; Upper Level: 298 square feet
Lower Level: 896 square feet; Total: 2,090 square feet

● Three level living results in family living patterns which will foster a delightful feeling of informality. Upon arrival at this charming second home, each family member will enthusiastically welcome the change in environment – both indoors and out. Whether looking down into the living room from the dormitory balcony, or walking through the sliding doors onto the huge deck, or participating in some family activity in the game room, everyone will count the hours spent here as relaxing ones. Study the plan carefully. Note the sleeping facilities on each of the three levels. Two bedrooms and a dormitory in all to sleep the family and friends comfortably. There are two full baths, a separate laundry room and plenty of storage. Don't miss the efficient U-shaped kitchen.

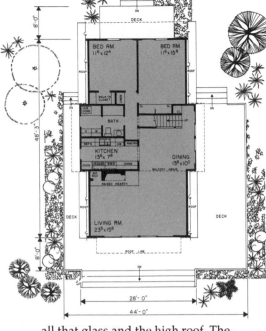

Design W1451

First Floor: 1,224 square feet
Second Floor: 464 square feet
Total: 1,688 square feet

● This dramatic A-frame will surely command its share of attention wherever located. Its soaring roof and large glass area put this design in a class all of its own. Raised wood decks on all sides provide delightful outdoor living areas. In addition, there is a balcony outside the second-floor master bedroom. The living room will be the focal point of the interior. It will be wonderfully spacious with

all that glass and the high roof. The attractive raised-hearth fireplace will be a favorite feature. Another favored highlight will be the lounge area of the second floor where it is possible to look down into the living room. The work center has all the conveniences of home. Note the barbecue unit, pantry and china cabinet.

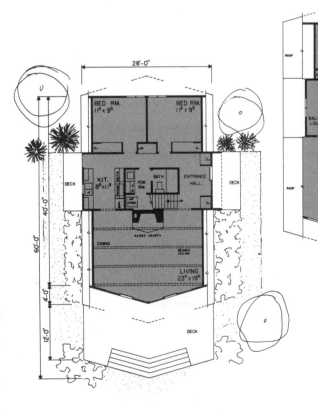

Design W2431

First Floor: 1,057 square feet
Second Floor: 406 square feet
Total: 1,463 square feet

● A favorite everywhere, the A-frame vacation home is easily recognizable. Inside, the beauty of architectural detailing is apparent. The living room sports a high ceiling which slopes and has exposed beams. The second-floor master suite has a private balcony, private bath and lounge. Don't miss the raised-hearth fireplace for cozy winter nights.

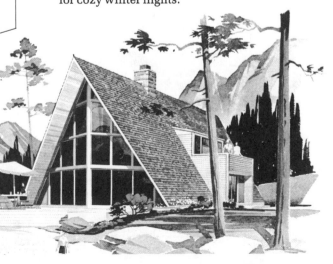

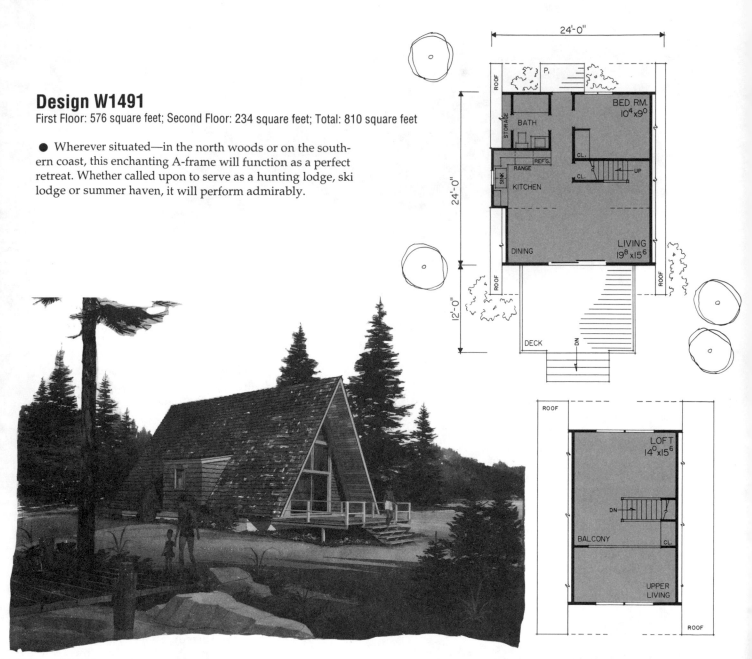

Design W1491

First Floor: 576 square feet; Second Floor: 234 square feet; Total: 810 square feet

● Wherever situated—in the north woods or on the southern coast, this enchanting A-frame will function as a perfect retreat. Whether called upon to serve as a hunting lodge, ski lodge or summer haven, it will perform admirably.

24'-0"

ROOF
P.
STORAGE
BATH
BED RM.
10⁴x9⁰
REF'G.
CL.
RANGE
SINK
CL.
UP
KITCHEN
24'-0"
DINING
LIVING
19⁸x15⁶
ROOF
ROOF
12'-0"
DECK
DN

ROOF
LOFT
14⁰x15⁶
DN
BALCONY
CL.
UPPER
LIVING
ROOF

24'-0"

BED RM.
11⁶x10⁰
BED RM.
11⁶x10⁰
CL.
CL.
36'-0"
AIR COND.
BATH
RANGE REF'G.
SLOPED CEILING
KIT.
8⁴x12⁸
LIVING RM.
15⁰x17⁰
PANTRY
12'-0"
TERRACE

Design W2423

Square Footage: 864

Design W1424

First Floor: 672 square feet
Second Floor: 256 square feet
Total: 928 square feet

● This chalet-type vacation home with its steep, overhanging roof, will catch the eye of even the most casual onlooker. It is designed to be completely livable whether the season be for swimming or skiing. The dormitory of the upper level will sleep many vacationers, while the two bedrooms of the first floor provide the more convenient and conventional sleeping facilities. The upper level overlooks the living and dining area with its beamed ceiling. The lower level provides everything that one would want for vacation living.

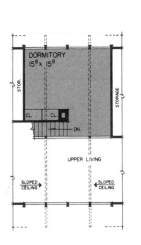

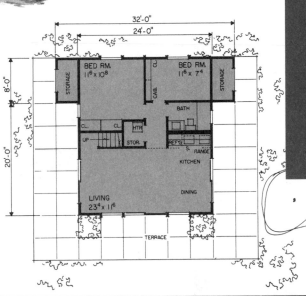

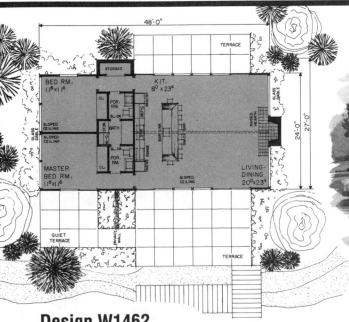

Design W1462

Square Footage: 1,176

● A second home with the informal living message readily apparent both inside and out. The zoning of this home is indeed most interesting – and practical, too. Study the plan carefully.

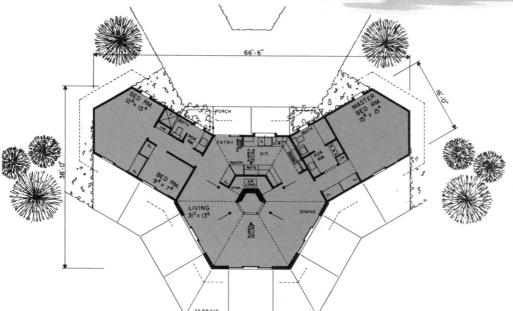

Design W2461
Square Footage: 1,400

● If you have the urge to make your vacation home one that has a distinctive flair of individuality, you should give consideration to the three designs illustrated here. Not only will you love the unique exterior appeal of your new home; but, also, the exceptional living patterns offered by the interior. The basic living area is a hexagon. To this space conscious geometric shape is added the sleeping wings with baths. The center of the living area has as its focal point a dramatic fireplace.

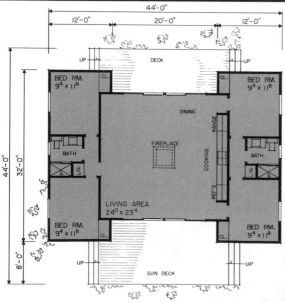

Design W1440
Square Footage: 1,248

● Here's a clever design that separates the sleeping areas into two wings, each with its own bath. The living area radiates around a central fireplace and has two deck options — one to the front, the other to the rear. Kitchen chores are accomplished along one long wall of the living area.

Design W1404
Square Footage: 1,336

● Here is an exciting design, unusual in character, yet fun to live in. This design with its frame exterior and large glass areas has as its dramatic focal point a hexagonal living area which gives way to interesting angles. The spacious living area features sliding glass doors through which traffic may pass to the terrace stretching across the entire length of the house. The wide overhanging roofs project over the terraces, thus providing partial protection from the weather. The sloping ceilings converge above the unique open fireplace. The sleeping areas are located in each wing from the hexagonal center.

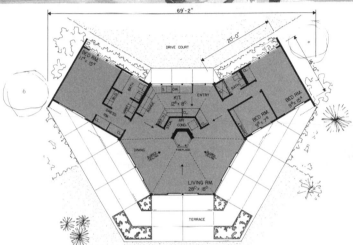

Design W2457
Square Footage: 1,288

● Leisure living will indeed be graciously experienced in this hip-roofed second home. Except for the clipped corner, it is a perfect square measuring 36 x 36 feet. The 23-foot-square living room enjoys a great view of the surrounding environment by virtue of the expanses of glass. The wide overhanging roof affords protection from the sun. The "open planning" adds to the spaciousness of the interior. The focal point is the raised-hearth fireplace. The three bedrooms are serviced by two full baths which are also accessible to other areas. The kitchen, looking out upon the water, will be a delight to work in. Observe the carport, the big bulk storage room and the dressing room with its stall shower.

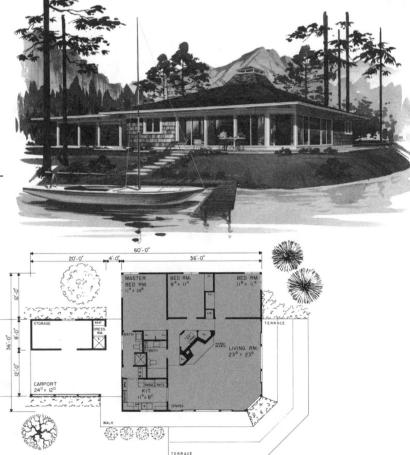

283

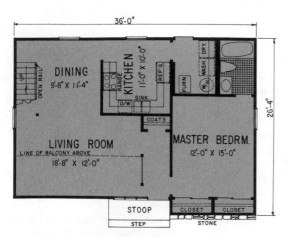

DINING
9'-8" X 11'-4"

KITCHEN
11'-0" X 10'-0"

RANGE

REF'G

SINK

D/W

WASH DRY

FURN

COATS

LIVING ROOM
LINE OF BALCONY ABOVE
18'-8" X 12'-0"

MASTER BEDRM.
12'-0" X 15'-0"

STOOP

STEP

STONE

CLOSET

CLOSET

36'-0"

26'-4"

Design W4153 First Floor: 893 square feet
Second Floor: 549 square feet; Total: 1,442 square feet

L **D**

● The rectangular shape of this design will make it an economical and easy-to-build choice for those wary of high construction costs. The first floor benefits from the informality of open planning; the living room and dining room combine to make one large living space. The partitioned kitchen is conveniently adjacent yet keeps the cooking process out of the living area. Also downstairs is the master bedroom and bath. The second floor houses two large bedrooms, a full bath, and a balcony over the living room. Notice the skylights.

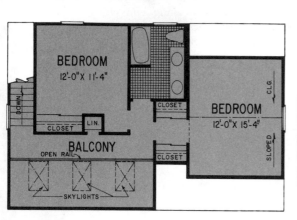

BEDROOM
12'-0" X 11'-4"

DOWN

CLOSET

LIN.

CLOSET

BALCONY

OPEN RAIL

SKYLIGHTS

BEDROOM
12'-0" X 15'-4"

CLG.

SLOPED

CLOSET

L
**LIFESTYLE
HOME PLANS**

Design W4114

Main Level: 852 square feet
Upper Level: 146 square feet
Total: 998 square feet

● This home was designed with the outdoors in mind. A large, wraparound deck provides ample space for sunning and relaxing. Huge windows and sliding glass doors open up the interior with lots of sunlight and great views—a must in a vacation home. Open planning makes for relaxed living patterns; the kitchen, living, and eating area flow together into one large working and living space. An upstairs loft provides added space for a lounge or an extra sleeping area.

L
**LIFESTYLE
HOME PLANS**

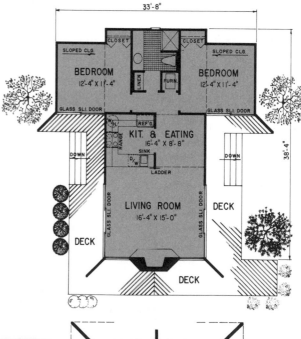

33'-8"

CLOSET

CLOSET

SLOPED CLG.

SLOPED CLG.

BEDROOM
12'-4" X 11'-4"

LINEN

FURN.

BEDROOM
12'-4" X 11'-4"

GLASS SLI DOOR

GLASS SLI DOOR

REF'G

RANGE

KIT. & EATING
16'-4" X 8'-8"

SINK

D/W

LADDER

DOWN

DOWN

LIVING ROOM
16'-4" X 15'-0"

GLASS SLI DOOR

GLASS SLI DOOR

DECK

DECK

DECK

38'-4"

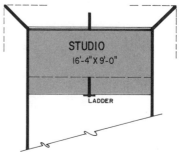

STUDIO
16'-4" X 9'-0"

LADDER

● Drama is a key element in the attraction of this bold contemporary. Though compact in size, it offers great living potential. The front entry opens directly to the great room/dining room combination. Close by is an L-shaped kitchen with a laundry area. The master bedroom upstairs has a balcony overlook to the great room below. It shares the second floor with two family bedrooms. Note that the carport has two large storage areas for tools or gardening equipment.

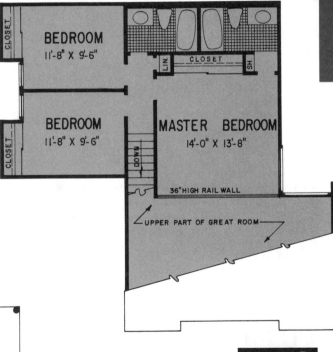

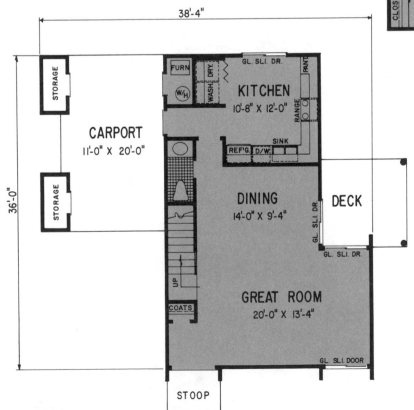

Design W4154

First Floor: 730 square feet
Second Floor: 665 square feet
Total: 1,395 square feet

D

When You're Ready To Order . . .

Let Us Show You Our Home Blueprint Package.

Building a home? Planning a home? Our Blueprint Package contains nearly everything you need to get the job done right, whether you're working on your own or with help from an architect, designer, builder or subcontractors. Each Blueprint Package is the result of many hours of work by licensed architects or professional designers.

QUALITY

Hundreds of hours of painstaking effort have gone into the development of your blueprint set. Each home has been quality-checked by professionals to insure accuracy and buildability.

VALUE

Because we sell in volume, you can buy professional-quality blueprints at a fraction of their development cost. With our plans, your dream home design costs only a few hundred dollars, not the thousands of dollars that custom architects charge.

SERVICE

Once you've chosen your favorite home plan, you'll receive fast efficient service whether you choose to mail your order to us or call us toll free at 1-800-521-6797.

SATISFACTION

Our years of service to satisfied home plan buyers provide us the experience and knowledge that guarantee your satisfaction with our product and performance.

ORDER TOLL FREE 1-800-521-6797

After you've studied our Blueprint Package and Important Extras on the following pages, simply mail the accompanying order form on page 301 or call toll free on our Blueprint Hotline: 1-800-521-6797. We're ready and eager to serve you.

Each set of blueprints is an interrelated collection of floor plans, interior and exterior elevations, dimensions, cross-sections, diagrams and notations showing precisely how your house is to be constructed.

Here's what you get:

Frontal Sheet
This artist's sketch of the exterior of the house, done in realistic perspective, gives you an idea of how the house will look when built and landscaped. Large ink-line floor plans show all levels of the house and provide a quick overview of your new home's livability, as well as a handy reference for studying furniture placement.

Foundation Plan
Drawn to 1/4-inch scale, this sheet shows the complete foundation layout including support

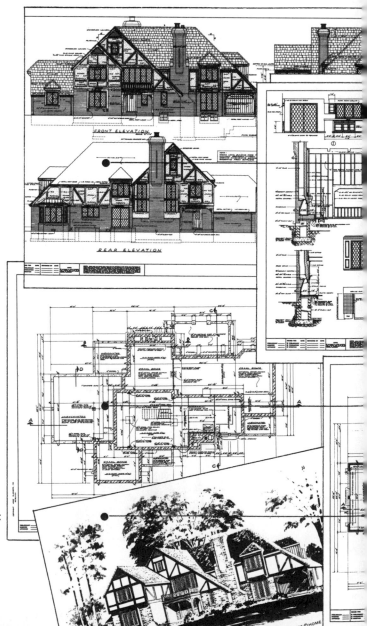

walls, excavated and unexcavated areas, if any, and foundation notes. If slab construction rather than basement, the plan shows footings and details for a monolithic slab. This page, or another in the set, also includes a sample plot plan for locating your house on a building site.

Detailed Floor Plans
Complete in 1/4-inch scale, these plans show the layout of each floor of the house. All rooms and interior spaces are carefully dimensioned and keys are provided for cross-section details given later in the plans. The positions of all electrical outlets and switches are clearly shown.

House Cross-Sections
Large-scale views, normally drawn at 3/8-inch equals 1 foot, show sections or cut-aways of the foundation, interior walls, exterior walls,

floors, stairways and roof details. Additional cross-sections are given to show important changes in floor, ceiling or roof heights or the relationship of one level to another. Extremely valuable for construction, these sections show exactly how the various parts of the house fit together.

Interior Elevations
These large-scale drawings show the design and placement of kitchen and bathroom cabinets, laundry areas, fireplaces, bookcases and other built-ins. Little "extras," such as mantelpiece and wainscoting drawings, plus moulding sections, provide details that give your home that custom touch.

Exterior Elevations
Drawings in 1/4-inch scale show the front, rear and sides of your house and give necessary notes on exterior materials and finishes. Particular attention is given to cornice detail, brick and stone accents or other finish items that make your home distinctive.

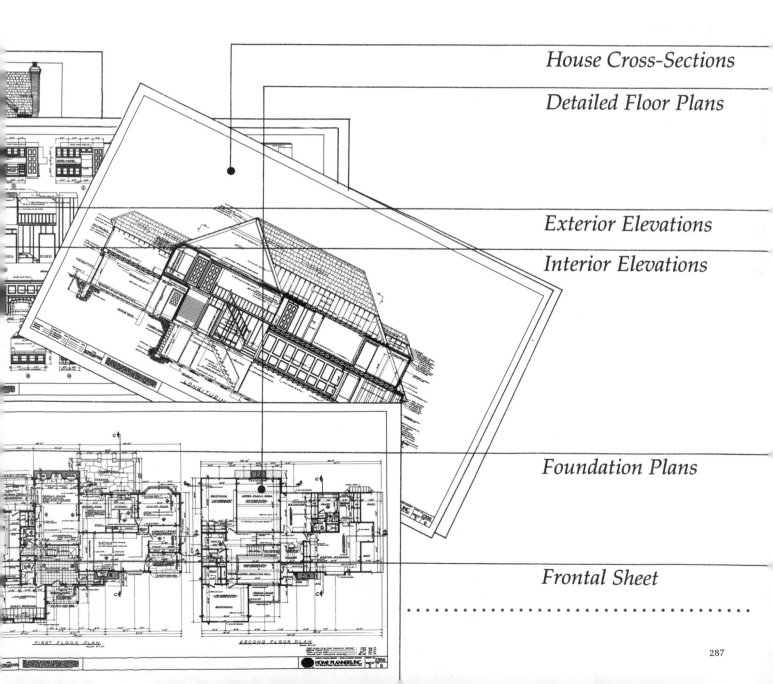

House Cross-Sections

Detailed Floor Plans

Exterior Elevations

Interior Elevations

Foundation Plans

Frontal Sheet

Important Extras To Do The Job Right!

Introducing seven important planning and construction aids developed by our professionals to help you succeed in your home-building project.

To Order, Call Toll Free 1-800-521-6797

To add these important extras to your Blueprint Package, simply indicate your choices on the order form on page 301 or call us Toll Free 1-800-521-6797 and we'll tell you more about these exciting products.

MATERIALS LIST

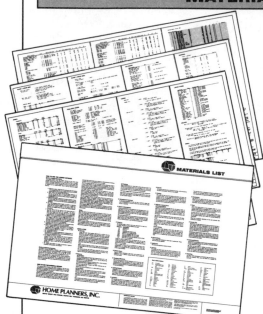

For many of the designs in our portfolio, we offer a customized materials take-off that is invaluable in planning and estimating the cost of your new home. This comprehensive list outlines the quantity, type and size of material needed to build your house (with the exception of mechanical system items). Included are:

- framing lumber
- roofing and sheet metal
- windows and doors
- exterior sheathing material and trim
- masonry, veneer and fireplace materials
- tile and flooring materials
- kitchen and bath cabinetry
- interior drywall and trim
- rough and finish hardware
- many more items

(Note: Because of differing local codes, building methods, and availability of materials, our Materials Lists do not include mechanical materials. To obtain necessary take-offs and recommendations, consult heating, plumbing and electrical contractors. Materials Lists are not sold separately from the Blueprint Package.)

This handy list helps you or your builder cost out materials and serves as a ready reference sheet when you're compiling bids. It also provides a cross-check against the materials specified by your builder and helps coordinate the substitution of items you may need to meet local codes.

SPECIFICATION OUTLINE

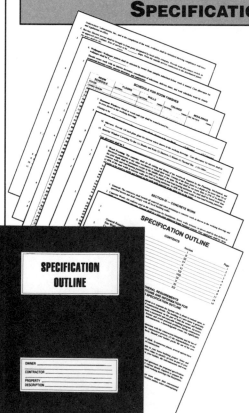

This valuable 16-page document is critical to building your house correctly. Designed to be filled in by you or your builder, this booklet lists 166 stages or items crucial to the building process.

For the layman, it provides a comprehensive review of the construction process and helps in making the specific choices of materials, models and processes. For the builder, it serves as a guide to preparing a building quotation and forms the basis for the construction program.

Designed primarily as a reference for the homeowner, this Specification Outline can become a legally binding document. Once it is filled out and agreed upon by owner and builder, it becomes a complete Project Specification.

When combined with the blueprints, a signed contract and schedule, the Specification Outline becomes a legal document and record for the building of your home. Many home builders find it useful to order two of these outlines—one as a worksheet in formulating the specifications and another to be carefully completed as a legal document.

DETAIL SHEETS

If you want to know more about techniques—and deal more confidently with subcontractors—we offer these remarkably useful detail sheets. Each is an excellent tool that will enhance your understanding of these technical subjects.

Plan-A-Home®

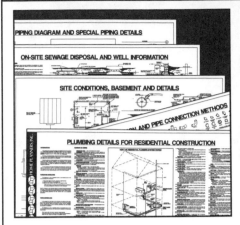

PLUMBING

The Blueprint Package includes locations for all the plumbing fixtures in your new house, including sinks, lavatories, tubs, showers, toilets, laundry trays and water heaters. However, if you want to know more about the complete plumbing system, these 24x36-inch detail sheets will prove very useful. Prepared to meet requirements of the National Plumbing Code, these six fact-filled sheets give general information on pipe schedules, fittings, sump-pump details, water-softener hookups, septic system details and much more. Color-coded sheets include a glossary of terms.

ELECTRICAL

The locations for every electrical switch, plug and outlet are shown in your Blueprint Package. However, these Electrical Details go further to take the mystery out of household electrical systems. Prepared to meet requirements of the National Electrical Code, these comprehensive 24x36-inch drawings come packed with helpful information, including wire sizing, switch-installation schematics, cable-routing details, appliance wattage, door-bell hookups, typical service panel circuitry and much more. Six sheets are bound together and color-coded for easy reference. A glossary of terms is also included.

Plan-A-Home® is an easy-to-use tool that helps you design a new home, arrange furniture in a new or existing home, or plan a remodeling project. Each package contains:

- More than *700 peel-off planning symbols* on a self-stick vinyl sheet, including walls, windows, doors, all types of furniture, kitchen components, bath fixtures and many more. All are made of durable, peel-and-stick vinyl you can use over and over.

- A reusable, transparent, *1/4-inch scale planning grid* made of tough mylar that matches the scale of actual working drawings (1/4 -inch equals 1 foot). This grid provides the basis for house layouts of up to 140x92 feet.

- *Tracing paper* and a protective sheet for copying or transferring your completed plan.

- A *felt-tip pen*, with water-soluble ink that wipes away quickly.

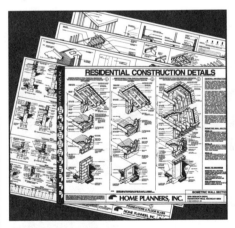

CONSTRUCTION

The Blueprint Package contains everything an experienced builder needs to construct a particular house. However, it doesn't show all the ways that houses can be built, nor does it explain alternate construction methods. To help you understand how your house will be built—and offer additional techniques—this set of drawings depicts the materials and methods used to build foundations, fireplaces, walls, floors and roofs. Where appropriate, the drawings show acceptable alternatives. These six sheets will answer questions for the advanced do-it-yourselfer or home planner.

MECHANICAL

This package contains fundamental principles and useful data that will help you make informed decisions and communicate with subcontractors about heating and cooling systems. The 24 x 36-inch drawings contain instructions and samples that allow you to make simple load calculations and preliminary sizing and costing analysis. Covered are today's most commonly used systems from heat pumps to solar fuel systems. The package is packed full of illustrations and diagrams to help you visualize components and how they relate to one another.

With Plan-A-Home®, you can make basic planning decisions for a new house or make modifications to an existing house. Use with your Blueprint Package to test modifications to rooms or to plan furniture arrangements before you build. Plan-A-Home® lets you lay out areas as large as a 7,500 square foot, six-bedroom, seven-bath house.

⌐ The Landscape Blueprint Package

For the homes marked with an ⌐ in this book, Home Planners has created a front-yard landscape plan that matches or is complementary in design to the house plan. These comprehensive blueprint packages include a Frontal Sheet, Plan View, Regionalized Plant & Materials List, a sheet on Planting and Maintaining Your Landscape, Zone Maps and Plant Size and Description Guide. These plans will help you achieve professional results, adding value and enjoyment to your property for years to come. Each set of blueprints is a full 18" x 24" in size with clear, complete instructions and easy-to-read type. See the following pages for 40-different front-yard Landscape Plans to match your favorite house.

Regional Order Map

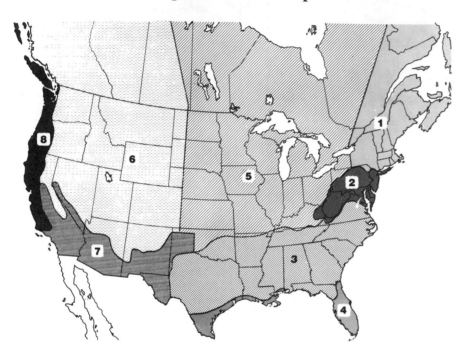

Most of the Landscape Plans shown on these pages are available with a Plant & Materials List adapted by horticultural experts to 8 different regions of the country. Please specify Geographic Region when ordering your plan. See pages 296-301 for prices, ordering information and regional availability.

Region	1	Northeast
Region	2	Mid-Atlantic
Region	3	Deep South
Region	4	Florida & Gulf Coast
Region	5	Midwest
Region	6	Rocky Mountains
Region	7	Southern California & Desert Southwest
Region	8	Northern California & Pacific Northwest

CAPE COD TRADITIONAL
Landscape Plan L200

WILLIAMSBURG CAPE
Landscape Plan L201

CAPE COD COTTAGE
Landscape Plan L202

GAMBREL–ROOF COLONIAL
Landscape Plan L203

CENTER–HALL COLONIAL
Landscape Plan L204

CLASSIC NEW ENGLAND COLONIAL
Landscape Plan L205

SOUTHERN COLONIAL
Landscape Plan L206

COUNTRY–STYLE FARMHOUSE
Landscape Plan L207

PENNSYLVANIA STONE FARMHOUSE
Landscape Plan L208

RAISED–PORCH FARMHOUSE
Landscape Plan L209

NEW ENGLAND BARN–STYLE HOUSE
Landscape Plan L210

NEW ENGLAND COUNTRY HOUSE
Landscape Plan L211

TRADITIONAL COUNTRY ESTATE
Landscape Plan L212

FRENCH PROVINCIAL ESTATE
Landscape Plan L213

GEORGIAN MANOR
Landscape Plan L214

GRAND–PORTICO GEORGIAN
Landscape Plan L215

BRICK FEDERAL
Landscape Plan L216

COUNTRY FRENCH RAMBLER
Landscape Plan L217

FRENCH MANOR HOUSE
Landscape Plan L218

ELIZABETHAN TUDOR
Landscape Plan L219

TUDOR ONE–STORY
Landscape Plan L220

ENGLISH–STYLE COTTAGE
Landscape Plan L221

MEDIEVAL GARRISON
Landscape Plan L222

QUEEN ANNE VICTORIAN
Landscape Plan L223

GOTHIC VICTORIAN
Landscape Plan L224

BASIC RANCH
Landscape Plan L225

L–SHAPED RANCH
Landscape Plan L226

SPRAWLING RANCH
Landscape Plan L227

TRADITIONAL SPLIT–LEVEL
Landscape Plan L228

SHED–ROOF CONTEMPORARY
Landscape Plan L229

WOOD–SIDED CONTEMPORARY
Landscape Plan L230

HILLSIDE CONTEMPORARY
Landscape Plan L231

FLORIDA RAMBLER
Landscape Plan L232

CALIFORNIA STUCCO
Landscape Plan L233

LOW–GABLE CONTEMPORARY
Landscape Plan L234

NORTHERN BRICK CHATEAU
Landscape Plan L235

MISSION–TILE RANCH
Landscape Plan L236

ADOBE–BLOCK HACIENDA
Landscape Plan L237

COURTYARD PATIO HOME
Landscape Plan L238

CENTER–COURT CONTEMPORARY
Landscape Plan L239

For Landscape Plan prices and ordering information, see pages 296-301.

 Or call **Toll Free,**
1-800-521-6797.

▣ *The Deck Blueprint Package*

Many of the homes in this book can be enhanced with a professionally designed Deck Plan. Those home plans highlighted with a ▣ have a matching or corresponding deck plan available which includes a Deck Plan Frontal Sheet, Deck Framing and Floor Plans, Deck Elevations and a Deck Materials List. A Standard Deck Details Package, also available, provides all the how-to information necessary for building *any* deck. Our Complete Deck Building Package contains 1 set of Custom Deck Plans of your choice, plus 1 set of Standard Deck Building Details all for one low price. Our plans and details are carefully prepared in an easy-to-understand format that will guide you through every stage of your deck-building project. See these pages for 25 different Deck layouts to match your favorite house.

SPLIT–LEVEL SUN DECK
Deck Plan D100

BI–LEVEL DECK WITH COVERED DINING
Deck Plan D101

FRESH–AIR CORNER DECK
Deck Plan D102

BACK–YARD EXTENDER DECK
Deck Plan D103

WRAP–AROUND FAMILY DECK
Deck Plan D104

DRAMATIC DECK WITH BARBECUE
Deck Plan D105

SPLIT–PLAN COUNTRY DECK
Deck Plan D106

DECK FOR DINING AND VIEWS
Deck Plan D107

BOLD, ANGLED CORNER DECK
Deck Plan D108

SPECTACULAR "RESORT–STYLE" DECK
Deck Plan D109

TREND–SETTER DECK
Deck Plan D110

TURN–OF–THE–CENTURY DECK
Deck Plan D111

WEEKEND ENTERTAINER DECK
Deck Plan D112

STRIKING "DELTA" DECK
Deck Plan D113

CENTER–VIEW DECK
Deck Plan D114

KITCHEN–EXTENDER DECK
Deck Plan D115

BI–LEVEL RETREAT DECK
Deck Plan D116

SPLIT–LEVEL ACTIVITY DECK
Deck Plan D117

OUTDOOR LIFESTYLE DECK
Deck Plan D118

TRI–LEVEL DECK WITH GRILL
Deck Plan D119

CONTEMPORARY LEISURE DECK
Deck Plan D120

ANGULAR WINGED DECK
Deck Plan D121

DECK FOR A SPLIT–LEVEL HOME
Deck Plan D122

GRACIOUS GARDEN DECK
Deck Plan D123

TERRACED DECK FOR ENTERTAINING
Deck Plan D124

For Deck Plan prices and ordering information, see pages 296–301.

 Or call **Toll Free**, **1-800-521-6797**.

Price Schedule & Plans Index

House Blueprint Price Schedule
(Prices guaranteed through December 31, 1993)

	1-set Study Package	4-set Building Package	8-set Building Package	1-set Reproducible Sepias
Schedule A	$210	$270	$330	$420
Schedule B	$240	$300	$360	$480
Schedule C	$270	$330	$390	$540
Schedule D	$300	$360	$420	$600
Schedule E	$390	$450	$510	$660

Additional Identical Blueprints in same order...............$50 per set
Reverse Blueprints (mirror image)....................................$50 per set
Specification Outlines ....$7 each
Materials Lists:
      Schedule A-D $40
      Schedule E $50
Exchanges ....$40 exchange fee for the first set; $10 for each
      additional set
      $60 total exchange fee for 4 sets
      $90 total exchange fee for 8 sets

Deck Plans Price Schedule

CUSTOM DECK PLANS

Price Group	Q	R	S
1 Set Custom Plans	$15.00	$20.00	$25.00
Additional identical sets:	$5.00 each		
Reverse sets (mirror image):	$5.00 each		

STANDARD DECK DETAILS
1 Set Generic Construction Details $14.95 each

COMPLETE DECK BUILDING PACKAGE

Price Group	Q	R	S
1 Set Custom Plans			
1 Set Standard Deck Details	$25.00	$30.00	$35.00

Landscape Plans Price Schedule

Price Group	X	Y	Z
1 set	$35	$45	$55
3 sets	$50	$60	$70
6 sets	$65	$75	$85

Additional Identical Sets ....$10 each
Reverse Sets (Mirror Image)..$10 each

These pages contain all the information you need to price your blueprints. In general the larger and more complicated the house, the more it costs to design and thus the higher the price we must charge for the blueprints. Remember, however, that these prices are far less than you would normally pay for the services of a licensed architect or professional designer.

Custom home designs and related architectural services often cost thousands of dollars, ranging from 5% to 15% of the cost of construction. By ordering our blueprints you are potentially saving enough money to afford a larger house, or to add those "extra" amenities such as a patio, deck, swimming pool or even an upgraded kitchen or luxurious master suite.

Index

To use the Index below, refer to the design number listed in numerical order (a helpful page reference is also given). Note the price index letter and refer to the House Blueprint Price Schedule above for the cost of one, four or eight sets of blueprints or the cost of a reproducible sepia. Additional prices are shown for identical and reverse blueprint sets, as well as a very useful Materials List for some of the plans. Also note in the Index below those plans that have matching or complementary Deck Plans or Landscape Plans. Refer to the schedules above for prices of these plans. Some of our plans can be customized through Home Planners' Home Customizer® Service. These plans are indicated below with this symbol: 🏠. See page 301 for more information.

To Order: Fill in and send the order form on page 301—or call toll free 1-800-521-6797.

DESIGN	PRICE	PAGE	CUSTOMIZABLE	DECK	DECK PRICE	LANDSCAPE	LANDSCAPE PRICE	REGIONS
W1223	C	46						
W1305	A	29		D106	S			
W1307	A	66		D114	R	L226	X	1-8
W1357	A	54						
W1379	A	54						
W1382	A	29		D106	S			
W1383	A	29		D106	S			
W1387	A	22		D101	R			
W1388	A	22		D101	R			
W1389	A	22		D101	R			
W1396	B	28						
W1404	A	283						
W1424	A	281						
W1440	A	282						
W1451	A	279						
W1462	A	281						
W1491	A	280						

DESIGN	PRICE	PAGE	CUSTOMIZABLE	DECK	DECK PRICE	LANDSCAPE	LANDSCAPE PRICE	REGIONS
W1499	B	278						
W1704	B	165						
W1726	B	259						
W1754	B	260		D100	Q			
W1783	C	104						
W1820	C	64						
W1877	B	110		D114	R			
W1884	B	58						
W1891	B	28						
W1908	A	91						
W1947	B	67						
W1948	B	67						
W1994	D	49						
W2114	C	31						
W2123	C	110						
W2135	C	261						
W2173	D	149						

DESIGN	PRICE	PAGE	CUSTOMIZABLE	DECK	DECK PRICE	LANDSCAPE	LANDSCAPE PRICE	REGIONS
W2182	B	261						
W2199	A	25						
W2205	B	147						
W2213	C	168						
W2226	D	65						
W2229	C	263						
W2247	C	169						
W2248	C	141						
W2251	D	200						
W2255	C	32						
W2256	C	44						
W2272	B	146						
W2303	C	33						
W2304	C	47						
W2329	C	30						
W2330	B	36						
W2339	B	106						
W2343	D	267						
W2347	C	211						
W2351	B	24		D101	R			
W2377	A	97						
W2379	B	103		D120	R	L212	Z	1-8
W2386	B	259				L238	Y	3,4,7,8
W2390	C	107		D101	R			
W2392	D	16						
W2393	B	165						
W2417	B	277						
W2423	A	280						
W2431	A	279						
W2439	A	274						
W2457	A	283						
W2461	A	282						
W2464	A	277						
W2483	B	276						
W2488	A	233	🏠	D102	Q			
W2490	A	95	🏠					
W2502	C	140				L212	Z	1-8
W2504	C	143						
W2505	A	57	🏠	D113	R	L226	X	1-8
W2511	B	171		D108	R	L229	Y	1-8
W2528	B	23		D100	Q			
W2529	C	37						
W2530	B	86						
W2532	B	37						
W2534	D	45				L227	Z	1-8
W2536	C	136						
W2548	C	137						
W2549	C	150						
W2552	C	137						
W2557	B	50						
W2562	D	92		D122	S			
W2565	B	52		D101	R	L225	X	1-3,5,6,8
W2579	D	145						
W2580	C	136						
W2581	C	89						
W2583	C	142						
W2588	C	164						
W2591	A	36						
W2594	C	236		D120	R			
W2595	C	42						
W2602	B	104						
W2608	A	167		D112	R	L228	Y	1-8
W2628	A	166		D105	R			
W2646	B	239		D114	R	L224	Y	1-3,5,6,8
W2647	D	239				L224	Y	1-3,5,6,8
W2670	D	197		D105	R	L236	Z	3,4,7
W2671	B	11		D114	R	L234	Y	1-8
W2679	C	130						
W2702	B	62						
W2703	A	64		D113	R			
W2704	B	59		D107	S	L225	X	1-3,5,6,8
W2705	B	59		D107	S	L217	Y	1-8
W2706	B	59		D107	S	L225	X	1-3,5,6,8
W2708	C	102		D112	R			
W2711	B	112	🏠	D105	R	L229	Y	1-8
W2715	C	144						
W2716	C	170				L229	Y	1-8
W2717	C	20						
W2719	C	148						
W2720	B	43						
W2721	C	48						
W2729	B	101				L234	Y	1-8
W2730	C	20		D124	S			
W2734	C	158						
W2735	C	163						
W2741	B	50		D114	R			
W2743	B	259						
W2744	A	63						
W2748	A	91						
W2753	B	23		D112	R			
W2754	B	62						
W2756	C	41		D101	R	L234	Y	1-8
W2759	C	85						
W2761	B	12		D105	R	L229	Y	1-8
W2763	C	152						
W2764	C	30						
W2765	D	263		D106	S			
W2771	C	88						
W2772	C	97						
W2780	C	86						
W2781	C	6		D121	S	L230	Z	1-8
W2782	C	93		D101	R			
W2789	C	19		D117	S	L228	Y	1-8
W2790	B	27						
W2791	D	196						
W2792	B	55						
W2793	B	26						
W2795	B	18						
W2796	B	40						
W2797	B	21						
W2802	B	56	🏠	D118	R	L220	Y	1-3,5,6,8
W2803	B	56	🏠	D118	R	L225	X	1-3,5,6,8

DESIGN	PRICE	PAGE	CUSTOMIZABLE	DECK	DECK PRICE	LANDSCAPE	LANDSCAPE PRICE	REGIONS
W2804	B	56	🏠	D118	R	L232	Y	4, 7
W2805	B	35		D113	R	L220	Y	1-3, 5, 6, 8
W2806	B	35		D113	R	L220	Y	1-3, 5, 6, 8
W2807	B	35		D113	R	L220	Y	1-3, 5, 6, 8
W2809	B	55						
W2818	B	8	🏠	D101	R	L234	Y	1-8
W2819	C	40		D113	R			
W2822	A	114				L229	Y	1-8
W2823	B	100		D112	R	L229	Y	1-8
W2824	B	264						
W2826	B	219	🏠	D116	R			
W2827	C	15				L229	Y	1-8
W2828	B	14						
W2829	D	240		D113	R	L219	Z	1-3, 5, 6, 8
W2830	C	177						
W2831	C	98		D113	R			
W2832	C	265		D113	R			
W2833	C	271						
W2834	D	177						
W2835	C	176						
W2838	C	270						
W2846	C	159						
W2848	C	178						
W2856	C	160						
W2857	D	267				L239	Z	1-8
W2858	C	266						
W2860	C	270						
W2861	C	269						
W2862	C	268						
W2864	A	61	🏠	D100	Q	L225	X	1-3, 5, 6, 8
W2866	C	39						
W2868	B	162						
W2871	B	264		D117	S			
W2872	D	237						
W2873	C	48						
W2874	D	238						
W2875	B	53		D113	R	L236	Z	3, 4, 7
W2876	B	231						
W2877	C	236		D114	R			
W2879	D	203						
W2881	C	262						
W2882	C	262						
W2883	C	235						
W2884	B	84						
W2886	B	272						
W2887	A	111						
W2892	B	34						
W2893	C	157		D120	R			
W2894	C	156						
W2895	D	151						
W2896	C	161						
W2900	C	265						
W2901	C	155				L229	Y	1-8
W2902	B	272				L234	Y	1-8
W2903	C	268						
W2904	C	87						
W2905	B	90		D121	S	L229	Y	1-8
W2906	C	107		D114	R			
W2910	B	115						
W2912	B	51						
W2913	B	61		D124	S			
W2915	C	9		D114	R	L212	Z	1-8
W2917	B	60						
W2918	B	38		D124	S			
W2920	D	206	🏠	D104	S	L212	Z	1-8
W2925	B	100						
W2926	D	193						
W2927	B	218	🏠	D100	Q			
W2928	C	234						
W2930	B	60	🏠					
W2934	D	199		D109	S			
W2936	C	131						
W2937	C	13				L229	Y	1-8
W2938	E	202						
W2944	C	154						
W2948	B	250	🏠					
W2949	C	245		D123	S			
W2950	C	224						
W2952	E	194				L235	Z	1-3,5,6,8
W2956	E	195						
W3163	B	58						
W3311	D	208		D109	S	L220	Y	1-3,5,6,8
W3319	C	253	🏠	D112	R	L217	Y	1-8
W3321	C	252	🏠	D116	R	L209	Y	1-6,8
W3322	C	251	🏠	D118	R	L234	Y	1-8
W3330	A	217						
W3331	A	221						
W3336	B	216						
W3338	B	94						
W3341	B	218						
W3342	B	221						
W3344	D	241						
W3346	B	220	🏠					
W3347	D	96						
W3352	B	113		D108	R	L229	Y	1-8
W3357	D	10		D115	Q	L211	Y	1-8
W3361	D	198						
W3362	D	129						
W3364	D	201						
W3368	C	17		D104	S	L220	Y	1-3,5,6,8
W3400	C	242	🏠					
W3401	C	243	🏠					
W3402	D	244	🏠					
W3403	C	5		D115	Q	L237	Y	7
W3404	D	207		D106	S	L230	Z	1-8
W3405	D	246	🏠			L236	Z	3,4,7
W3408	D	4						
W3409	C	209						
W3410	D	105						
W3416	A	228	🏠					
W3418	A	108	🏠					
W3419	B	228	🏠					

DESIGN	PRICE	PAGE	CUSTOMIZABLE	DECK	DECK PRICE	LANDSCAPE	LANDSCAPE PRICE	REGIONS
W3424	B	109	🏠					
W3425	C	225	🏠					
W3426	C	254	🏠					
W3428	C	222	🏠					
W3429	C	223	🏠					
W3432	C	249	🏠			L233	Y	3,4,7
W3433	C	248	🏠			L213	Z	1-8
W3434	D	247	🏠					
W3435	D	255	🏠	D104	S	L227	Z	1-8
W3438	C	7				L209	Y	1-6,8
W3439	C	213	🏠					
W3441	C	257	🏠					
W3449	C	256	🏠					
W3450	C	212	🏠	D106	S	L229	Y	1-8
W3556	D	81						
W3557	D	227						
W3560	B	226						
W3562	B	210						
W4012	A	273						
W4015	A	275						
W4019	A	120				L229	Y	1-8
W4027	A	275						
W4036	B	105		D112	R			
W4052	B	191						
W4090	B	190						
W4095	A	180				L229	Y	1-8
W4101	B	187						
W4102	B	175				L230	Z	1-8
W4114	A	284						
W4115	B	174						
W4122	B	182		D106	S			
W4124	B	72						
W4129	A	173						
W4141	C	153						
W4153	A	284		D115	Q	L202	X	1-3,5,6,8
W4154	A	285		D111	S			
W4155	A	70		D115	Q	L229	Y	1-8
W4157	A	71						
W4160	B	138						
W4162	B	139						
W4168	A	181		D108	R			
W4175	A	185						
W4183	B	77				L231	Z	1-8
W4186	B	68						
W4196	B	69		D114	R			
W4197	B	183						
W4199	B	132						
W4203	A	75						
W4214	B	117		D114	R			
W4216	A	122				L229	Y	1-8
W4224	A	121				L229	Y	1-8
W4225	A	119						
W4226	A	118						
W4227	A	123						
W4232	A	78				L229	Y	1-8
W4240	C	184		D112	R			
W4241	C	135				L230	Z	1-8
W4242	A	79						
W4247	B	124		D116	R	L229	Y	1-8
W4248	A	125		D116	R	L229	Y	1-8
W4254	B	172						
W4261	D	126				L212	Z	1-8
W4264	B	116		D105	R			
W4293	B	80		D120	R			
W4300	B	186						
W4307	B	82						
W4308	C	204				L231	Z	1-8
W4313	B	99						
W4317	B	73		D117	S			
W4323	A	76				L231	Z	1-8
W4327	C	133		D109	S			
W4328	C	128		D112	R	L229	Y	1-8
W4330	C	127						
W4331	C	134				L231	Z	1-8
W4334	B	83				L231	Z	1-8
W4340	B	74				L231	Z	1-8
W4354	C	189						
W4365	C	189		D112	R			
W4376	C	189		D112	R			
W4382	A	238				L224	Y	1-3,5,6,8
W4386	B	229				L220	Y	1-3,5,6,8
W4389	C	214						
W4390	B	230						
W4391	B	215						
W4406	B	232						
W4408	C	192						
W4548	E	205						

Before You Order . . .

Before completing the coupon at right or calling us on our Toll-Free Blueprint Hotline, you may be interested to learn more about our service and products. Here's some information you will find helpful.

Quick Turnaround
We process and ship every blueprint order from our office within 48 hours. On most orders, we do even better. Normally, if we receive your order by 5 p.m. Eastern Time, we'll process it the same day and ship it the following day. Because of this quick turnaround, we won't send a formal notice acknowledging receipt of your order.

Our Exchange Policy
Since blueprints are printed in response to your order, we cannot honor requests for refunds. However, we will exchange your entire first order for an equal number of blueprints plus the following exchange fees: $40 for the first set, $10 for each additional set; $60 total exchange fee for 4 sets; $90 total exchange fee for 8 sets.... *plus* the difference in cost if exchanging for a design in a higher price bracket, or *less* the difference in cost if exchanging for a design in a lower price bracket. (Sepias are not exchangeable.) All sets from the first order must be returned before the exchange can take place. Please add $8 for postage and handling via ground service; $20 via 2nd Day Air.

About Reverse Blueprints
If you want to build in reverse of the plan as shown, we will include an extra set of reversed blueprints (mirror image) for an additional fee of $50. Although lettering and dimensions appear backward, reverses will be a useful visual aid if you decide to flop the plan. Right-reading reverses of Customizable Plans are available through our Customization Service. Call for more details.

Modifying or Customizing Our Plans
With such a great selection of homes, you are bound to find the one that suits you. However, if you need to make alterations to a design that is customizable, you need only order our Customizer® kit or call our Customization representative at 1-800-322-6797, ext. 800, to get you started (see additional information on next page). It is possible to customize many of our plans that are not part of our Home Customizer® Service.

If you decide to revise plans significantly that are not customizable through our service, we strongly suggest that you order reproducible sepias and consult a licensed architect or professional designer to help you redraw the plans.

Architectural and Engineering Seals
Some cities and states are now requiring that a licensed architect or engineer review and "seal" your blueprints prior to construction. This is often due to local or regional concerns over energy consumption, safety codes, seismic ratings, etc. For this reason, you may find it necessary to consult with a local professional to have your plans reviewed. This can normally be accomplished with minimum delays, for a nominal fee. In some cases, Home Planners can seal your plans through our Customization Service. Call for more details.

Compliance with Local Codes and Regulations
At the time of creation, our plans are drawn to specifications published by Building Officials Code Administrators (BOCA), the Southern Standard Building Code, or the Uniform Building Code and are designed to meet or exceed national building standards. Some states, counties and municipalities have their own codes, zoning requirements and building regulations. Before starting construction, consult with local building authorities and make sure you comply with local ordinances and codes, including obtaining any necessary permits or inspections as building progresses. In some cases, minor modifications to your plans by your builder, local architect or designer may be required to meet local conditions and requirements. Home Planners may be able to make these changes to Customizable Plans providing you supply all pertinent information from your local building authorities.

Foundation and Exterior Wall Changes
Most of our plans are drawn with either a full or partial basement foundation. Depending upon your specific climate or regional building practices, you may wish to convert this basement to a slab or crawlspace. Most professional contractors and builders can easily adapt your plans to alternate foundation types. Likewise, most can easily convert 2x4 wall construction to 2x6, or vice versa. If you need more guidance on these conversions, our handy Construction Detail Sheets, shown on page 289, describe how such conversions can be made. For Customizable Plans, Home Planners can easily provide the necessary changes for you.

How Many Blueprints Do You Need?
A single set of blueprints is sufficient to study a home in greater detail. However, if you are planning to obtain cost estimates from a contractor or subcontractors—or if you are planning to build immediately—you will need more sets. Because additional sets are cheaper when ordered in quantity with the original order, make sure you order enough blueprints to satisfy all requirements. The following checklist will help you determine how many you need:

_____Owner

_____Builder (generally requires at least three sets; one as a legal document, one to use during inspections, and at least one to give to subcontractors)

_____Local Building Department (often requires two sets)

_____Mortgage Lender (usually one set for a conventional loan; three sets for FHA or VA loans)

_____TOTAL NUMBER OF SETS

Toll Free 1-800-521-6797
Normal Office Hours:
8:00 a.m. to 8:00 p.m. Eastern Time
Monday through Friday
Our staff will gladly answer any questions during normal office hours. Our answering service can place orders after hours or on weekends.

If we receive your order by 5:00 p.m. Eastern Time, Monday through Friday, we'll process it the same day and ship it the following business day. When ordering by phone, please have your charge card ready. We'll also ask you for the Order Form Key Number at the bottom of the coupon. Please use our Toll-Free number for blueprint and book orders only.
For Customization orders call 1-800-322-6797, ext. 800.

By FAX: Copy the Order Form on the next page and send it on our International FAX line: 1-602-297-6219.

Canadian Customers
Order Toll-Free 1-800-848-2550
For faster, more economical service, Canadian customers may now call in orders on our Toll-Free line. Or, complete the order form at right, and mail with your check indicating U.S. funds to:

 Home Planners, Inc.
3275 W. Ina Road, Suite 110
Tucson, AZ 85741

By FAX: Copy the Order Form on the next page and send it on our International FAX line: 1-602-297-6219.

The Home Customizer®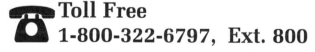

Many of the plans in this book are customizable through our Home Customizer® service. Look for this symbol on the pages of home designs. It indicates that the plan on that page is part of The Home Customizer® service.

Some changes to customizable plans that can be made include:

- exterior elevation changes
- kitchen and bath modifications
- roof, wall and foundation changes
- room additions
- and much more!

If the plan you have chosen to build is one of our customizable homes, you can easily order the Home Customizer® kit to start on the path to making your alterations. The kit, priced at only $19.95, may be ordered at the same time you order your blueprint package by calling on our toll-free number or using the order blank at right. Or you can wait until you receive your blueprints, spend some time studying them and then order the kit by phone, FAX or mail. If you then decide to proceed with the customizing service, the $19.95 price of the kit will be refunded to you after your customization order is received. The Home Customizer® kit includes:

- instruction book with examples
- architectural scale
- clear acetate work film
- erasable red marker
- removable correction tape
- ¼" scale furniture cutouts
- 1 set of Customizable Drawings with floor plans and elevations

The service is easy, fast and *affordable*. Because we know and work with our plans and have them available on state-of-the-art computer systems, we can make the changes efficiently at prices much lower than those charged by normal architectural or drafting services. In addition, you'll be getting custom changes directly from Home Planners—the company whose dedication to excellence and long-standing professional experience are well recognized in the industry.

Call now to learn more about how simple it can be to have the *custom home* you've always wanted.

**☎ Toll Free
1-800-322-6797, Ext. 800**

ORDER FORM

**HOME PLANNERS, INC., 3275 WEST INA ROAD
SUITE 110, TUCSON, ARIZONA 85741**

THE BASIC BLUEPRINT PACKAGE
Rush me the following (please refer to the Plans Index and Price Schedule in this section):

_____ Set(s) of blueprints for plan number(s) _____.	$_____
_____ Set(s) of sepias for plan number(s) _____.	$_____
_____ Additional identical blueprints in same order @ $50.00 per set.	$_____
_____ Reverse blueprints @ $50.00 per set.	$_____
_____ Home Customizer® Kit(s) for Plan(s)_____ @ $19.95 per kit.	$_____

IMPORTANT EXTRAS
Rush me the following:

_____ Materials List @ $40 Schedules A-D; $50 Schedule E	$_____
_____ Specification Outlines @ $7.00 each.	$_____
_____ Detail Sets @ $14.95 each; two for $22.95; three for $29.95; any four for $39.95 (Save $19.85). ❏ Plumbing ❏ Electrical ❏ Construction ❏ Mechanical (These helpful details provide general construction advice and are not specific to any single plan.)	$_____
_____ Plan-A-Home® Kit @ $29.95 each.	$_____

DECK BLUEPRINTS

_____ Set(s) of Deck Plan _____.	$_____
_____ Additional identical blueprints in same order @ $5.00 per set.	$_____
_____ Reverse blueprints @ $5.00 per set.	$_____
_____ Set of Standard Deck Details @ $14.95 per set.	$_____
_____ Complete Deck Building Package (Best Buy!) Includes Custom Deck Plan _____ (see Index and Price Schedule) Plus Standard Deck Details.	$_____

LANDSCAPE BLUEPRINTS

_____ Set(s) of Landscape Plan _____.	$_____
_____ Additional identical blueprints in same order @ $10.00 per set.	$_____
_____ Reverse blueprints @ $10.00 per set.	$_____

Please indicate the appropriate region of the country for Plant & Material List. (See Map on page 290): Region _____

SUB-TOTAL — $_____

SALES TAX (Arizona residents add 5% sales tax; Michigan residents add 4% sales tax.) — $_____

POSTAGE AND HANDLING	1-3 sets	4 or more sets	
COMMERCIAL SERVICE (Requires street address - No P.O. Boxes)			
•Ground Service Allow 4-6 days delivery	❏ $6.00	❏ $8.00	$_____
•2nd Day Air Service Allow 2-3 days delivery	❏ $12.00	❏ $20.00	$_____
•Next Day Air Service Allow 1 day delivery	❏ $22.00	❏ $30.00	$_____
POST OFFICE DELIVERY If no street address available. Allow 4-6 days delivery	❏ $8.00	❏ $12.00	$_____
OVERSEAS AIR MAIL DELIVERY Note: All delivery times are from date Blueprint Package is shipped.	❏ $30.00	❏ $50.00	$_____
	❏ Send COD		

TOTAL (Sub-total, tax, and postage) — $_____

YOUR ADDRESS (please print)

Name _____

Street _____

City _____ State _____ Zip _____

Daytime telephone number (_____) _____

FOR CREDIT CARD ORDERS ONLY
Please fill in the information below:

Credit card number _____

Exp. Date: Month/Year _____

Check one ❏ Visa ❏ MasterCard ❏ Discover Card

Signature _____

Please check appropriate box:
❏ Licensed Builder-Contractor
❏ Home Owner

Order Form Key
TB28

 **ORDER TOLL FREE
1-800-521-6797**

Additional Plans Books

THE DESIGN CATEGORY SERIES

1.

ONE-STORY HOMES
A collection of 470 homes to suit a range of budgets in one-story living. All popular styles, including Cape Cod, Southwestern, Tudor and French. **384 pages. $8.95 ($10.95 Canada)**

2.

TWO-STORY HOMES
478 plans for all budgets in a wealth of styles: Tudors, Saltboxes, Farmhouses, Victorians, Georgians, Contemporaries and more. **416 pages. $8.95 ($10.95 Canada)**

3.

MULTI-LEVEL AND HILL-SIDE HOMES 312 distinctive styles for both flat and sloping sites. Includes exposed lower levels, open staircases, balconies, decks and terraces. **320 pages. $6.95 ($8.95 Canada)**

4.

VACATION AND SECOND HOMES 258 ideal plans for a favorite vacation spot or perfect retirement or starter home. Includes cottages, chalets, and 1-, 1½-, 2-, and multi-levels. **256 pages. $5.95 ($7.50 Canada)**

THE EXTERIOR STYLE SERIES

9.

THE ESSENTIAL GUIDE TO TRADITIONAL HOMES
Over 400 traditional homes in one special volume. American and European styles from Farmhouses to Norman French. "Readers' Choice" highlights best sellers in four-color photographs and renderings. **304 pages. $9.95 U.S. ($11.95 Canada)**

10.

THE ESSENTIAL GUIDE TO CONTEMPORARY HOMES More than 340 contemporary designs from Northwest Contemporary to Post-Modern Victorian. Four-color section of best sellers; two-color illustrations and line drawings throughout the remainder. **304 pages. $9.95 U.S. ($11.95 Canada)**

11.

VICTORIAN DREAM HOMES 160 Victorian and Farmhouse designs by three master designers. Victorian style from Second Empire homes through the Queen Anne and Folk Victorian era. Beautifully drawn renderings accompany the modern floor plans. **192 pages. $12.95 ($15.95 Canada)**

12.

WESTERN HOME PLANS
Over 215 home plans from Spanish Mission and Monterey to Northwest Chateau and San Francisco Victorian. Historical notes trace the background and geographical incidence of each style. **208 pages. $8.95 ($10.95 Canada)**

OUR BEST PLAN PORTFOLIOS

NEW ENCYCLOPEDIA OF HOME DESIGNS
Our best collection of plans is now bigger and better than ever! Over 500 plans organized by architectural category including all types and styles and 269 brand-new plans. The most comprehensive plan book ever.

15. **352 pages. $9.95 ($11.95 Canada)**

AFFORDABLE HOME PLANS For the prospective home builder with a modest or medium budget. Features 430 one-, 1½-, two-story and multi-level homes in a wealth of styles. Included are cost saving ideas for the budget-conscious.

16. **320 pages. $8.95 ($10.95 Canada)**

LUXURY DREAM HOMES At last, the home you've waited for! A collection of 150 of the best luxury home plans from seven of the most highly regarded designers and architects in the United States. A dream come true for anyone interested in designing, building or remodeling a luxury home.

17. **192 pages. $14.95 ($17.95 Canada)**

HOME IMPROVEMENT AND LANDSCAPE BOOKS

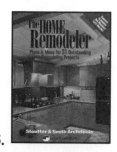

5.

THE HOME REMODELER
A revolutionary book of 31 remodeling plans backed by complete construction-ready blueprints and materials lists. Sections on kitchens, baths, master bedrooms and much more. Ideas galore; helpful advice and valuable suggestions. **112 pages. $7.95 U.S. ($9.95 Canada)**

6.

DECK PLANNER 25 practical plans and details for decks the do-it-yourselfer can actually build. How-to data and project starters for a variety of decks. Construction details available separately. **112 pages. $7.95 ($9.95 Canada)**

7.

THE HOME LANDSCAPER
55 fabulous front and back-yard plans that even the do-it-youselfer can master. Complete construction blueprints and regionalized plant lists available for each design. **208 pages. $12.95 ($15.95 Canada)**

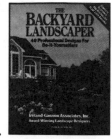

8.

BACKYARD LANDSCAPER
Sequel to the popular *Home Landscaper*, contains 40 professionally designed plans for backyards to do yourself or contract out. Complete construction blueprints and regionalized plant lists available. **160 pages. $12.95 ($15.95 Canada)**

INTRODUCING THE NEW BLUE RIBBON DESIGNER SERIES

13.

200 FARMHOUSES & COUNTRY HOME PLANS Styles and sizes to match every taste and budget. Grouped by type, the homes represent a variety from Classic Farmhouses to Country Capes & Cottages. Introductions and expertly drawn floor plans and renderings enhance the sections. **224 pages. $6.95 ($8.95 Canada)**

14.

200 BUDGET-SMART HOME PLANS The definitive source for the home builder with a limited budget, this volume shows that you can have your home and enjoy it, too! Amenity-laden homes, in many sizes and styles, can all be built from our plans. **224 pages. $6.95 ($8.95 Canada)**

Please fill out the coupon below. We will process your order and ship it from our office within 48 hours. Send coupon and check for the total to:

HOME PLANNERS, INC.
3275 West Ina Road, Suite 110, Dept. BK
Tucson, Arizona 85741

THE DESIGN CATEGORY SERIES—A great series of books edited by design type. Complete collection features 1376 pages and 1273 home plans.

1. ____One-Story Homes @ $8.95 ($10.95 Canada)	$ _____
2. ____Two-Story Homes @ $8.95 ($10.95 Canada)	$ _____
3. ____Multi-Level & Hillside Homes @ $6.95 ($8.95 Canada)	$ _____
4. ____Vacation & Second Homes @ $5.95 ($7.50 Canada)	$ _____

HOME IMPROVEMENT AND LANDSCAPE BOOKS

5. ____The Home Remodeler @ $7.95 ($11.95 Canada)	$ _____
6. ____Deck Planner @ $7.95 ($9.95 Canada)	$ _____
7. ____The Home Landscaper @ $12.95 ($15.95 Canada)	$ _____
8. ____The Backyard Landscaper @ $12.95 ($15.95 Canada)	$ _____

THE EXTERIOR STYLE SERIES

9. ____Traditional Homes @ $9.95 ($11.95 Canada)	$ _____
10. ____Contemporary Homes @ $9.95 ($11.95 Canada)	$ _____
11. ____Victorian Dream Homes @ $12.95 ($15.95 Canada)	$ _____
12. ____Western Home Plans @ $8.95 ($10.95 Canada)	$ _____

THE BLUE RIBBON DESIGNER SERIES

13. ____200 Farmhouse & Country Home Plans @ $6.95 ($8.95 Canada)	$ _____
14. ____200 Budget-Smart Home Plans @ $6.95 ($8.95 Canada)	$ _____

OUR BEST PLAN PORTFOLIOS

15. ____New Encyclopedia of Home Designs @ $9.95 ($11.95 Canada)	$ _____
16. ____Affordable Home Plans @ $8.95 ($10.95 Canada)	$ _____
17. ____Luxury Dream Homes @ $14.95 ($17.95 Canada)	$ _____
Sub-Total	$ _____
Arizona residents add 5% sales tax; Michigan residents add 4% sales tax	$ _____
ADD Postage and Handling	$ 3.00
TOTAL (Please enclose check)	$ _____

Name (please print) _____

Address _____

City _____ State _____ Zip _____

CANADIAN CUSTOMERS: Order books Toll-Free 1-800-848-2550. Or, complete the order form above, and mail with your check indicating U.S. funds to: Home Planners, Inc. 3275 W. Ina Road, Suite 110, Tucson, AZ 85741.

TO ORDER BOOKS BY PHONE CALL TOLL FREE 1-800-322-6797

TB28BK

303

Where The Heart Is

Home Planners' Featured Home Design

Design W2781
First Floor: 2,132 square feet
Second Floor: 1,156 square feet
Total: 3,288 square feet

L **D**

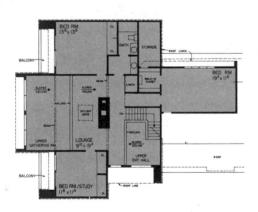

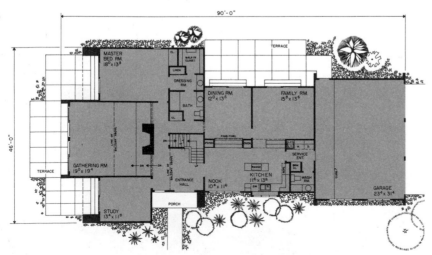

Tony and Penny Wastcoat of Bozeman, Montana wasted no time in getting right to work on their impressive contemporary—Design W2781. They purchased the plans in the fall of 1989, began building in October of that year and by March 31st of the following spring were moved into their new home. Nice work considering how brutal the winters can be in that part of the country!

Though they are pleased with the outcome of their home and achieved the bold contemporary look that first attracted them to the home, the Wastcoats made some changes to the original floor plan that allowed the house to be more livable for their family. The open area and lounge on the second floor became two full baths and walk-in closets for two of the secondary bedrooms. The original bath and storage area became a fourth bedroom. A laundry room was added behind the linen closet and the large bedroom was extended another four feet. Downstairs, the original laundry became a coat closet and the family room was expanded by four feet. By shifting the position of the stairs, a half-bath was added contiguous to the master bath and dressing area.

By personalizing their home, the Wastcoats turned what might have been just another house into their own special space! Home Planners salutes the effort they put into their home-building project and is happy to have been a part of it. ■